Cynthia J. Giachino

# BETWEEN LINES

**BETWEEN LINES**

Copyright © 2025 **Cynthia J. Giachino**

ISBN (Paperback): 979-8-89672-168-0
ISBN (Ebook): 979-8-89672-169-7
ISBN (Hardcover): 979-8-89672-173-4

All rights reserved. No part of this book may be used or reproduced by any means, graphic, electronic, or mechanical, including photocopying, recording, taping or by information storage and retrieval system without the written permission of the author except in the case of brief quotations embodied in critical articles and reviews.

Names and identities have been changed or are composites. This is my rendition and recollection of events, written as fiction. I have related them to the best of my knowledge. This book is not intended to hurt or harm anyone. Rather, its purpose is to teach, learn and give hope.

Because of the dynamic nature of the Internet, any web addresses or links contained in this book may have changed since publication and may no longer be valid. The views expressed in the work are solely those of the author and do not necessarily reflect the views of the publisher, and the publisher hereby disclaims any responsibility for them.

Printed in the United States of America.

PROMINENT
BOOKS
EDGE

5830 E 2nd St, Ste 7000 #9983
Casper, WY 82609
USA

Dear Readers,

    It's exciting to have you join me on this journey of truth and deception, friendship, and discovery.

    The year 2024 was a challenging one for me, particularly with the release of my first book, <u>Quiet. Fear</u>. Toward the end of the year, I uncovered that the majority of my marketing plans and expenses had been exploited in what I can only describe as several elaborate scams. Not only were they financially draining, but it also left me feeling angry and humiliated. Despite pursuing every possible avenue to fix the situation, I remain trapped in the aftermath.

    Feeling alone, and embarrassed, I slowed myself down for reflection. During that time I thought about the young man who had played a key role in the last scam. Something about him sparked intrigue —questions that went beyond the fraud itself, and delved into the who, what, when, where, why, and how of this individual. He was undoubtedly an intriguing mystery.

    From these questions, extensive research, and my own personal experiences, <u>Between Lines</u> was born. And a personal goal was accomplished; that of helping readers explore and become knowledgeable of the complex world of scams through an exciting, whirlwind of adventure among friends.

    I hope Between Lines ignites as many questions and meaningful conversations for you as it did for me and I'm thrilled for you to dive in!

Thank you,
Cynthia J. Giachino

# Chapter 1

# HARRIS

*March 2024*

"Now departing, Flight H204V to Bangkok. Now departing, Flight H204V to Bangkok."

"Mom, that's my flight." Harris, a striking young Asian American man in his mid-twenties, reached for his worn leather duffel bag. Saying goodbye to his mother was always hard, but this farewell felt unbearable to him. His body felt nervous; as well as excited. He gently took his mother's hands in his, hoping to ease their worries.

"I promise that the job in Bangkok will be temporary—a steppingstone. A year from now, I will have enough money to come home and get you the care you need. Moreover, the experience I'll gain from working at a large international corporation will make it much easier to secure a job back home in London."

She squeezed his hand in hers, her voice trembling. "I understand, Harris, but this is the first time in twenty-five years that we will be so far apart—and I have nobody but you!"

Harris looked into her teared eyes, searching for the resilience he'd admired his entire life. "Mom, it's time for me to stand on my own—and for you to do the same. We will both make new friends and have new experiences. There will be so much to talk about. Remember the notebook I left for you? I did that because it makes me feel better about leaving, and I know that it will help you see that I am never truly gone."

Her lips quivered into a faint smile. "Yes, your notes and drawings about bills and payments, contacting people, and getting around. It was thoughtful of you. Thank you. I am sure I will be using it every day for a few months."

"No matter the time of day or night, you can call or text. We can Zoom too. You will enjoy seeing me as much as I will seeing you! Staying connected will make the days pass more easily and keep our bond strong, no matter the distance." He spoke with conviction, though fear gnawed at him. What if she struggled being alone? After Dad died, she leaned heavily on her only child. Now Harris hoped their neighbors would step in, and maybe his new boss would allow an occasional long weekend home.

"Mom, I've got to go—you wouldn't want me to miss my flight!"

With a sly tilt of her head, she teased, "Well, that wouldn't be the worst!" her smile softened the moment. She smoothed the lapel of his suit, pretending to find a wrinkle.

"You look so handsome in this new suit!"

He laughed gently and asked, "You remember how to get home, right?"

She nodded, finally shooing him off with both hands.

"Yes, yes—now go!"

**Harris approached the boarding line**, its length stretching far ahead, but he paused despite his priority access as a business-class passenger. The flight would be long enough— twelve hours to Bangkok. There was no rush to be seated immediately. Standing for a while longer seemed preferable. Next to him was another young man, dressed in a suit. He turned to Harris and inquired, "Is this your first trip to Bangkok?"

Harris, enjoying the thoughts in his own mind, but not wanting to be rude, politely answered, "I have been there once before with friends during a college spring break. How about you, is this your first?"

"It is! I have a job interview at one of their hospitals."

"Interesting!" Replied Harris. "I recently completed college and have landed a job in my major, computer science, in Bangkok. The arduous days of working full-time, taking night classes, and caring for my mother have finally come to a closure! I look forward to the rest of my life. How about you? What position are you seeking in the hospital?"

"I am an internist. I understand the long haul of college and family. My wife and I thought Bangkok's opportunities were far better than staying in Europe, so I am going to scout it out. Are you from London?" the stranger asked.

"I was born in Chicago and moved to London when I was fifteen years old."

"Why would you leave Chicago? I love that city!"

Harris introduced himself to the stranger. "By the way, my name is Harris." He offered his hand.

The stranger took it and gave a firm handshake. "My name is Robert. It's been fun talking with you. Where are you seated? We could sit together. Looks like we are coming up next for boarding." And with that he moved ahead of Harris.

Harris grinned, "I'm flying business."

Robert replied, "Me too. Do you mind if we sit together?"

"Not at all," replied Harris, thinking the trip may feel shorter with someone to talk to.

The stewardess addressed him. "Ticket, please."

Harris dug deep into his pants pocket and retrieved the folded ticket, embarrassed, as she smoothed it for scanning.

"Thank you. Nice suit!" She smiled, returning the ticket in better condition.

Harris blushed. Dating hadn't been a priority, and compared to his peers, he was shy—particularly around women his age.

Walking onto the plane, Harris was greeted by a middle-aged steward, whose warm, sincere smile seemed as universal as the airline's greeting itself. "Welcome aboard. Please use the overhead bin closest to your seat."

Harris immediately saw Robert sitting in the aisle seat, but he didn't mind the window. He shoved his duffel bag in the overhead, keeping his laptop and neck pillow close in hand. He greeted Robert, "So we meet again!"

Robert smiled, stood up and gave Harris room to sidestep to the window seat.

**"Would you like a drink?"** asked Robert.

"No thanks," replied Harris.

Robert then turned to Harris, "So why did the family leave Chicago?"

"We loved Chicago. My dad was an orthopedic surgeon. We had a grand home on Lake Michigan. My mom worked part time at the National Archive which is why I minored in literature. She had me reading when I was three. Life was wonderful and then all that secure comfort of home changed in a few heartbeats. One morning, while having coffee at a small café with other doctors, while attending a convention in London, a terrorist hurled an IED bomb into the building."

"Wow! Harris, I'm so sorry! Man, that had to be horrible. I mean, it still is!" Robert moved nervously in his seat shaking his head. "Maybe we should change the subject?"

"Robert, it's okay. Talking about dad makes me feel as if he is still here. I like remembering him. It's more difficult for my mother. She wanted to leave the memories in Chicago and be closer to his soul in London. She believed Dad's spirit would find us there and we would be together forever—a belief that offered her comfort after such a devastating loss. That's how I ended up being part British! How about you? Were you born in London?"

"I was! I am a full British Londoner with an only child spoiled life. My dad is also a doctor. He spent his single years working as a Doctor without Borders, and then he met my mother, who is also a Londoner. They married overseas, returned to London to raise a family, and that's about it."

"What a small world!" Harris shifted in his seat. "My dad was also a member of Doctors without Borders, and he met my mom in the Philippines. They came to Chicago to raise a family, and they only had me! We are both "only children." Maybe they knew each other!"

Robert sat up excitedly, "They certainly could have! This is remarkable. I feel like you are a brother!"

"One big difference," added Harris, "I wasn't a spoiled child after we moved to London." My mom sank into a deep depression. The move was expensive, and my mother was frugal. When I turned sixteen I found a part-time job in a well-known publishing company and from then on life was a juggling act of school, work, and home."

Robert listened attentively. "This is a big deal for you… leaving home and going to Bangkok to work! How do you think your mom will handle it?"

"It will be hard at first, but she's an intelligent woman and I left specific requests with the neighbors to help her out. We both love flowers, and I hope that she will find a flower shop to work in and help her days go by. I asked her to come with me. Bangkok is vivid, bustling, and alive! The tropical plants and flowers would keep her busy! But she can't leave dad's spirit." For the first time Harris turned his head away from Robert and looked out over the sun clouds.

"Hey, how about a cold beer?" asked Robert.

Harris looked at Robert, "That sounds good! And maybe a snack to go with it?"

Both young men smiled and pressed the service button.

**The plane touched down at 6:30 a.m., Bangkok time.** Harris and Robert exchanged cell phone numbers, and each began their own journey. He without his wife, and Harris without his mother.

Harris retrieved his duffel bag and joined the slow-moving line of passengers disembarking. He followed the crowd to the pickup zone, scanning the line of drivers who were holding cards of their passenger's last name printed on them. Harris saw the name "Smythe;" that was him. Harris looked further down the line to see if there was another "Smythe," as this driver looked out of place wearing a discolored white shirt that clung to his body from the morning heat and humidity, paired with black athletic pants and worn sneakers—a far cry from the tailored suits worn by the other drivers. Harris hesitated briefly, noting the oddness, but shrugged it off and walked toward him, relieved that the company hadn't forgotten to send someone.

"Hi, I am Harris Smythe." Harris held out his hand, only to receive a cold stare in return. The driver did not shake his hand; instead, his eyes narrowed, studying Harris with unsettling scrutiny. Harris's apprehension sent a shudder down his spine.

"I will take your luggage, Mr. Smythe. Is this all?" the driver asked, his gaze lingering on the well-used duffel bag.

"Yes, this is it. But I'll carry my laptop," Harris replied firmly, clutching the bag's strap. Trust didn't come easily when faced with the driver's sly demeanor, and the laptop felt too valuable to leave in his hands.

The driver smiled—a slow, slippery smile that made Harris's apprehension deepen. "Follow me, Mr. Smythe."

As they approached a dark blue Toyota with heavily tinted windows, the driver asked, "How was your flight?" his voice smooth, bordering on arrogance.

"Long but comfortable," Harris replied, keeping his answers brief to curtail any further small talk.

"That's what they all say!" The driver chuckled devilishly. "Hopefully, you won't have to make the flight again!"

The words hung in the air like a sharp blade. Harris's unease deepened. New city, new job, and now an oddball driver whose creepy behavior was unraveling his nerves.

The driver opened the door and gestured to Harris to enter. "I haven't asked you your name," Harris said, pausing before stepping in.

"It's Somsak," he replied.

"Thank you, Somsak," Harris slid into the back seat, watching as Somsak placed his duffel bag in the trunk.

Feeling relief from the air-conditioned vehicle, Harris settled himself and immediately thought of sending a text to his mother. *Landed safely. Met another young man traveling to Bangkok for a job interview. We talked a long time and then fell asleep, which helped make the trip feel shorter. I am now in a company car heading to the apartment. I forgot how hot and humid Bangkok is! Love you.*

The chilled bottle of water on the seat caught his eye, a welcome relief in the stifling heat. He took a sip and removed his suit coat, draping it neatly beside him. Bangkok's tropical warmth was a sharp contrast to London's damp, cooler climate.

As the car pulled away from the airport, Harris took a few deep breaths and focused his attention on the world outside his window.

He had visited Bangkok once before during a spring break with three of his college friends. It was a vibrant city that left a mark on his memory—a mix of ancient beauty and modern energy. It was that visit that had drawn him back and fueled his decision to start anew—in a place that always felt alive.

Harris gazed out at the cityscape. Towering palms, sprawling banyan trees, and lush coconut and rain trees lined the sidewalks, many of which were ancient. Shopkeepers prepared for the day, each storefront offering its own unique charm while street vendors expertly arranged baskets overflowing with ripe papayas, golden mangoes, fresh shiitake mushrooms, and sticky rice. The scent of grilled pork glazed with palm sugar drifted its scent through the air, pulling him back to fond memories of his previous trip. Harris could taste the smells.

He was looking forward to dusk when he would walk back to the street vendors. Bangkok's illuminated nightlife flashed bright colors when the sun began to set, creating a party-like atmosphere that was hard to resist, even for the shy, introverted Harris. He leaned forward to address Somsak. "Would you please drop me off at the Nong Noch Tropical Garden? It is such a beautiful morning, I would like to take a walk through the gardens before it gets too warm."

Somsak replied, "I was given orders to take you directly to your apartment."

"Yes, I understand, but no worries. I have the address with me, and I will use Grab later," Harris confidently replied.

Grab was a ride service much like Uber and Lyft.

"Just a minute," Somsak replied, visibly agitated. He texted someone on his phone then glanced into the review mirror, his eyes flashing with anger. "I'll drop you at the entrance," he offered.

And he did just that. The car came to a screeching halt. Somsak opened Harris's door, went to the trunk to retrieve the duffel bag, and then dropped it at Harris's feet, who was now standing on the sidewalk. Somsak squealed the tires while speeding away.

Harris watched the car navigate down the busy street, recklessly weaving in and out of lanes and traffic. "I am glad to be rid of that man!" Harris muttered to himself. He slung his coat over his arm, placed the laptop in his duffel bag, and then hung the strap over his shoulder. He began walking toward the tropical gardens main entrance.

Since his last trip, he had learned that Nong Noch Tropical Garden was known as one of the most stunning botanical gardens in the world. He scanned its beauty saying to himself, "My mother taught me about every flowers' history that she would bring home. And from that flowers remind me of her love. How I wish she were here, right next to me, seeing nature's beauty from a different country with a vastly different environment."

As he followed the garden's paths, he used his cell phone camera and snapped pictures of unbelievably gorgeous and rare roses, orchids, blue lotuses, and chrysanthemums to share with her. He sent them with a message: "I will bring you here someday soon. You won't believe the beauty of these tropical flowers and plants! It is true what you said, 'Their colors are more vivid than any other flowers of the world'!"

Minutes later, his mother responded in a text: "How beautiful they are! I will look forward to joining you! I am doing well. My neighbor dropped in with his grandson who is four. Imagine that! Love you. Send pictures of the apartment. Love, Mom."

Harris smiled. All was good! The fresh air and fragrant scents, Robert's companionship, and the successful long twelve-hour flight. Except for the creepy driver, he now felt reenergized and focused. It was time to see his apartment, unpack, check in with his company, and explore the city.

**He called Grab, and within minutes,** a driver arrived. Harris greeted the driver and slid into the back seat, noticing a bottle of water was waiting for him once again.

He was parched from the walk. "Excuse me," he addressed the driver, "is this water for me?"

"Yes, yes…water…for you!" the driver replied in broken English.

Just as Harris reached for the bottle, the back door on the opposite side of the car flew open. A man in a black suit, his head covered in a black ski mask, slid in, his movements swift and deliberate.

Before Harris could react, the man lunged at him, wrapping his hands around Harris's throat. Harris kicked and clawed, grabbing at the man's hair in a desperate attempt to fight back; but his attacker was trained, and Harris's attempt was fruitless. A sharp prick in his neck sent a wave of numbness through his body. His vision blurred as he slumped into the seat. The last words he heard were "Welcome to your new job."

**Hours later, a cattle prod poked into** Harris's back, jolting him awake with a scorching pain. He tried to move, but his body was bound tightly, his arms and legs hog-tied. His mouth was taped shut, and every muscle ached from the unnatural position. His clothes were gone and replaced by a red prison-like jumpsuit.

Booted feet shoved him forward, sliding his body across a grimy tiled floor until he collided with the metal legs of a chair. A soldier untied his legs and arms. "Get up! Sit!" he ordered.

A deep, English-speaking male voice followed, speaking slowly. "Welcome, Ricco R. Smith," he said with a mocking tone and then addressed a militia soldier. "Take the tape off his mouth. Let's hear what he has to say."

The tape was ripped away, leaving Harris wincing in pain. His legs felt disconnected from his brain - the lingering effects of a drug flowing through his system. Disoriented and terrified, he struggled to piece together what had happened. The body of the voice stood inches behind him, staying invisible.

"My name is Harris, not Ricco, Harris Smythe, not Smith," he stammered, his voice trembling. "You have the wrong person! I am nobody! How long have I been out? Where am I?" Harris demanded, his fear mounting.

"You've been out for two days," the voice replied, its tone dripping with mockery. "I bought you today and gave you your life back. Like a newborn baby!" The man laughed, clearly amused by his own twisted humor. "And where are you? You're at my cyber camp. This is your new job. Your new beginning."

The voice was eerily familiar, as though Harris had heard it before—on television, the news, or the radio. Two days! That wasn't possible. "Where are my clothes, my phone, my laptop, my passport, and my watch? This isn't funny. There's no joke here!" Harris spoke, his voice shaking. "That watch belonged to my father!"

The voice, cold and unyielding, thundered, "It is noble to honor your father. But he is gone, Ricco Smith. And now, so are you. Your passport, watch, and every possession of value have been sold to the highest bidders. That suit you wore—fine craftsmanship, much like your father's watch—will feed you for weeks. You should be grateful. Others don't have such luxuries to barter. What you wear now is your uniform, your only need for as long as you remain here. Your identity is erased, so I suggest you learn to accept Ricco R. Smith. It is a clever, sexy name. Don't you agree?"

Harris blinked, his mind spinning. "Please listen. I came to Bangkok from London to work for a tech company. I am not who you think I am." His voice pleading with desperation.

The deep voice snickered, a sound that sent shivers down Harris's spine. "Let me see. Six feet tall, black wavy hair, boyish face, lives with his mother in London. Graduated in the top ten of his class. Sound familiar?" A soldier shoved a stack of papers into Harris's face while the voice continued, "You did an excellent job filling out every form sent to you. Impressive work, Ricco! Welcome!"

Harris's desperation grew into a flaring anger. "You cannot keep me here! People will know I am missing! Especially my mother."

The voice leaned in, growling the words into Harris's ear. "Your mother will miss you, no doubt, but when she reports you missing, she will hit a dead end as well as the police. It has already been over forty-eight hours. The chances of finding you alive are very slim, and soon, those agencies quit looking and asking."

Then the voice stepped directly behind Harris and placed a lanyard around his neck, dangling against his chest and holding six cards. "When you have completed your assignments, we will discuss your release. We paid thousands for you, Ricco. If you perform well, we might even triple our investment. Your first task is Irene Watkins—a retired schoolteacher publishing her first book. Books, Ricco! One of your joys! Be happy! You might even like it here! Now, any questions?"

Harris stared, his throat dry, his mind screaming. He said nothing.

A soldier struck him across the back of his head. "Answer!" he demanded.

"I'm not working to help you build an army!" Harris spat, his voice trembling with fury and disbelief. This had to be some drug-induced nightmare.

"Take him to his room. Make sure he eats. Tomorrow, he begins training, five a.m. sharp!" The voice snapped like a whip.

**The soldiers grabbed Harris and** marched him down a maze of dim, narrow hallways.

"Who are you people?" he asked the two soldiers dragging him down a narrow hallway lined with doors, their faded numbers barely visible beneath layers of cheap yellow paint.

"At least tell me where I am!" Harris shouted but neither soldier flinched. They kept even steps as they walked down the dated black and white tiles, making an echo from their heavy boots, an unnerving sound.

Harris looked up. The suspended ceiling squares were stained with dull yellow patches, showing where water leaks were or still remain. "Is this an old hostel?" he tried again to get some clue as to where he was, but the soldiers continued to look straight ahead and follow their orders, as if he weren't there.

Finally, they stopped at one of the narrow doors. A soldier unlocked the door and shoved Harris inside. He stumbled, crashing onto a stained, dirty mattress on the floor. The door slammed shut, and he heard the lock slide into place, bolting his fate.

**Harris sat up, his chest tightening**, stomach churning from the smell of the mattress. He quickly crawled off of it and scurried to the opposite wall. He saw the window and thought he may be able to open it, but it was coated with black, not allowing any natural light or air and no lock. It was stationary.

"I think I am going to vomit!" he said aloud, with no one to hear him. "Is this where they are going to keep me?" He looked around. At one time, the walls were blue, but now, the paint was peeling, revealing a dirty, grayed plaster with desperate messages.

"What are those messages? Maybe they will tell me where I am?"

He walked over to the wall and observed the scratches, like tally marks. They were names of loved ones, crude calendars, and a fading plea to someone's mother. Each whispered a story of those who had been trapped here before him. Chills ran down his spine. This was real.

"I need some water." He noticed a rust-stained sink, barely attached to a wall, which had a sign that read, "Not Safe for Drinking." "I just need a splash in my face." Out of instinct, and with a hint of hope, Harris turned the handle, no water. He felt water hadn't left the faucet in an exceptionally long time. Harris stood in the center of the small room. A simple metal desk with a single drawer and an equally unforgiving chair completed the bleak décor.

His stomach churned. "What am I going to sleep on? Not that mattress – if you can call it that." Its foam oozed from the torn seams, the fabric covered by years of filth and stains. He frantically scanned the room, looking for sheets, towels, a blanket, anything that would cover the overwhelming filth of what he had for a bed. And there was nothing.

"Mom, how did this happen! I can't call you for help. I can't call Robert. The pictures from the garden will be the last glimpse of me smiling and being free. How will you cope? Please, mom, stay strong. I will come back. I will!" Harris sat on the floor, his head between his knees and cried.

He was a caged animal. They stripped him of his identity and of the outside world. He was owned, a possession, a tool in someone else's hands. And what would they do to him? And who was Irene Watkins?

## Chapter 2

# IRENE AND BETTY

*March 2025*

Irene opened the drapes of her patio doors and gazed upon the bouquet of purple lilacs sitting on the outdoor coffee table. "Flowers can heal the soul, but I'm afraid my soul is too broken to heal. I will never be the same. This publishing scam has robbed me of much more than money. I trust no one. My hands shake. My mind scatters, unable to stay focused on one thing. In life we should have three wishes that would get us out of a terrible situation. I should be shopping with Betty, my closest friend, but instead I sit in doom and gloom."

Betty, Irene's long-time friend, met on the first day of sixth grade. Irene was walking off the bus when she saw a girl her age standing under a tree. She was wearing the custom school plaid skirt, a white blouse, and navy-blue sweater. Her Mary-Jane shoes were shinier than the sun that day, and her backpack was navy to match her outfit. She was meticulously put together; however, she did not look happy. In fact, she looked downright upset. Irene was always reaching out to those in trouble or hurt or plain lonely. She introduced herself and offered to walk her to her first hour class, and ever since, they had a sister-like relationship.

Irene paced back and forth in front of her patio windows. "Betty has never abandoned me. We have been through hard times from middle school through college, and we found solutions."

"I remember when Russ and I went through our divorce. Betty told me divorce is too expensive, and she knew that Russ and I still had feelings for one another, but not the kind that keeps two people married. She was right, and we separated instead. Russ went one way, and I went another. We sold the house and split our money. It's going smoothly. Betty is a problem solver, which is exactly what I need."

"Why am I so decisive? I'm scared and embarrassed. Pathetic! That's what I am, pathetic." Irene forcibly walked over to her cell phone, which was on the charging dock, picked it up, typed in her pin, and pressed Betty's picture.

Betty had taken the road of divorce and now lived in her own apartment in downtown Chicago, just two blocks from Irene. It was a modern apartment with a stunning view of Lake Michigan. It came as part of her divorce settlement. She and her husband had two homes. The other was in Arizona. He was a golfer, and she was more of an intellect and historian. It made sense for him to stay where it was warm and for her to be near the opportunities and the beauty of the Great Lakes and the culturally rich city of Chicago. The divorce was cordial, with no children involved.

They had their differences - Betty was short, petite, and curvaceous. Irene was a pleasant five feet, eight inches with long legs and a shorter torso. Irene had a model's figure, whereas Betty's was an hour glass. Betty's shoulder-length hair was thick, honey blonde, and cut with a sharp blunt style. Irene had long straight hair that was usually unmanageable and ended up as a twisted bun on top of her head. Betty chose fabrics of silk; Irene chose cotton. Betty preferred high heels while Irene preferred flats. Irene didn't want to draw attention to herself, while Betty would feel comfortable in a Broadway play. Being opposites could have been their reason for such a long fruitful friendship.

**"Hello Betty, it's me." Irene's voice came across forlorn.**

"Well hello 'me.' Please do tell what is going on! You sound miserable!"

"I have fallen into the rabbit hole of depression. I called Russ last week and he is having one good art show after another. That's just what I wanted to hear after feeling like a failure for months."

"Why on Earth haven't you been telling me this? I could use a challenge!" stated Betty.

"I didn't want to bother you," answered Irene.

"Nothing is as important as our golden friendship. I truly do mean that! Would you like to walk over to my apartment, or I could walk to yours?" asked Betty.

"Oh Betty, I knew I could depend on you, like old times. I'll wrap myself up in a warm sweater and come over." "I'll be waiting to buzz you up," replied Betty.

**The walk to Betty's was a long two blocks**, but Irene savored every step, breathing in the crisp lake air. Winter was at its end, and the winds off Lake Michigan were not forgiving to the arrival of spring. Her spirits lifted and she felt as though she could walk forever.

When she arrived at Betty's apartment, the usual breathtaking awe fell over her. It was a newer high-rise built with a modern twist, showing off massive windows and displaying a balcony in every unit.

"Good morning ma'am." The doorman greeted her. "Can I please have your name?"

"Of course. I am Irene Watkins. Here to see Betty Ovalang." It was obvious he knew every person who came in and out of the building, and she was not one of them. The security impressed her.

Looking up from his clipboard he responded, "Here you are." He crossed off her name and opened one side of the double doors.

As Irene entered the lobby, she thought its cleanliness was meticulous. A serial-killer clean. The simple décor displayed a large fireplace with a U-shaped navy-blue leather couch. White conversation chairs were scattered about and a sharply dressed female clerk stood behind a small front desk. The entire building reeked Betty.

Betty was wealthy. Her divorce took five years to come to fruition because of money issues and a rare African bird that they shared. Her husband knew how much she loved that bird and would never give the bird to her. Ever. She knew he was being mean, just to stir her up. That was the kind of jerk he was. Eventually, she let the bird go and settled for the two Maltese poodles they also shared.

"Good morning, and you are Irene, here to visit Betty," the sharply dressed desk clerk confirmed.

"Yes, that is correct," replied Irene.

The clerk handed her a key card. "This is for the elevator. Betty is in apartment number 32. Enjoy your day!"

Irene walked to the elevator, slid in her key card, and pressed the button numbered thirty-two. The sleek, stainless-steel interior was deadened with silence, and the elevator moved swiftly, like a stealth bomber. When the doors opened, Irene felt as if her feet were still on the ground floor. She grinned, thinking of it as a carnival ride. Betty was there to greet her.

"Irene!" Betty reached out and gave her friend an enormous warm hug. "How was your walk?" she asked as she began leading Irene to the apartment.

"I could have walked forever. It is a perfect day to enjoy the cool air of spring."

"Well, if you don't mind, I called my bakery and Phil reserved the quaint little table near the back for us to talk, have coffee, and a sweet roll. I can call my Uber driver."

"Please allow me to split the cost," Irene didn't ask, she politely insisted.

"There's the Irene I grew up with! Yes, we'll split the cost. I'll grab my wrap and be right back." Betty went to her main bedroom to grab a warm cloak.

Irene's eyes went directly to the wall of floor-to-ceiling windows that framed a stunning view of Lake Michigan. Her feet followed her eyes. "Betty, what a view! I never tire from it!" she said as she gazed at the lake.

Bundled in her cashmere wrap, Betty approached Irene. "It grabs my heart and takes my breath away several times a day," she spoke softly as she joined Irene in admiration of the lake.

"I can see how that would happen! I bet it is spectacular during a storm!"

"Oh, it is! And a bit scary too! The water turns dark in color, and with the white caps, it feels like it is calling you to join her in play. But that's a façade. It is really an angry sea of water."

"Hmm." Irene turned to face the rest of the apartment.

It, too, was simply decorated, but comfy with oversized cushions on the two-charcoal gray midsized couches, the fireplace framed with a white sparkly brick, and the two stressless sleek chairs facing the fireplace topped it off. Above, hung a new modern art painting with colors of black, gray, and lavender. "This is gorgeous Betty! I haven't seen it before. Is it new?"

"Yes and thank you." Betty acknowledged Irene's compliment. "My designer found it. She knows me well! I like to decorate for the season, but planning on how to put a room together, that's all her! How do you like your new apartment, Irene?"

"Small apartment, small budget, makes it perfect! I love the roomy kitchen, and you know how I cook and bake often. The building security is sufficient and how can I complain about its location? I am only two blocks from you, and across my street is a local corner grocer. Betty, how did you find that for me? Did you pay someone to move out?" laughed Irene.

"That's exactly what I did! Who told you? I bet it was the door man," Betty joked and noticed Irene's face was blank and her hands were shaking. "Would you rather walk along the lake today? You mentioned that you felt like walking forever."

"Betty, I have been a nervous, anxious wreck. I was so stupid and trusting! Russ can never find out what a horrible mistake I made. But it wasn't all my fault. I—"

Before Irene could say another word Betty interrupted. "Goodness grief, girl! What in heaven's name are you being so frantic about?"

"Betty, I can't say the word. It makes me sick. What am I going to do?" Irene's agitated demeanor was not a trait of hers, creating worry in Betty.

"Listen, Irene, tell me with one word what is going on?" Betty spoke slowly and calmly.

There was a deep breath, and then Irene spoke quickly and quietly, changing her demeanor to being more like herself, "I was scammed!"

Betty kept her cool, understanding how frightening a scam can be and she needed to gather more information before a reaction. "Did you lose any money?" she tried to ask calmly.

"I made such a mess of my life. I lost fifty thousand dollars. My entire savings account. Stupid me! I should have taken up knitting and not writing! I don't understand this world!" Irene's voice started off with volume but ended in a whisper.

"Irene, how can I help?" Betty asked sincerely.

"I don't know. I need to sleep, but I can't. I'm hungry, but when I make my meal I lose my appetite. It's hopeless, like me." Irene put her trembling hands in her pockets.

"This is what we are going to do. We will take that walk. I will cancel the reserved table at the bakery. Then we'll come back to my apartment and have an early dinner together. Something simple, soul food, like mac and cheese with apple pie!" Betty tried her hardest not to be overly pushy, yet firm. "And we have the night to talk more."

Irene walked up to Betty and gave her a tight hug. "Thank you, Betty. I need someone to help me get out of this hopeless feeling. I would love to walk and eat dinner with you afterwards, but then I want to go home. We can talk more in the morning, at my house. Is that okay with you?"

"Absolutely! Now let's get in this crisp spring air before it's gone! And I can drive us to the beach. It's only two blocks." Betty took Irene by the hand.

**This is a good parking spot**, and we don't have far to walk before we reach the beach." Betty turned off the car and looked over at Irene. "Are you sure you want to continue?"

"I am sure. I know that you won't judge me and talking is helping me see reality more clearly. Facing it straight on is my way out."

"Talking can help connect the dots! Now bundle up! The lake winds create quite a chill!" Betty reminded Irene of lake effects.

Irene wrapped the scarf she was wearing around her neck and tightened up her sweater. "They say keeping your neck warm is healthy. Have you heard that before?"

"I have. It goes back to ancient Egypt and Rome. In Egypt, it was the queen making a fashion statement. In Rome, it was the men. They called them sweat cloths as they helped them stay cool and dry. Other cultures, such as Italy, say a scarf around the neck keeps cold-related illnesses at bay. Such a simple piece of cloth, and it has remained a part of culture over time."

"Interesting! You love history," remarked Irene as she took hold of Betty's arm and walked down to the golden sandy beach that was catching the fall of each rhythmic wave. "Isn't this lovely?" Irene asked as she stood still soaking in the panoramic view. Betty nodded in agreement. "It never gets old. I love the smell of the air and the water. It is captivating!" Betty and Irene stood facing the lake for several moments, absorbing its beauty.

Irene sighed, "I find it freeing. Moving water does that to me."

They began walking along the shoreline.

**After a few minutes, Betty opened the door for conversation.** "Now, tell me about this scam. How did it begin? How long has it been going on?" Betty asked.

This moment was what had kept Irene up all night. She began with a slow casual tone. "You know I have been drafting a novel about my life," she began.

"Yes, it's what brought you to Chicago, but, Irene, I remember you talking about it in high school. The experiences you had with your godparents, right?"

"Correct, I knew it would inspire a story. Ideas for the plot constantly swirled in my mind but an excuse always got in the way—college kept me too busy, teaching filled every day and night, followed by the exhausting pursuit of my master's degree. Time was not plentiful. However, when I moved here, everything changed. I have been writing daily, even with my part-time job at the library. Several months ago, I ran off a few manuscripts and shared them with three library employees. Their feedback was positive. That same night, energized by their encouragement, I decided to take the leap of faith and self-publish."

"That doesn't surprise me. You really have a talent for bringing stories to life," said Betty. "Back in school, English was everyone's most dreaded subject—but it was where you shined."

"English and Literature classes were easy for me. However, drafting an autobiographical novel is considerably more difficult than any class I have taken. And publishing is beyond my experiences, but after this fiasco, I may be an expert."

"What exactly is 'this fiasco'?" a curious Betty encouraged an answer.

"I'm getting there, but first you need to travel the same road as I did, or you won't understand. I called four self-publishing companies that had incredible reviews to inquire about their pricing. I did not feel the story needed developmental editing since I have an editing degree. And copyediting was not a concern since the three people who read the novel stated I had done a fine job with detail, description, flow, and grammar. However, I did feel the need for one word-by-word edit."

"Must you do all that editing? Trust yourself, Irene. It's your gift," reminded Betty.

"Thanks for believing in me, but I felt it in my gut that one more read, one by a true editor, was needed. The publishing companies did not take kindly to that idea. They were relentless about having all three edits professionally completed by *their* team. It made no sense to me to have every level of editing repeated on my dime," explained Irene.

"Wait! The publishing companies want you to pay for each type of editing?" Betty appeared shocked at such a request.

"They do! Four cents per word for developmental, 25 dollars per one thousand words for copyediting, and 40 dollars per hour for proofreading. The grand total to publish was $17,500, but because they liked my story, they offered to invest $5,000, reducing the cost to $12,500—which was out of line! Besides, how can I be sure their proofreaders are professionals? For all I know, it could be someone they hired fresh out of high school! How could I trust them?"

"Really, Irene, I don't think you should pay them for another full round of editing!" Betty was firm in her tone.

"I am only getting started! I spoke with a big-name publisher who took me through a lengthy process of what I needed to get my name on the waiting list. One needed request was having proof of three thousands sales—with no invoices I couldn't do that! The mid-tiered publishers were bombarded with contracts but one eagerly took my call. They assigned me a young man who had recently graduated with a literature degree. He was thoughtful, genuinely interested in my story, and eager to hear about my writing struggles. I vented all my frustrations out to him, and he listened. He agreed that there are no real watchdogs for publishing—it was 'a sea infested with sharks!' Irene chuckled. That made me laugh out loud—it truly felt that way!"

Irene continued. "I asked him if I could handle the editing myself, and he agreed, but there is always a 'but'…

he offered to proofread for me without charge. When I asked him what college he attended, he politely explained he couldn't disclose confidential information. I did not find that strange—it actually seemed smart of him to protect his privacy. He emailed me daily until I mentioned feeling pressured whenever he discussed marketing and book fairs. He explained that marketing is costly and urged me to start considering it as part of the publishing process. What do you think, Betty?"

Betty paused, giving it deep thought. "I don't think that it is unusual to keep one's personal life private. That sounds normal, and books do need marketing, which can be costly!" Betty pointed out.

"Agree!" Irene remarked. "Our friendship continued and one day, I decided to take the plunge, and I purchased a $1,200 publishing package. It covered proofreading, ISBN numbers, the cover design, formatting, and a press release for social media—a real bargain! I felt a wave of relief and excitement as I embarked on this new journey. It was coming to life! Soon after he presented me with a cover. Surprisingly, I loved it. The cover and the editing was done. Now we need to complete the interior and synopsis."

"Was that near Christmas? You were in such a joyous mood! I was thrilled to see you being happy with the move and your work at the library!" commented Betty.

"Yes! It was near Christmas and the New Year! Then in January came all the extras and my excitement quickly turned into worry about money and my budget."

"What kind of extras?" asked Betty.

"More marketing, paid for reviews…the entire 'get your book up and running' package."

"How did you pay for this?" inquired Betty.

"I used credit cards. My gut told me to stop. The cost was becoming outrageous! The company said I could pay with a 3-month plan. That was doable. But what I didn't know was that in the publishing world, they only begin the project after they have received full payment. They have you by the neck. The only way to solve that is to pay the entire amount upfront. I should have had more patience. When Russ and I were building our house: we paid a third of the money in the beginning, a third halfway, and the final payment was when we went to the bank for closing. Now it is pay up front with no guarantees that the work will be completed or fulfilled to satisfaction!"

Betty lit up. "That happened to me! I had a young man do some house painting for me, and the contract said the payment had to be paid up front, so I paid him. He did wonderful work. Very neat and he used brushes. Then one day, he called and said he was ill. 'No problem,' I thought, but he never returned. He took all the money upfront and completed only 80 percent of the job. Finding someone to come in and finish someone else's work was difficult. I ended up paying double. Some things of our past were wiser and better than how we do things today."

"Then you understand that my first big mistake was stopping monthly payments. I could do them with a small budget adjustment but not with the entire payments. Therefore, I began loading up my credit cards so the job would be completed in three months instead of six!"

"That's a questionable process in my opinion. So what happened in February?" asked Betty.

"They disappeared! They had published several popular names. I believed they were solid. Their ratings on the internet were good. They were founded by an author, but internally they were in financial trouble. My rep disappeared.

The contracts I signed for thousands of dollars would never be fulfilled. Banks refused to credit my account due to the fact that the company wasn't listed as being bankrupt. But they were nonexistent! Ratings were taken off the internet. Their building was closed. No phone calls or emails were returned. I made 33 phone calls in one month. I have the list from the phone company, and not one reply. I was duped!"

"This is where I believe the scamming began. Perhaps my representative sold my information—or maybe he was the first scammer, the one who kept me under their control for a year. I have no proof, but it feels like the truth in my mind. I was sunk from here on out. I believe he is receiving all the royalty income illegally." Irene stopped walking and with tears in her eyes, faced Betty.

Seeing her friend's tears angered Betty. "Well, that is unreal. And the fact that you have reached out for help and no one cooperates with you blows my mind. What did you do? What *could* you do?"

"I moved on to another company, paid for a signing in the LA Festival of Books, and reprinted Quiet. Fear. I wasn't going to give up on my story. I believe it has a strong message the world should hear. You know how determined I am when I strongly believe in something," Irene chuckled through her tears.

"I sure do!" giggled Betty. All those marches we did in college! You're stronger than you think! I would have given up and walked away, calling it an honest try. But knowing you…you would grow more determined and stubborn! Did the new company stay true to their word?" added Betty.

"Kind of. They helped me build confidence, but their work brought little profit, and I wasn't receiving any invoices. Without invoices you can't tell which marketing tools work. Sadly, I had to leave and move on…again." Irene began to flush. "There is…more. A lot more." Irene bowed her head in shame, her breathing fast and shallow. "This is my secret life of shame and guilt. Please be patient if I need to stop and gather my wits."

"There's more? Irene, how can there be more? What you have explained is enough to break anyone!" exclaimed Betty. "This is terrible!" Those people need to be investigated and charged with a crime! They are stealing money! Ruining people lives!"

"How about we continue in the morning. I'm ready for that apple pie!" Irene wanted to end the discussion. After hearing it aloud, she felt nauseated. She grabbed Betty's hand. "Let's get back to the car before we get any colder."

They both picked up their pace and headed for the parking lot, each feeling a pain that was difficult to describe.

A pain that kept their nerves imprisoned.

## Chapter 3

# SCAM CAMP

*Ricco*

**The old, dilapidated building** felt like it would fall over one day, taking the lives within its walls. Ricco wished those walls could talk. He needed to find answers for all of his questions. Here, in this camp, he had no friends. He was not allowed to talk to anyone, so becoming his own best friend, or worst enemy, was a necessity to staying sane.

"It's been almost a year in this hell hole, forced to work seventeen hours a day, sometimes longer, destroying the lives of the innocent to aid militia armies with weapons, and to help pay for human trafficking to fill these camps." Ricco paced in his small cell, occasionally stopping to kick a wall, venting his anger as he spoke only to himself.

"Watchful eyes staring at me. They must see my hate and I hate them all. This is my life sentence for having a dream to succeed. To make my mother proud. I wanted to work hard and be someone. Now I work hard to destroy others making me less of a human every day. If I live through this, I will not ever be able to forgive myself for believing in something that sounded too good." Ricco grabbed onto the newly placed bars that kept him from the window of escape and tried to move them. It was hopeless. His world was hopeless.

"I don't know for certain where I am, but it is hot and humid. I could still be in Thailand. I heard rumors that there were others being held in a bigger camp nearby. How can the world allow this to happen? Do they know and not care, or don't they know? Breathe Harris, yes, Harris! That's my real name. I say it often, so I do not forget who I am." He heard the clanking of keys opening his lock. He scuttered to his mattress on the floor.

"Time for your shower," the soldier said in a forceful monotone. "Get up!" he ordered and poked Ricco with the tip of his gun.

They were herded, like animals, to the front of the building and then lined up in two rows. With their orange jumpsuits on they were hosed down. Other soldiers dumped cleaning powder over them from above. They scrubbed their clothing and bodies with their hands. Then they were hosed again, sometimes the water power was so strong it would knock many of the workers over. That was their shower. When they had hard rains they were often taken out to the yard and made to stand still as the rain pelted like leather straps against their bodies.

The laborers rarely spoke to one another; instead, they used other means of communication that were safer, such as facial expressions, hand signals, a cough, or a gesture. Occasionally, there were times when the soldiers left, and talk took place, but it was always in fear. Fear was the air that they breathed. Today, after the shower, the soldiers stood in a circle, laughing while sharing a story.

Ricco looked to his left and gave the young man next to him a 'heads-up' nod. The young man rubbed his hands over his stomach. Ricco nodded yes and rubbed his stomach too. They were all hungry and thirsty.

Today he could smell the cool salty air of a nearby ocean or bay and could see a thick, jungle-like canopy of trees and greenery. From time to time, he was able to hear the sound of a big engine. Maybe a jeep or a truck. One thing was for certain—they were somewhere in Southeast Asia. Cambodia, Thailand, Myanmar, or Vietnam…it could be any of them.

Ricco scanned the group. He noticed that a few were missing. "I can't get sick. The sick and the weak are never seen again. My dad would stay strong, and I have that in me. No matter how badly I feel, I force myself to eat what I am given. That gives me strength mentally and physically."

Meals were at set times and always consisted of the same food: rice, fruit, and raw vegetables. At breakfast, each laborer also received three bottles of water, and the constant heat quickly taught them how to ration it.

Ricco observed every moment of the day with precision and memory. "I am determined to get out of this camp and back to freedom or die trying. I will not die here. My life will not end in my twenties. I will see my mother. I pray for her health. I pray for another chance to prove myself to her."

Next they were herded to their breakfast, fed, given their water and then taken to the workstations. Once everyone was seated, the constant clicking of the keyboards and soft muttering of others speaking were the only sounds allowed in the room. Ricco would visualize a happy scene, such as being in downtown Bangkok at night to get himself pumped up to trick and steal from the innocent.

Suddenly, Ricco's attention zoned in on a new sound. That of slow, heavy footsteps entering the workroom and the smell of marijuana mixed with aftershave. A new more intense fear filled the room as well as his own being. As much as he wanted to turn his head, he kept his focus on his computer screen. He was not one to cause trouble or draw extra attention to himself. Attention lowered his chance of ever escaping.

The footsteps stopped close to his desk.

"You Ricco?" a soldier asked in a gnarly tone.

Ricco looked up. "Yes." *The less said, the better*, he thought.

"You're coming with us." His gnarly tone grew louder.

Ricco began feeling his body temperature rise. His heart thumped in his chest, his mouth as dry as a cotton ball. "I will need to shut down my station," he swallowed his fear and forced the words out.

"Wrong answer. We don't wait," said the soldier, kicking the chair out from under Ricco.

The soldiers grabbed him from under the arms and dragged Ricco out of the workroom down several hallways and stopped at a room with a large door and faded yellow walls.

There, directly in front of him, on one of those faded yellow walls was the angry black symbol that he had seen on his first day. Now he had recognized it on the soldiers' wrists too. He had no idea what the symbol meant to the militia, but it appeared to empower them. They sat him down in the same metal chair he sat in on the first day at the camp. Then they waited in silence.

Again, he heard heavy footsteps coming his way. They hit the floor in uniform timing, then stopped. "Well, well, what have we got here? Mr. Ricco. The talented young man from London." It was the voice. He approached from behind, like before, stopping just short of being in front of him.

Ricco began breathing rapidly. He feared that they would find his mother and bribe her for money to release him, but he didn't want that to happen. The militia were merciless. Ricco never wanted her to smell their staunch or feel the back of their hand. Yet here he was, helpless and pathetic. The only way to protect her was to keep her in the dark. Help her believe he was gone.

"Ricco, I have been watching your work with Ms. Watkins. Would you say it is proceeding as expected?"

*Voice man has a good vocabulary,* Ricco took a mental note and tried to show that he was fearless, but as soon as he talked, it was obvious he was scared to death. "It is… moving…s-s-slowly," Ricco stammered. "She is nibbling but not biting. I do believe that once the interior of the book is complete, I will be able to convince her to have us pitch her book at the London Book Fair. That will bring in thousands of dollars."

"Hmmm, thousands. And what has she invested to this day?"

Ricco had not been pushy or aggressive with Irene, not as much as he was with the other fifty authors who were more business orientated. He and Irene had developed a trusting comfortable relationship, and now he believed he was going to experience the repercussions for doing so. "Seven grand for the publishing and release in the US, Canada, and internationally. She also paid for the book reviews, sir."

The voice man did not move. He stood still, exactly at the point of not being seen.

"You have six weeks. Then we meet again to determine our next move. Toughen up. No more nibbling. Get the interior done. Understood? Your ransom is looking dim."

*Who is this guy? He sounds American. And why me? Why was I sold to this guy? How did this happen?* Ricco's mind flooded with "what ifs" and how he could do what was being asked of him without proper food, water, or sleep.

Then his head jolted forward, and all thoughts quickly diverted to the pain he now felt on the back of his head. The soldier blasted him with the butt of a rifle.

"Answer!" the soldier commanded.

Barely breathing, Ricco pushed his words out. "Yes, sir. Six weeks. London Book Fair. Complete project. Get tough," Ricco shakily replied as his head throbbed, and the room spun in slow motion.

The hit knocked away his fear of dying and allowed a new feeling to emerge—the anger. The anger he swallowed every day and night. The anger that filled his belly and kept him alive. The anger that lived in the air blended with fear.

The voice man was the commander, no doubt about that. He walked out using the same number of steps with which he had entered. The soldiers untied Ricco's hands, grabbed him under the arms, and dragged him back to his workstation. He fought for consciousness. Once they reached the workroom, they threw him on the floor and gave a clear loud order, "Work!" The soldiers laughed at Ricco, then each gave him a solid kick to the gut, turned, and walked out.

**Minutes went by as Ricco laid** on the floor coming in and out of consciousness. When the room returned to the normal daily sounds, a worker near Ricco quietly came to his side. "Ricco, are you all right?" he whispered.

"My head hurts, and I can't focus," a disorientated Ricco whispered back.

Blood pooled on the floor from the back of his head. The worker gently lifted Ricco's head. "You have a large gash back here. Put pressure on it," his colleague whispered while helping him up to his chair and then gently gliding him back toward his desk. "Pretend you are working and try to keep your eyes still for a while." He patted Ricco on the back, helped him get his hands up to the keyboard, and swiftly returned to his own station.

Foggy-minded and with blurred vision, Ricco tried to read the screen, but the words looked like tiny black ants. He took his old sweat rag, folded it into layers, and pushed it against the gash on the back of his head. He clenched his teeth so as not to scream from the pain. Then he sat. Useless and thinking. *They did this so I would not succeed. Then they could get rid of me and assign someone more ruthless to do my work. That is not going to happen. I am my father's son. He did not fail. If I could send a message to Irene, she would report it to the authorities.* Then Ricco recalled the money. *He mentioned ransom money. Irene has enough money to get me out of here, if getting out is even real.*

He opened one eye and looked at the screen, which was now a blur of black and white. He opened the other eye; it gave him enough sight to ping out a short email. Steadying his breathing, he lightened his fight-or-flight tension, placed his hands on the keyboard, and began typing.

> Hello Irene,
>
> I hope this email finds you well and enjoying spring in Chicago. In my youth, I visited the "Windy City." It has fond memories.
>
> I've been dealing with a personal matter that doesn't allow me to complete my work as expected The company is in a remote and poor area. It is hot and humid with jungle-like conditions and few fans.
>
> While I am healing, please give thought to the marketing plan for the book fair. Trust me. It is great for exposure, attracting thousands of people from all over the world.
>
> Best regards,
> Ricco Smythe

He pushed send and tried to close his eyes, but that made the spinning in his head worse. His head throbbed to the beat of his heart. It was maddening. At least the bleeding had stopped. He released a sigh. For now, staring at the white screen was all he could manage. He overlooked the fact that he had used his legal last name.

He knew that Irene was his way out. He hoped she could read between lines.

## Chapter 4

# THERE'S MORE

**Irene woke up feeling like she couldn't breathe.** She took several deep breaths trying to slow down her racing heart. Morning anxiety had become part of her daily life. "Betty is coming over this morning! I need to put myself together. Let's see, Betty likes frothed cream." Irene walked over to the fridge and looked for cream; there was none. "I have time to run across the street to the corner grocer." She threw a light coat over her sweatshirt and pants to make the quick run.

"I hope Harry isn't too cheerful this morning. I feel like biting someone's head off!" Irene mumbled as she got into the elevator and pushed the button for the lobby.

The door opened, and sure enough, there was Harry, a handsome middle-aged man and the apartment's door attendant. He began working there twenty years ago. Now he was known as an entity to the building. Irene enjoyed talking with Harry, but not today. Today, she was in a constant panic attack. She wanted to get the cream and return home as fast as she could. Something told her that was not going to happen.

"Good morning, Ms. Irene. Going to the library this morning?" Harry cheerfully asked.

"Not today, Harry. Betty is coming over and I need cream. I am going to the corner market," Irene replied sharply.

"Cross at the light, Irene! This is not 1965!" yelled Harry.

"Thank you for reminding me!" she shouted back as she jaywalked across the street. Irene grabbed a pint of the Irish Cream coffee creamer and immediately checked out. She dashed across the street and back to Harry, who was opening the door for her.

"Thank you, Harry." She flew past him like a paper airplane.

"One day I'll be calling 911 instead of opening the door for you, if you don't start walking up to the corner crossing, Ms. Irene!"

"Got it, Harry! I will start practicing, I promise," she shouted back as the elevator door closed. It was an older elevator, and lately, she wondered if she could jog up the steps and get to her apartment faster.

Feeling safer and more comfortable in her apartment she immediately began to put together a morning platter and drinks to share with Betty. No sooner had the froth machine stopped, than there was a knock on her door. Irene walked to the door, and without thinking, asked, "Who is it?"

"It's me, silly girl," said Betty, looking into the peephole that she knew Irene was looking out of.

Irene opened the door. Her eyes quickly scanned Betty's casual wear. A deep purple, almost black, top, and bottom pant set made of an interesting material. Irene wanted to touch it out of curiosity. Betty handed her a small white bakery box.

"Those are scones, fresh from this morning's shift. The new girl that works at the counter is sweet as candy! She always greets me and tells me which pastries are the freshest."

"Thank you for picking these up. You know what my relationship is with scones, and I can really use one today!"

"Your scones are my dark chocolates!" responded Betty.

Irene opened the box, and her face lit up. Right next to the scones were four dark chocolate truffles. "Why does this not surprise me?" asked Irene.

"Because it is me! Where I go, so does chocolate. We will never divorce one another! That is a lasting relationship! Even if I develop diabetes—you will find me a fine low sugar or no sugar dark decadent chocolate, won't you, Irene?"

"Yes, my dear, I will do that and hand me your wrap. The coffee is ready."

**Irene returned carrying a shiny**, well-polished silver plate with the scones and napkins arranged in a half-circle and two borosilicate coffee glasses she used only with her special friends. They were the most expensive belongings in her apartment and Betty was all about presentation.

"This is such a welcoming arrangement!" commended Betty.

"Take a scone or truffle or both and be careful. The coffee is hot!" replied Irene.

"What is the flavor of the day?" smiled Betty.

"Irish cream!" answered Irene.

"Wonderful! How lovely!" Betty reached out first, anxious to have a cup of Irene's coffee. She steamed the cream and added a dab of butter to make it smooth and less bitter.

"Are you ready?" asked Irene after eating a scone and a truffle. I do need to bring you to my ending."

"I'm all ears!" Betty nestled herself on the living room couch, on the opposite end of Irene.

Irene smiled, imagining Betty with more than two ears. "I will begin after the LA Book Festival and when I decided to leave the second publishing company."

"Let me do a re-cap and see if I am getting this right," added Betty. "The publisher kept selling your book, taking the royalties and sale numbers to benefit themselves while using your marketing and footwork. The more you tried to sell *Quiet Fear*, the more money the scammers made. Neither the large printing press nor the popular online book selling sites would hear you out, respond, or offer help."

"You have condensed my situation well," complimented Irene.

"Did your sales go up after LA?" Betty asked with caution.

Irene slowly shook her head no. "That is where the problem still lies. I have no idea of book sales because I have never received quarterly invoices. Those invoices give you the data you need to move forward with more wisdom. The only people that made money were the large publishing company and the bankrupt company taking my royalties and possibly the new publisher."

Betty broke in, "This is unbelievable! Publishing and printing a book is like playing a game without instructions!"

Irene tried to smile, but each sentence explaining how she got to where she was, ached.

"These fast, sweet-talking young men and women who scam others know a great deal about psychologically getting into another's head and heart. They are experts on how to gain trust and friendship over the phone or through an email. The pressure is horrendous! I was convinced that if I did not invest immediately, I would lose my spot for the 'deal of the day.' I thought that because there are millions of books and authors, it made sense when they said they couldn't hold a spot for me—because they would naturally move on to the next. Now I know better. A 'deal' can wait for tomorrow! There have been a lot of hard lessons learned."

"It hurts to see you hurt." Betty's face expressed concern and sadness.

"Oh Betty, I wasn't thinking realistically. I was stupid and now the guilt weighs on my heart. I am a prisoner in my own body."

"No, you are not! I know you, Irene. I understand how going through this was like an assault, an attack on you and your book. That brings shame and embarrassment, which is why people often don't report. It would be too painful. But you are here, reporting to me. You are already headed toward healing."

There was a brief pause as both friends looked upon one another. Slowly, Irene began to smile, which made Betty follow suit.

Irene rolled her neck and head, releasing tension. "I needed a company that was transparent with invoices. I had to know what marketing methods were working, and which weren't, and I needed help with social media."

Sympathetically, Betty agreed. "I know! Recently, I took a class to learn how to use my Apple phone! And I forgot half of what they said. You know me. I sat there acting like everyone else when I should have been taking notes! My memory failed me, as I knew it would, but I wanted to blend in. So yes, I understand some of your feelings, especially when it comes to technology!"

"I still take notes, but not as well as in my younger years!" responded Irene. "Those were the days when life was all on paper! For me, it's more complicated with computers, emails, and texts. But only we mid-lifers know that! I print out my contracts, but there have been times I didn't do it immediately and then lost them. I did save all my receipts but paying before you see the finished product doesn't help the consumer. That's what I have come to believe."

"How did you choose another company?" an interested Betty inquired as she moved forward, leaning closer to Irene on the couch.

"I did a lot of deep thinking. I kept a book of contacts and people that worked for me, and I recalled their demeanors. One particular young man stood out. He was with a relatively new and small publishing company. He had an old soul, but he was wise about the present also. When I asked him if he would republish my story, he sounded surprised and happy. He promised quarterly invoices, which was my number one requirement. He started the process immediately without putting any pressure on me, saying things such as 'You should buy a marketing program also' or 'We have a special going on and it will not be available after today'! No more pressure! As soon as someone calls and becomes pushy, I lose interest and wish them a nice life. My book finally landed in the right place with the new company."

"*That* brings us up to today. Right?" asked Betty.

"I wish! There was a large hiccup in-between signing with my current publisher and the present." Irene looked away from Betty, not wanting to see the dissatisfaction in her face.

"You have to be kidding, Irene! What more could you possibly get wrapped up in?"

Irene shrugged. "You're right to feel surprised because it was a surprise. I received a call from a secretary who worked for an executive director of a small, yet successful film company. We all know their name. The secretary set a date for me to talk with him. I could hardly breathe. I was hopeful, nervous, and anxious. I would be able to pay off my debt. It was glorious!"

"And what happened?" Betty asked cautiously, knowing it didn't turn out good.

"The executive director had a sexy British accent! He asked friendly get-to-know-you questions, and then he talked about the contract and how making a movie worked. He said an employee bought a copy of *Quiet Fear* in LA at the book festival and read it. She was inspired by the story and could see it on the big screen, which led him to check it out. He did, and from there, he contacted me. He said I was one of the lucky people to be picked up by film in that manner."

Irene was on a roll, wanting to finish this failure as fast as she could. "I asked him for three days to read over the contract, which he agreed to. At that time, I was not very trusting, so I hired an entertainment lawyer to look over the contract and advise me on my next move. She called back and said it was a good contract with a normal timeline, and it was safe to sign. So I did. Betty, it was a happy day!"

"Until...?" Betty drew the word out to create suspense.

"Until a couple months went by and I spent another 14 thousand dollars."

"No, you didn't! You wouldn't!" a surprised Betty responded.

"I did. When he received the signed contract, he introduced me to *his* publishing company, the one the film company used for their movie releases and trailers. I told him about Dillon, my new publisher, and that I just paid for reprinting, and I asked if he could work something out between the two of them. He said he could, but it would slow the process down. Then he gave me examples, and it all made sense."

Betty interrupted. "Boy, they are good imposters!"

"And fast talkers! He guaranteed me that the movie's publishing company was professional and efficient. The only glitch was with payments. They always had a challenging time with my credit cards, asking for a different card or a bank account. That was a red flag. I felt waves of doubt, but the lawyer gave me the green light, so I did what they asked."

"What did they ask for?" inquired a puzzled Betty.

"They suggested I have chapter summaries professionally written—needed for acquisitions, so they said. Next came the all-important query letter. Followed by the book being translated into Spanish. And the priciest of all—a book-to-movie treatment and a script."

"Why on Earth would you need a book-to-movie treatment? And a script? The author rarely writes a script! That sounds excessive! And how did you even afford all that?" Betty's skepticism was tangible.

"I couldn't! I maxed out my charge cards. I had five of them." Irene answered with her eyes closed. "Meanwhile, I was truthful with Dillon and told him what had happened. Dillon warned me. He told me there was a scam out there with that particular movie industry. I half-believed him, and what kept me from dropping everything was the lawyer's approval. I know Dillon was frustrated but also inquisitive, asking for details which he later researched.

As Dillon was working on one end to protect me from more fraud, my new representative was doing their best to drag me into their scam deeper. And just when I began to think this was not real, they sent me a thousand-dollar advancement for a contract with Sims and Son. Why would a fraudulent company *pay me*? That made no sense. They had to be real. Right?"

"Wait now." Betty paused to pull her thoughts together. "So you are saying the movie deal was a scam? The lawyer said it was legit! Oh, Irene, I am so sorry!"

"Scammers are trained professionals today, Betty. They can change the color of a logo by a few pixels, and it looks the same unless you are a graphic computer expert and put it under a microscope. They call them criminal actors, and they are!"

Betty was befuddled. "I don't know what to say. What did you do to end this nightmare?"

Collecting herself, Irene explained her next move. "There was a man I knew that I felt comfortable enough with to ask for help. He came over, and within ten minutes, he found the proof that I needed. The domains of the company I was working with were different from the *real* film company. It was a small difference but made a huge tell-all. The scammers domain had a hyphen, whereas the real company did not. Then the computer technologist dug a little deeper and found that it was originating from overseas. They were not in America. My heart sank. I was pig butchered!"

Now Betty felt completely overwhelmed. "Wait! Explain, 'pig butchered.'"

"Pig butchering is when a scammer works with his or her victim for a period of time, building trust, friendship, and even romance. That's called 'feeding the pig.' The end deal is to steal the victim's money over and over. That is when 'the pig is butchered.' I read that this type of scamming began in scam camps around 2020, during the COVID period, mainly in Southeast Asia, but now it is global. It replaced a lot of on-line gambling. The United States is not protected from it." Irene closed her eyes and took a deep breath. "It is maddening to understand what they were doing and that I fell for it. I want to ring their necks." Her shame was now anger and she couldn't look at Betty.

Betty understood and let it be. She asked, "How long have you been communicating with this scam company?"

"Months longer than I should have!" admitted Irene.

Betty's heart felt heavy for her friend. "After all this and you still want to get your book out there? You are one resilient and determined author! What about your lawyer? Have you told her?"

"No, not yet. When I have more strength in myself, I will, but I did call Dillon. He was sympathetic and thank goodness he did not say 'I told you so.' That would have broken me. Telling the family that the contract wasn't real was embarrassing enough, and I felt like a complete failure in doing so.

My entire life, I budgeted paycheck to paycheck and was proud of my money management, and then this! Pig butchered! Do you have any idea how those two words are destructive to one's thinking process? I can see the scammers laughing at me and celebrating how easy I was to feed. But I was changing. I no longer cared about the movie, the new book, and the other lies. In my head, I wanted to keep them hanging on a little longer. Two could play this game!"

"Now wait a minute. You are leading them on? Have you lost your mind?" Betty was ready to throw the room at Irene.

"Hear me out and you will understand. There is this relationship I developed with Ricco, my rep, that keeps eating away at me. Between lines he is trying to tell me something, maybe a warning."

"Hold on, Irene! His job is to get into your head, and that is exactly what he has done. A criminal actor!" Betty reminded Irene about those who scam.

"I know you want to wring his neck," Irene shot back.

"No, I want to ring *your* neck!" Betty rebounded.

"Hold on a minute, Betty! When I look back at the other scammers, Ricco doesn't fit the profile. We emailed daily. He had questions about a sentence or a paragraph. He was actually reading the manuscript. Another time, he had an idea about a character. Then it was the cover. After a couple months, my suspicion began to grow that Ricco was the only person working on my story. There was not a team or subcontractors. There probably was no publishing company. Then one morning I was determined to talk to him, to actually hear his voice. Email was not working for me anymore, and there was no other way possible to get a hold of him. That is when my gut feeling kicked in that he was reaching out, more than he was scamming me."

Betty froze like a statue. "If I followed your story correctly, you have spent over fifty thousand dollars with four publishers and a film company, but you have only what you started out with...and that is your book."

For a minute or two, Irene was quiet. The two friends stood in silence; eyes locked on one another.

Irene broke the silence. "Yes, as sick as it is, that's right. Pig butchered. I feel awful about myself, my choices, my banks that paid the scammers instead of me, but then, I reverse the negatives and look at the situation in real time, and in doing that, I realize we all have a fairly good chance at being scammed—at least once in our lifetime. I went beyond that, but time cannot be turned back. I desperately wanted my book to be successful and still do! Now, I have no one to turn to but you, Betty. I don't blame you for not trusting me."

Betty stopped her pacing and gave Irene a tight hug. "Listen, girl. We've been through hard times before, and we can get through this. For starters, you must bury these scammers and work only with Dillion."

"Betty, I couldn't agree more, but I have this strong feeling that Ricco is truly in trouble. He and I communicate like a mother and son. He cannot be one of the bad guys. But I do not blame you for not believing me! After hearing this story, I am sure you see me as a nutty fruitcake and an easy target, too trusting, too much of a worn-out hippie. Love and peace to everyone!" She waved a scornful peace symbol with her fingers.

Sincerely, Betty responded, "Not a fruitcake. Not a hippie. But a lonely woman who wanted this book to have some success, more than money itself. You wanted to own who you are and instead, you lost yourself. Your identity was stolen. Your mind has been twisted and turned, feeling a loss of direction."

"You always 'get me,' Betty. Everything you said is true. But just for a moment, can we *assume* that Ricco *is* a fraud and not being forced to work for a fraudulent company. He is really a part of it. How do you explain why it feels as if he is trying to tell me something? And why is he working so hard to earn my trust in his abilities rather than selling me packages? Something is wrong, and I want to figure it out. He has manners, he is bright, and his devotion to literature is highly noted." Irene was now letting out her true concern—the actual reason she opens the daily emails. She wanted to save Ricco and in doing so, save herself.

"That is what a good scam artist will do, Irene! They play with your psyche, find the weakest link, and build the relationship. You mentioned that he gives you big discounts. What is a few thousand dollars if he can get twenty thousand? At least they are not the type to kidnap you or get into your bank account."

"Someone has tried to get into my bank account," admitted Irene. "But I have too many warnings, and the bank followed secure measures," Irene informed Betty.

"Smart move, Irene! Let me make sure I have this right...you have not seen this man, nor have you spoken to him. Ricco only exists in an email," reconfirmed Betty.

"Yes, that is correct. But, Betty, how many people have you talked to in various businesses, and you have no idea what they look like? Besides, the voice is not reliable anymore because a voice can be replicated with artificial intelligence. The film producer stole an identity. Pictures can be fake. What is a person to do? How can I trust anyone?"

Silence, once again, filled the space between the two friends.

Irene felt this was the right time to throw out the last bit of information that she was keeping to herself. "As strange as it may be, please be patient. I think Ricco may be one of those young professionals tricked into a job position after college. They send you an unbelievable contract with benefits, a flight ticket, and a hotel reservation. They fly you to a country far away, pick you up, drug you, and then...they sell you to a scam labor camp. Betty, that really happens to thousands of young people! And I sense that Ricco is one of those, and he is asking for help."

Betty put her arm around her friend's shoulder. "My dear Irene, if you feel this strongly about Ricco, then you must talk to the police and see if they can help. It is time to put all this behind you. Only move forward with people you have trusted and will continue to trust. You are jumping out of one fire and landing in another—we could even inform the FBI!"

"I reported it to the police, and the way they looked at me, I doubt much was done. The officer typed up a report and filed it. I tried calling the company number on the website, and there was no answer. The phone rang, but like he said, they had no secretaries or answering machines. There's always a dead end. And I filed a report with the US government."

Betty gently but directly responded, "I am proud of you for doing that. It will help others. And you still feel strongly that Ricco is a prisoner of scams, like you?"

"Yes, I truly do! I believe it with my whole heart. He needs help, just as I do."

"Can you share the emails with me? I can try to see what you are feeling and seeing," offered Betty.

"Of course I will!"

Betty sat shaking her head in disbelief. "I can't believe this!" Betty gave her friend a gentle pat on the back for comfort. "Irene, I think this is enough for today. Why don't we go for lunch? I do need a few glasses of wine!"

## Chapter 5

# STELLA

"**A table for two, please.** A quiet area if possible, thank you!" Betty requested with authority as if she visited the restaurant daily. She not only looked important and wealthy; she sounded that way too. Irene was more reserved, fearful of doing wrong, and calculating.

"This way," the host led them to a small corner table.

"Thank you, this is perfect," responded Irene.

The hostess began her presentation, "Our specials today are basil tomato soup and the BLT." She handed out the menus, poured the water, and left.

Betty reached out to Irene. "Do you think we should give Stella a call and see if she could meet us? You cannot keep her in the dark about this, Irene. She is a dear friend, and she can be helpful! Stella is rough around the edges, but her heart is made of gold."

"I've been wanting to, but humiliation has kept me away from friends until today, Betty," confessed Irene. "I feel foolish being scammed more than once, and I am not a stupe! But what I did reflects that word—which makes my life pretty messed up at the moment. I failed but I don't want to fail Ricco too."

"No, you have not failed, Irene! We are going to get to the bottom of your gut feelings about Ricco, then we will work at getting your money back and do a worthy printing for *Quiet Fear*. The first step is not to spend one dollar more until Stella, and I, check this publishing company out," Betty stated sternly.

"I am grateful for any help you offer," agreed Irene, "but I am going to need support and a semi-truck full of encouragement. Once I feel I am back to owning my life again, I will have the strength to rebound on all levels. It's getting started on the right path that is so darn tough!"

"That is why we need Stella. If anyone can put someone back on track, it's her!" Betty giggled.

Irene chuckled too. "It won't hurt. Give her a call!"

**Stella was different from Betty and Irene.** She was a tough ex-military and said what she felt with little filter. Betty was always well-dressed, even when she went to bed. Irene dressed casually and comfortably, but when she had to, she could clean up to meet any competition. Whereas Stella stayed focused on the color black, the fabrics leather and lace, and regardless of how she wore it, she always drew attention. When all three were together, there had to be wonderment as to how three such unique people could be close friends, but they were.

Stella answered Betty's phone call. "It's me. What's up?" she asked Betty.

"Irene and I are having lunch at our usual spot. We began discussing a particular subject, and we're wondering if you could join us. We would like to have your input," informed Betty.

"It's a perfect day to meet. Blizzard and I were bored silly, and I have a few weeks off. I will get ready and be there in about twenty," answered Stella.

"Wonderful! We can't wait to see you! We are in the back corner," confirmed Betty.

"Soon! Thank you." And with that, Stella hung up.

"It sounds like Stella is coming and bringing Blizzard too." Irene paused. "Do they allow dogs in here? I have never seen one."

"They don't allow dogs, but Stella pays no attention to that law. Blizzard isn't a dog. Blizzard is some Greek mythological creature that appears to be a dog but is a princess of some faraway land." Betty cracked herself up thinking of Blizzard as a Greek goddess.

Irene joined in the laughter. "Should we order a glass of wine as we wait?"

"What a nice thought! Yes, we should do that. I'll try to get someone's attention to order."

Sitting in their quiet corner, Betty and Irene became lost in their wine sipping and storytelling as they waited for Stella.

"When she gets here," mentioned Betty, "she will scan the entire room in a minute and be able to tell you where the bar is, the bathrooms are, exits, creepy people she does not want to encounter, and where her friends are," Betty informed Irene. "Speaking of our pretty tall devil, she has arrived!" Betty spotted Stella's tangled white mess of hair and smiled at Irene while stating a warning, "She's here! Be prepared!"

Irene gave a heads-up and responded, "I wish I could be a little bug and live in that head of hair! Stella is full of surprises and adventure. I hope she never changes—she is everyone's hero."

"She sure is! And she's loved just the way she is!" added Betty as her facial expressions exhibited worry. "She has Blizzard…let the fireworks begin!"

"And they will!" Irene laughed. "That must be what she has begun to argue about with the host. I can see Blizzard's little white head too. So darn cute!"

Stella hovered over the host. "Please allow me to explain. Blizzard is a well-trained service dog. I have her in this cute, stylish doggie carrying case that doubles as my purse. She weighs five pounds, has no teeth, and cannot bark. Jesus, son of Mary, I cannot leave her in the car! Would you leave your two-legged child in the car alone on a chilly day like today? I do not think so, and no way in hell will I leave my little four-legged furry child in the car either!"

Stella lifted the carrying case up to her face and gave Blizzard a comforting pat and kiss on the head.

The host tried to respond, but Stella would not stop long enough for her to do so.

"You know that is illegal, whether they have two legs or four legs, if they die in a locked car, you are going to jail. It is that simple. Now, if you would please excuse me, I see that my party is waiting." Stella flung the carrying case strap over her shoulder. Blizzard stared at the host and showed off her throaty growl.

Heads turned as Stella walked tall and confident across the dining room. Stella was six feet tall and built like a person who knows the gym very well. Her legs were as long as Betty was tall. She had high cheekbones, a chiseled nose, full lips, and a wild head of dyed white hair. Even with her natural height, Stella loved wearing heels. On this day, she displayed a three-inch wooden heel on an ankle height set of black boots. Stella's outfit always had a weapon of sorts, just in case.

She wore a black sports bra with a sheer black tank over it. Skintight black yoga pants, with a meshing going up on the side of each leg. She loved to show off her body, and she had one to do so! Her silver arrow earrings dangled about three inches below her earlobe and the three necklaces fell perfectly over her neck and chest area. One a choker, the other a dainty thin chain of silver with a small "S" right in the middle; and the last one, a large white opal, which laid about an inch above her cleavage.

"There you are! My two most favorite people!" She approached Irene first and then moved to Betty, giving them both a kiss on each cheek. "It's been too long!" she said to both. Her joy spread throughout the room as she settled herself in at the table. "I am so happy you called. The day was stifling for Blizzard and me. No excitement at all! Then the phone rang—Betty, that was perfect timing!" She rested Blizzard's carrying case on the empty chair and opened the top for the tiny Maltese-poodle to stick her head out. "What are you gals, ordering?" She looked up for a menu when a man approached, dressed in a sport coat and brown trousers.

On his lapel, he wore a badge that said "Manager."

"Oh, shit!" whispered Stella.

"Good afternoon, ladies. My name is David Spence, and I am the manager. I was informed that you have brought a dog into the restaurant. Is that correct?"

This was going to be Stella's fight. Irene and Betty refilled their wine glasses and sat back to watch the show.

"Are you blind? This right here is a dog." Stella pointed to Blizzard. "You can see she is not going to bother anyone. She will be a better customer than the spoiled brats you have screaming and throwing food right behind the hostess's desk. Not a good look for business, don't you think? Maybe they should have them caged, like mine is."

Irene's eyes were bigger than usual as she looked over at Betty. Betty had a little smirk on her face as she obviously was enjoying the scene.

"Ma'am, I will call the police. Your dog cannot be in the restaurant. It is a law."

"First, Mr. Manager, my name is Stella, not 'ma'am.' Second, this is Blizzard." She then reached into the carrying case, pulled out her black, studded wallet, opened it, and pulled out a card the size of a driver's license. Then she stood up to face off her enemy, who now faced Stella at the level of her breasts. "Are you looking at my opal or my breasts?" Stella asked. "Because you should be looking at this card here!" The manager became voiceless.

But Stella's voice remained firm and in full gear. She continued to hammer the manager: "You know you should always ask if the dog is a licensed service dog before you begin your speech about the law." She held up the license, but the manager's eyes had a difficult time leaving where they were. "Hey, this is what you are to be looking at." She held the card about half of a foot from his face. "I should report you to upper management for sexually assaulting me."

"Umm, no, ma'am, I mean, Stella. I see that the dog, I mean Blizzard, is a service dog. I am dreadfully sorry to have caused you stress. All three of you enjoy a free lunch! What do you say?" He was pathetically excited.

Stella sat gracefully and placed the card back into her wallet. "Thank you. That is the least you could do. For starters, you can send another bottle of wine to the table." Blizzard was staring the manager in the eyes, giving him a long drawn-out deep growl. "Now, now, Blizzard. The man is not going to hurt me, but you feel his bad juju, don't you?" Stella patted Blizzard's head as she looked cruelly at the manager who was scuttling away.

"No wonder why he has the day manager job!" huffed Stella.

"That was quite the performance. Have you ever tried for a role in the theater?" asked Betty jokingly.

"Oh, hell no! Me? Acting? That would be a nightmare," Stella defended herself.

"Did you not just do a performance?" inquired Irene.

Stella looked confused. "No, that wasn't a performance. That was me, being me. I can't stand when people tell me to take Blizzard out of their business, and they have not inquired if she could possibly have the right to be there. Enough of that—what are you two chatting about?"

Betty and Irene brought Stella up to date about the scams. Irene explained her feelings about Ricco being in a scam camp and needing help.

Stella sat quietly, taking in every word and expression on their faces. She only began to speak when they were both finished. And only then did she respond. Slowly and with purpose, Stella advised, "Girls, this publishing charade must come to an end…now!" her voice filled with authority.

In defense, Irene looked at Stella and said, "How do I do that without feeling guilt about Ricco? You know I cannot let that go."

"Irene, I am not suggesting you don't do *anything*," responded Stella. "I agree with you. We should at least see if there is any truth to him being in one of those filthy labor camps. But here is what I think we should do."

Betty and Irene leaned in toward Stella in anticipation.

Stella continued, "We need to plan a trip!" she exclaimed.

"Where to? We have not a clue where he is!" an anxious Betty responded as she sat back in her chair.

"Betty dear"—Stella placed her hand on top of Betty's in a calming manner—"that is exactly what we need to find out. We will gather his emails and read through them for clues. I am good at that! The military taught me how to locate missing…missing…missing equipment and such." Stella caught herself being too loose with her lips. Her military life was private and rarely spoken about.

Irene looked carefully at Stella. Then Betty. Then Blizzard. "I need to calm down and relax. Can we talk about this tomorrow? I mean, this is not a little spring fling vacation about which we are talking."

"A wonderful idea," a relieved Betty agreed. "Besides, you look exhausted, Irene."

"I know, I am. Does tomorrow work for you, Stella?"

"It does! I am going to find the monster who holds these kids as prisoners so they can scam people, making the monsters rich to supply weapons to their army and make human trafficking affordable for their labor! I would like to—"

Betty interrupted, fearing what was going to come out of Stella's angry loud voice, creating more trouble. "Stella, I understand that you want to punish these thugs, but let's not take it that far…at least for now. Okay?"

Stella was grateful for Betty. Betty could press a wrinkle out of anything! She sat back, relaxed, and felt more positive. "You are right, Betty, I am jumping the gun about this. We will continue tomorrow and see where it goes from there. And I must add that the soup and sandwich was superb, as well as the extra bottle of wine!"

Betty smiled. "You're a stinker, Stella! Now let's throw in a decent tip for our waitress."

They all reached into their wallets. Stella threw out a twenty, Betty followed, and Irene laid down a ten. "Is that enough?" she asked.

"It's perfect, Irene," replied Stella.

"To both of you, thank you," added Irene. "You have made me laugh, cry, and fill a hole of loneliness. I look forward to tomorrow. Does three o'clock work? If we need to go into the early evening, we can order take out from that tasty Korean restaurant a block away from me."

"I'm in," said Stella, getting Blizzard ready to carry.

"All good for me!" answered Betty, fussing over a wrinkle in her linen pants.

Irene felt her friend's sincere concern and willingness to work with her. They were there for one another when times were rough and when times were happy. However, this might be the first time things could become dangerous."

## Chapter 6

# NOWHERE MAN

**Ricco lost consciousness after he pressed the send button.** Every laborer in the room was too frightened to leave their station and help him. Fifteen minutes later, two soldiers entered the workroom and headed directly to Ricco's station. One soldier grabbed his arms while the other grabbed his feet. They carried him out without one spoken word. The laborers didn't stop, not for a second, as they stayed controlled by fear and glued to their dutiful work.

The soldiers carried Ricco to his room and dropped him onto his mattress, which he had covered with large fallen leaves he picked up from the ground on one of his breaks. He hid them in his jumpsuit, and when he returned to his room, he laid them on top of the filthy so-called mattress. The barrier gave him a feeling of separation from the others that had laid there before him. It released a miniscule of anxiety, helping him find some peace in his life, but not today, for today he had no feelings.

Being moved and then dropped increased the intensity of the throbbing pain in his head. His vision still blurred. He was unable to eat or drink. Shortly, he drifted back into his coma-like sleep.

Left there to die.

## Chapter 7

# GROUND ZERO

**Irene's table was ground zero for the next few days.** She added a leaf to make their space roomier and to handle sorting the emails. Scattered on the table were highlighters, notebooks, pencils, scissors, sticky notes, and tabs. It reflected Irene's teaching skills— gathering the materials—before beginning a project.

She also brewed fresh ground coffee and had a teapot filled with hot water. She set out raw sugar and cream. Her froth machine was plugged in and ready to go. A glass pitcher of ice water was set out on the counter along with coffee mugs, teacups, and water glasses. Next to the drinks, there were snacks: peanuts, walnuts, cheese squares, crackers, popcorn, pretzels, chocolate-flavored hummus, grapes, strawberries, bananas, and apples.

The intercom from the lobby buzzed. Irene anxiously went to answer it. She looked through the door's peephole and saw Stella and Betty waving at her. She laughed to herself and opened the door.

Stella entered first, dispersing an immense amount of energy. "Good morning, you international spy! Are you ready to investigate?" She gave Irene a smothering tight hug.

Betty followed. "We both gave Handsome Harry a tough time. He loves the attention, and we enjoy giving it to him! I also brought a huge map of the continents." She handed it to Irene. "Are you up for this?"

"Of course I am! My gut tells me this is a good start!" replied Irene. "How are *you* feeling, Betty?"

"I haven't been this excited about anything since my divorce!" she replied.

Irene looked at Stella, who was in the kitchen, checking out the display of drinks and finger foods. She was about to ask Stella the same question, but Stella beat her to the question.

"Where's the wine?" she asked, worrisome.

"Oh, I did not forget that! When we are almost done, I have two bottles chilling," Irene slyly replied. She didn't ask Stella how she felt about looking for Ricco because it was easy to see that Stella was in her element…rescuing people who needed to be rescued.

Stella moved to the table to check out the organized array of supplies. "Is this a homeschooling class?" she threw out with a chuckle.

Betty laughed at the thought of Irene teaching them. "I sure hope not!" she answered. "I don't think Irene has the patience to teach us, Stella."

"Oh, hell no! I would be sent to the couch immediately!" Stella reinforced Betty's idea.

Irene was smiling, but she was also ready to get going. "Okay, girls, I have a folder for each of you." She handed them out. "You can open them, and you will see emails I have received from Ricco. The oldest is on the left, and the newest is on the right."

"Damn, you're organized!" snapped Stella.

"Can I hang up the map before we begin?" inquired Betty.

"Absolutely," answered Irene. "Here, let me help you. We can hang it over this picture on the wall. I will get my double-sided tape."

She returned with a roll of clear, double-sided tape, and together, she and Irene hung the map while Stella was already skimming through the emails.

"Let's begin," Stella said, ready to dive in. "Do you all have a copy of the email that begins with 'It is always sunny…?'"

Betty and Irene responded in unison, "Yes!"

"Good!" continued Stella. "Grab a highlighter and a notebook. We will each read it to ourselves and highlight any words or phrases that you believe do not belong in a business letter. Don't worry about being right or wrong. Usually, your first impression is your most truthful. Then in your notebook, write the words and phrases down. Got it?"

"Got it!" Betty shot back quickly and seriously. She was always a good follow-the-directions student.

"We shouldn't stress over the accuracy," a dubious Irene stated as she was the student that needed reassurance and clarity.

"That is correct. Read it, highlight, record. Keep it simple. We will go over the lists later when we get into serious thinking, okay, Irene?" confirmed Stella.

*Email #1*

Hello Irene,

Where I am it is always sunny in the mornings, and I hope the sun is shining on Chicago too! It is a pleasure to have you on my client list, and I always look forward to the days we are working together.

Answering your question on how we communicate, I can tell you that we operate under a unique protocol—we do not share phone numbers due to the absence of a recording service. Without that, we would enter a realm of "he said, she said." Our communication is solely through our computers and email. Emails can be kept and referred back to. Rest assured, I am extensively trained to communicate through this setup, and I will stay in close contact with you to answer any questions.

The boss says that if he allowed me to talk on the phone, I would never get my work done, and that is bad for business. There is no waste of time at this bullpen. I work a set number of hours and talking needlessly would negatively affect my work. The rule is, "absolutely no socializing." But to be honest, I would love to socialize with you more as we share many common thoughts on various subjects!

Should you need clarification from an email, contact me immediately, and I promise to have an answer for you within the day. It is my job to be here for you as well as my other customers to answer questions, inform you on marketing promotions, and provide you with options for the printing of your story.

As always, it is a pleasure collaborating with you. Stay vigilant.

Sincerely,
Ricco Smith

**Ten minutes of silent reading** and scratching down notes went by quickly. Stella began to gather their responses. "Okay, stop here, and let's see what we have. Betty, you are first."

"From my first impression I chose the words *bullpen*, *vigilant*, and the phrase 'absolutely no socializing.'"

"Add those words to your list if they aren't already on it," directed Stella. "Irene?"

"I had *bullpen* and *vigilant*, added *no socializing*."

"Great! Thank you, Irene, and Betty." Stella continued, "I had all three and the phrase that stated, 'We do not share phone numbers due to the absence of a recording service.' Would you please add that to your list? Now move onto the next email.

*Email #2*

Hello Irene,

Hope you are well and enjoying your day. I am looking forward to retirement, and I just began my career!

Have you had a chance to verify the cover I sent yesterday? I am anticipating your input so we can move forward with its printing. It is one I see in my mind. Let me know if it is a green light. The blues reflect many scenes from the book, and your name looks sophisticated!

Nothing like the building I work in! It needs a complete workover. Being by the sea, the saltwater ages everything quicker. Hope that doesn't happen to me!

We need to keep track of time. You mentioned that you wanted to release your book no later than May. We may be cutting it close. I am productively busy with other authors who are taking advantage of our reasonable rates for a press release in Germany. We are waiting to hear your thoughts about that.

Enjoy spring in Chicago. It is extremely hot and humid here, and there is no air conditioning! A cool lake breeze would feel like heaven!

Sincerely,
Ricco Smith

"**Okay, here we go again,** looking for words or phrases that may or may not be clue words from Ricco to Irene."

They worked quietly, and if one finished, they would softly walk to the kitchen for a snack or a drink and then return to the table.

Stella took the lead. "Irene, did you find any word clues?"

"I sure did! *Extremely hot, no later than May, no air-conditioning, humid, saltwater, sea,* and *workover.*"

Stella then asked Betty, "How about you, Betty? Anything to add?"

Betty enthusiastically replied, "The only other words I had were 'need to keep track of time,' that's it!"

Stella remarked, "Interesting! I also chose *shades of blue*, *retirement*, and *aging quicker*. Ricco appears to be feeling old and tired, like a rusty hinge. Are we ready for number 3?" Both girls nodded in agreement.

*Email #3*

> Hi Irene,
>
> Attached is the final editing of the cover we agreed upon. Please review it for grammatical and spacing errors. Follow the correction worksheet I have sent to your email and return it to me when completed. I will then transfer the corrections for a final approval.
>
> Meanwhile, I will move forward editing the interior. Thank you for having worked on this as you drafted. Hopefully, it will move smoothly and without delay. Stay safe.
>
> Sincerely,
> Ricco Smith

**Once again, the room filled with silence,** but not for as long.

"This short email clearly states that he is working alone. There are no references toward a different department. It is you and him, Irene," Stella firmly stated.

"Yes, I agree. This is when I also confirmed my thinking that this poor young man is on his own, and because he is, I do not believe any of these books are printed in America. The company, if it exists, is overseas," added Irene.

Betty agreed, adding, "Something smells fishy in this email because a publishing company does not work in this manner. They have fulfillment centers that set up the printing format—artists for cover designs, editors for editing, and so forth. The lead representative is to see that all steps be done in a timely manner, and to sell their packages offering marketing ideas, but they do not do it themselves."

"So what words do you feel we should write down?" asked Stella.

"I will move forward with editing. I will move forward with the interior, I will transfer…does that work for everyone?" responded Irene.

"Works for me," replied Stella and Betty.

"Great!" complimented Stella. "Here is the last one for today. Then we will put our list together and see what it gives us. Ready?"

Irene and Betty were already reading.

*Email #4*

Hello Irene,

I hope this email finds you well and enjoying spring in Chicago. In my youth, I visited the "Windy City." One day, I may return, as it has fond memories of youth.

Forgive me for such a brief note; however, I have fallen ill and have not been well enough to accomplish my work duties. The company is in a remote and poor area with no available hospital or doctor and the jungle-like heat with no fans does not offer a pleasant place for recovery.

While I am healing, please give thought to the marketing plan for the book fair in Germany or/and London. Trust me. These book fairs are great for exposure as they attract thousands of people from all over the world. We will discuss the cost and payments at a later date.

Best regards,
Ricco Smythe

"**Immediately, I felt a different tone** in this email. It sounds like he is reminiscing, and then he tells Irene he is sickly. That is scary. Is he dying? Remember Stella picking up the idea that he was feeling 'old and tired, ready to retire'? That deeply concerns me! Other words I picked up were 'in my youth I visited the "Windy City," fallen ill, remote, and poor area…no doctors or hospitals, no fans, jungle-like heat.' Stress from not being able to work as he is expected to. I am worried about him!" Betty looked over at Irene. "No wonder why you are concerned!"

"All that is true, Betty," remarked Stella.

Irene added, "I have one more word I would like to add. He signed his last name as Smythe. I think that is his real last name, and being ill, he did not catch it."

"Wow! That is an important find! The more eyes we have on these emails, the better! Clever work, Irene." Stella was pumped with enthusiasm. "Now let's make one thorough list. Do you have a roll of wrapping paper and a black Sharpie, Irene?"

"I do! Just a minute." Irene ran to the spare bedroom closet, took out a roll of Christmas paper, then opened the desk drawer and grabbed three Sharpies. "Here," she said, laying them on the table.

"Thanks, I will cut off a long strip and tape it on the wall. I do not think the Sharpie will bleed through," commented Stella as she observed the paper.

"If it does," said Irene, "I will paint the wall. No worries." The list read…

| | | |
|---|---|---|
| bullpen | vigilant | workover |
| incredibly hot | no phones | no later than May |
| no air conditioning | no answering service | tracking time |
| humid | no socializing | shades of blue |
| saltwater | retirement | ill |
| sea | youth | Chicago |
| reminiscing | sickly | remote |
| poor | jungle-like | Smythe |
| working alone | overseas | alone |

The three friends stared at the words, looking for connections. The room was still, except for the hum of the refrigerator and the furnace fan turning on and off.

"Any thoughts you want to share? Irene? Betty?" asked Stella.

Betty replied, "He is in a bullpen. He did not refer to his place of work as an office, room, or building. He specifically said 'bullpen.' Bullpen is another word for camp. And that bullpen is hot with few fans, maybe none."

Irene nodded in agreement. "The camp, or bullpen, is in a location that is hot, humid, remote, jungle-like, poor, no phones. Those words tell me he is in a jungle, not America. It could be an Asian country, South America, Africa, India, Australia. We need more clues."

Stella agreed, "You're right. He's ill, in a camp, working his fingers off daily, vigilant, trying to be safe, or we need to be safe, not allowed to socialize, something regarding time and the month of May, he traveled to America, and his last name could be Smythe. Awesome! Let's take a break and move around. Maybe have something to drink… Does that sound good?"

Betty had one more question: "Stella, where is Blizzard? I just now realized she is not with us!"

Stella chuckled. "We were really concentrating! Blizzard is with my neighbor who adores her because she can bark and growl at anybody or anything she wants to when they are together. Plus, my neighbor loves to take Blizzard to the doggie spa. She will have videos for us to watch, and they are always a good laugh! I actually think that Blizzard's spa is better than mine! A spa day sounds good right about now, doesn't it?"

"It sure does! I haven't been to one for over a year. I did go every six weeks until the scamming took place. Now I need to plan my monthly budget carefully," added Irene.

Betty listened empathetically to Irene. She considered calling Russ to ask if he could help Irene financially for three months but rethought the idea. Irene might see it as none of her business, and it could strain their friendship. Betty decided against offering her own funds, thinking Irene wouldn't accept that kind of help. Stella's loud voice cut through the air and brought her back to the moment.

"Listen up!" Stella ordered as if she was in charge of an entire unit of soldiers. "I have friends that I served with, and I would like to show them the emails and the list to see what they say. Do you mind, Irene?"

"No, not at all. It would be helpful as I have no idea where to begin. I feel we need more clues. Especially about Ricco…his real first name and a country would be nice!"

Stella raised her glass of water. "Agree. He sounds more desperate, so maybe that will come soon. Keep us updated! Salute to a job well done!"

All joined in the toast and then Stella put her glass down.

"Wait! We forgot to do something extremely important!"

"What could that possibly be?" a concerned Irene asked.

Very slowly, Stella said, "The w-i-n-e!"

Irene laughed. "We've been thinking so hard that I totally forgot! I can fix that. Hold on for a few minutes!" Irene grabbed a wine bottle from the freezer and three glasses.

They toasted again, this time with wine.

Irene was physically present but emotionally she felt every minute of every day was a nightmare for Ricco. She wanted everything to move faster for his survival. Without sleep and the proper amount of food and water, getting ill was a realistic fear. She shuddered at the thought of *his* imprisonment.

## Chapter 8

# MAYA

**In the early morning hours,** Ricco felt a gentle hand trying to awaken him. He believed he was dreaming about his mother; he groaned and reached out for her hand. But the voice he heard was not that of his mother, but an unfamiliar voice of a woman. With much effort, he slowly pushed open his eyes.

An Asian woman near his age was leaning over him. Her long jet-black hair fell over her shoulders and down to her waist. Her eyes were like his, dark, and almond-shaped. Her nose, small and symmetrically pleasant, led him to her mouth. Her full lips moved with words that he could not hear. She dressed in camouflaged fatigues. Was she a foe or a friend?

She lifted Ricco's head and helped him drink from a water bottle. The cold, wet sensation was awakening and clearing. His foggy vision became clearer.

"That is a nasty cut on your head. I will need to treat it with antibiotics and clean bandages. My name is Maya. I am a nurse that was taken, much like you were. They allow me to help certain laborers. You are lucky that they put you on that list. Now, I am going to lift your neck up and slip this clean towel under it. Next, I am going to give you a shot of antibiotics. Do you have an allergy to any?"

Ricco scratched out a raspy "No."

"That is good! We have limited supplies. It will be painful, but I am going to lift your head up to clean the wound. Please do not scream! If you do, I must leave. Here is a rolled-up towel that you can bite down on. Do you understand? First the wound cleaning, then the shot."

"Maya?" Ricco's gritty voice called her name.

"Yes, Maya," she answered promptly.

"Are you…my angel?" he asked.

Maya grinned softly. "I could be! We will see how you feel about that after I clean you up!"

She went behind him and lifted his neck with one hand while slowly dripping clean water onto the wound with the other. Next, she took strips of white cloth and dabbed the dirt off. Then more water until she felt the wound looked clean and free of pus.

"You are doing great. I know this hurts, but the pain will lessen quickly. One day off in the labor room, and you will be ready to return. That is the order from the Bossman.

Now, bite down because I am going to put an ointment on your cut that I made. It will kill germs and take down the swelling, but it stings like a bee. Ready?"

Ricco nodded yes, closed his eyes tightly, and bit down on the rolled towel.

Maya quickly applied the tincture.

Never in his life had he experienced such intense pain. He could not help but scream as loud as he could on the inside. His entire body was wet with perspiration. He wanted to pull her hands away, but the intense pain lessened quickly, just as she said. The pain that stayed was tolerable. He spit the towel out. "Done?" he hopefully asked.

"I am wrapping it up and I will leave the bandage on. Tomorrow night I will return and put on a new one. Here, drink the rest of the water. I also brought you something to eat." She reached into a front pocket and pulled out two small bags of nuts and a banana.

"Will you get in trouble?" Ricco asked, his voice tinged with worry.

Maya smiled gently. "No, they have seen how I treat my patients. If I do anything beyond what is approved, then yes, I will receive punishment. I must have their permission for each patient. They want you back to work as soon as possible. You must heal. Think that way. You do not want to be eliminated. Do you understand, Ricco?"

"Yes, I do, and thank you, Maya."

She held his hand a little longer, a touch strong and comforting for both.

"I must go now. You have to eat, drink, and sleep. I will see you tomorrow."

She helped him up to a sitting position, smiled, and left as quietly as she came in, locking his door behind her.

**The only window in his room** was barred and covered with heavy black material. However, the material was not wide enough to cover the entire window, which allowed the morning sun to peek through the tiny slits on the sides. It awakened Ricco, and he appreciated knowing he was facing east and could keep track of each day and night.

Slowly, with sounds of painful straining, he pulled himself up into a sitting position. He felt the bandage wrapped around his head. "It wasn't a dream!" he said to himself. He attempted to stand, but his legs were wobbly. He looked around the dungeon-like room and noticed a bottle of water on the floor. He picked it up and took a few big gulps. Then he remembered the banana and protein bars.

He found them under the large leaves on his bed. Starving, he quickly peeled back the crinkly paper of the bar, and in two bites, it was gone. He grew angry with himself. Eating too fast was foolish. Not only could it give him stomach pains, but he also did not take time to enjoy it! He would not make that mistake with the second one.

Looking at the sunshine, he tried to remember Maya's face. She had petite features and a soft voice. Her touch was mystic. Wherever she placed her hands, there was heat and a feeling of wholeness. Ricco shook his head slowly, trying to get the images of the night to go away. For over a year, he thought only of terrible things the soldiers could do to him: of how hungry he was, the stench of all the laborers as they only showered at the end of the week, the smell of sewage in the halls, the lack of fresh air and water. There was nothing good to vision or dream of. Not until now. Maya filled his thoughts with a new joyous feeling of excitement. He let himself fall asleep to help time pass and his body to heal.

**Once again in the early morning hours** Maya entered Ricco's room quietly, locking the door behind her. The day had been incredibly hot and humid. The smell in Ricco's room held the scent of illness and injury. Old blood and sweat. She looked at the window; it was permanently closed. She took a strip of the rags, dabbed some alcohol on it, and waved it around the room hoping it would offer some disinfectant properties. Then she went to Ricco.

The banana and granola bars were eaten and the water bottle empty. "Good, very good," she said to herself. She leaned down and felt his forehead. "He is too warm. Infection must have set in."

"Ricco!" she gently called for him to awaken. "Ricco, time to wake up. It is Maya."

Slowly, Ricco responded, "Maya, it's good to see you." Ricco reached out for her hand. She allowed him to hold it. The sensation she felt was comforting. She had taken a liking to Ricco. Something she was forbidden to do…never was she to feel emotions.

"You have a fever, Ricco," she informed him. "Which means there is an infection setting in somewhere, and you are fighting it. It is a good thing that I gave you the shot when I did. I cannot give you another until next week, but I have herbs that I hope will help. Keep fighting. Do not let your body take over your mind."

"Those are wise words. On the happier side, my head feels better. I can sleep more because the pain has lessened. I sat up by myself for the first time today. Tomorrow I will stand." Ricco lowered his head. "I forgot. I must return to work tomorrow."

Maya stroked his shoulder-length hair out of his eyes. "I will do everything I can to try to get him to give you more rest. Three days?"

"You would do that for me?" he asked.

"Of course I would. You are fighting for your life right now. It is not a time to do an experiment on how strong or weak you may be."

He could hear the anger she held toward the Bossman. "Does he hurt you?"

"Not physically, not yet, but emotionally, he is a beast! He knows a great deal about the human body. I think he is British or Australian, maybe even American. He covers himself, so it is hard to say what he looks like, and he does not allow you to look at him."

"I saw that behavior from him too. He stood just a little behind me, and I was not allowed to turn my head. I had to stare at a symbol on the wall."

"One like this?" She rolled up her sleeve and exposed her forearm.

Ricco's eyes widened. "Yes! Yes, that is the same symbol! Are you one of them?"

"No! Absolutely not! But he wants the patients to believe I am. I woke up with it after they had taken me."

"What does it mean?"

"To them it means 'war against the rich.' It's a diamond with a parallelogram running through it. I think they made it simple so they can easily tattoo it on a person."

"And their purpose is to steal from those that have, but some do not have as much as they think. Many of my clients are elderly and others are just starting out. I have not had any wealthy people, like millionaires. Do you know what they do with it? The money?"

"No. If they are talking about business and I am near, they stop. I know only what I can see and nothing from what I hear."

"Where do you stay?"

"I stay with the militia. It is frightening, but the conditions are more agreeable." She looked over Ricco's dungeon. "We have better beds and linens and towels. We shower every other day. We have windows and freedom to move about the complex."

"Do they feed you well?"

"Yes, they do. I am so sorry to tell you these things. Only a few hundred feet away is a building that is maintained with supplies. And here you live in unhealthy conditions, but it is even worse for the field workers." Maya lowered her head in shame.

"There are different kinds of prisoners?"

"Yes, you are a laborer in technology. That has given you a better life. The laborers of the fields and property have it the worst. And those he allows in his complex, like me, have more comfort."

"Has anyone escaped?"

"Yes, but most are hunted down and killed. A few have made it out of Thailand, but the families had some kind of tie with the government, and there was a ransom."

"I am in Thailand!" Ricco was excited to be learning about his surroundings. He took everything in like a sponge and filed it in his "forever" files.

Maya placed her hand over her mouth. "I am not to tell anyone our location!" Her eyes flashed with fear. "I should be treating you and leaving." She began to unwrap his bandage.

Ricco carefully placed his hand on her arm. "You need not worry about me speaking to anyone about our conversations. I wouldn't put you in harm's way."

"Stay still as I unwrap the bandage." Maya carefully removed the white cloth and then observed his cut. "You should have had stitches, but it is too late now—it will heal as it is. There is no more odor, which means you're healing. I will treat it with my tincture again. Here is the rolled towel for you to bite down on."

Ricco took the towel. "On the count of three, I will bite down."

Maya began counting, "One, two, three!" She placed the soaked cloth on the wound with more pressure than the night before. "There," she said, showing a good feeling about the treatment. "This time, I was able to get deeper into the cut. I hope it will kill any infection that may be hiding. I believe that is why you have a fever."

She began to wrap a clean bandage around his head. "I will give you medication for pain." She went to her medical bag and returned with another bottle of water, protein bars, and the medicine.

"Here, swallow these. They will make you sleepy, but that is good."

Ricco tossed the pills into his mouth, took the water, and began gulping it down.

"Hey!" Maya scolded him. "It is not good to drink that fast. Take it easy. It is the only bottle I was able to spare! You will get another in the morning, right?"

His face was flushed, feeling embarrassed. "Yes, I get three bottles a day. I do not know why I gulped it like that! I am sorry."

"I am sorry that I cannot bring you more of what you need, and that is water. You have one more day and night of my care, and then you will have to go back to work. If you were fully hydrated, you would be stronger. Let me think on that thought." Maya was busy putting her med bag back together.

"Do you have to leave?" asked Ricco. "Can you stay five more minutes?" He wished she could stay the night, to lay next to him and feel her warmth, her wisdom, and her beauty.

She looked at her watch. "Five, that's it!" She smiled. Not any kind of smile, but a smile that was pure happiness. "I can give you a foot rub. That, too, is healing."

That was not what Ricco had in mind. His feet were a mess, and he had not showered in over a week. "No, no, no. Not my feet...why not my hands?"

Maya was already where she wanted to be, working on his pressure points to all major organs in his body. "Do not worry! I have seen feet much worse than yours. In fact, your feet look healthy and strong. Start walking tomorrow."

"I thought foot massages would tickle." He shyly smiled.

"You're ticklish?" she inquired.

"I am embarrassed to admit that I am. This is the first foot rub I have had. It is relaxing."

"Take care of your feet, young Ricco! They are our roots."

"Maya, you are wise beyond your age. Can I ask you one more question before you leave?"

"Yes, one more."

"Is your real name Maya?"

She stopped massaging his foot and slid over to the edge of his mattress. She picked up his hand and held it in hers. "No, they took my name away. My real name is Amber."

Ricco squeezed her hand tighter. "Amber, the gemstone, it is a beautiful, exotic name."

"How about you? What is your real name?" she asked in return.

"It is Harris. I was named after my grandfather, Harrison. It means 'son of Harry.' Nothing else. No gemstone or great warrior, just 'son of Harry'!" He tried to carry through a laugh, but it was too painful.

Maya filled in the laughter he lost. "I like Harris. I will call you Harry if I get mad at you." They both shared another short chuckle. "It is time for me to go. I will see you tomorrow. Please be stronger!"

"I will dream of tomorrow. Thank you, my golden Amber!"

She kissed his cheek. "I will also dream of tomorrow."

As she walked out, Ricco did not see a prisoner; he saw beauty, hope, and kindness.

# Chapter 9

# GAFFER, DOG, AND EDGE

**Irene looked out over the waters of the Great Lake of Michigan.** "Dear Ricco! Often, when I look out over the lake, it appears to be cold and dangerous. I can't see its beauty. I see fear and darkness. That is what you must see every day. I wish you could hear me. I have friends that are going to look into who you are and where you are. Hold on! We will come for you!" Irene pulled her sweater tightly across her body and began walking back to her apartment.

**Meanwhile, Stella met her team of friends** at the coffee shop on base. It was a safe haven for her kind. There was Dog, who spent his off-time training service dogs. Not married. No children. Stocky and strong. A fan of sports.

Edge, who was always on edge and had eyes like a fly. Tall, flexible, and athletic. Liked dating girls but had no interest to commit.

Lastly, there was Gaffer, an informal British term for "boss." He was the anchor of the group and played the part well as he rarely smiled, never laughed, and had too many dendrites in his brain. He was extremely conscientious and a recluse due to his work. He never mentioned family and remained single, even though he was eye candy.

Stella was the all-around go-to person. Fearless and skilled in many areas. She took no offense from anyone, as confidence was her middle name. She was definitely someone you would want on your team. Trusted and true. Together, the four had accomplished many dangerous, off-the-grid operations.

They were similar to mercenaries, funded by some of the richest people in the world, but their code was the complete opposite. They weren't in the business of rescuing people for money. Money was an acceptable donation to their labor, but they all shared one strong badge of honor, which was… do what is morally right.

"Thanks, guys, for meeting me today," a grateful Stella addressed her male friends.

"Yeah, well, get on with it. What is this about?" asked an ornery Edge.

"It is about helping two of my friends—one is being scammed and believes it is from a labor scam camp, and the other is helping her put the situation together." Stella offered the information in one swift sentence.

Gaffer shook his head. "No, no, no! Civilians doing espionage? Too dangerous, and it never ends well. Come on, Stella, you are our common-sense hero! How could you fall into this?"

Stella's body changed from relaxed to defiant in a minute. She leaned toward Gaffer, looking directly into his gorgeous green eyes. "First, they are my closest civilian friends. Second, one is in trouble, and third, after reading the emails, I do believe she may be right, and that young boy needs help! Gaffer, hear me out! Please?"

"I will hear you out, and I will offer advice, but no way am I going into the jungle. Never again," Gaffer replied.

"That is fine…no jungle…noted! Dog, are you okay with this?" Stella asked.

"I am okay with hearing you out. I hate those f——ing frauds."

"What about you Edge?" Stella waited for a response, which was rare.

"Scam camp…I want to hear more," he replied.

Taking a deep breath and composing herself, Stella handed them the word list. "Take a minute to read these words and tell me what you think. That is all I am asking."

The team took more time than Stella, Irene, and Betty. When it involves life and death, every word carried weight.

| | | |
|---|---|---|
| bullpen | alone | absolutely no socializing |
| incredibly hot | no phones | no later than May |
| no air-conditioning | no answering service | tracking time |
| humid | no socializing | shades of blue |
| green light | youth | Chicago |
| reminiscing | sickly | remote |
| poor | jungle-like | Smythe |
| vigilant | | |
| overseas | | |

Gaffer began, "Where did this list come from?"

"It comes from the emails this young man sent to my friend, Irene. She has authored a book, and this man's company is supposedly going to print it. She thinks he is sending clues of his trouble. They gave worked together for approximately six months." Stella stayed connected to Gaffer's face.

"Here's what I see," offered a serious Gaffer. "These are most likely clues. An editor or publishing company would not refer to their workplace as a bullpen or camp. That is the most important clue so far. Then I felt working alone, and absolutely no socializing sounded restrictive because printing requires collaboration. Remote, jungle-like, and the weather descriptions sound like Thailand, Cambodia, Vietnam…or a country in Southeast Asia. Having said that, I think it would be dangerous to get involved. Stop all communications." Gaffer sat back, pleased with his input.

Stella moved on.

"What about you, Dog? I have been watching, and you keep going over the words. What is puzzling you?" asked Stella.

"I ask myself, what words are or could be normal in conversation with an editor? I think *incredibly hot, no air-conditioning, humid, green light, youth, reminiscing, sickly, no later than May, tracking time, shades of blue,* and *Chicago* are all words that could be used in a communication letter with someone he would be familiar with. However, what is the name Smythe? It is supposed to be Ricco R. Smith. And the words *bullpen, vigilant, working alone, overseas, jungle-like, no phones,* and no answering service—that's a big red flag. This is a business that wants to sell books but has no verbal communication? Very weird. That is it. Interesting."

Stella replied, "Smythe, we believe, is his last name. And because of his illness, we think he was tired and weak and did not realize the mistake. Edge, I can see you are dying to jump in here! What is your say?" asked Stella.

"I agree with Dog and Gaffer on their word interpretations, but I also think we should investigate these cyber scam camps. Search and rescue, that is what we're about—right?" He looked at each person sitting at the table.

"It's not going to hurt, and it does make my blood simmer." Dog chuckled. "Not boil, and definitely not a hard boil, just a nice slow simmer for now."

"Time for a vote." Stella stood up directing her partners. "Taking some time to check these camps out would be helpful. Are we all in?" She laid her hand in the center of the table. Dog slapped his over Stella's, saying, "In." Followed by Edge, doing the same. Then it was Gaffer's turn.

He looked at his crew. It was hard turning Stella down; she had saved several missions from going bad. This was a little favor that she asked in return. He remained quiet and in thought, until his hand lifted, and he slapped it on top of Edge's. "In," he said. There was a cheer of approval and drinks were ordered. They didn't need an excuse to celebrate their unity, but they grabbed it if it was there.

**After their drinks, Gaffer** called another meeting. "I have a few questions for you, Stella."

"Go for it. What do you want to know?" she replied.

"Does your friend get calls and invoices?" Gaffer inquired.

"No verbal communication. Only emails. And yes, she has received invoices," Stella answered directly.

"How is his writing? Legible, correct grammar, familiar with English?"

"It is perfect. Irene, my friend who is concerned about this young man, believes he studied literature in college and may have been involved with a real publishing company. He is exceptionally knowledgeable."

"Is Irene gullible?" Gaffer continued to drill.

"No more than the rest of us. She separated from her husband and feels ashamed, but I think it's a well-planned scam. She was a protester back in the day, so I don't see her as exceptionally vulnerable!"

Gaffer gave her one of his rare, charming half-smiles. "I will want the team to see the emails, invoices, contracts, any communication she has with him."

"What are you looking for, Gaffer?" asked Stella.

"Email addresses, document signing programs, finance companies on the invoices. Even her bank checks that show who and where they were sent. Large legitimate companies do not use unsafe free programs."

"I will get everything I can and drop it off at your office. Thank you, Gaffer! I won't forget this!"

Gaffer, not one to show his emotions, shooed her away with his hand.

"When should we meet again?" she asked, turning halfway around to face Gaffer.

"In about a week, maybe sooner. I will let you know." He paused then continued, "Stella, retirement will look good on you!"

"You think so?" She struck a playful pose.

Back to his unemotional self, he replied, "Okay, you're dismissed."

Stella turned around and began to walk out of the room and back to the bar, feeling his eyes on her every step. *Interesting*, she thought to herself.

## Chapter 10

# STELLA, IRENE, AND BETTY

**The next day, Stella called** Irene and told her the good news.

"That means we need to do some research too! I have been looking into the last name *Smythe*. It has a strong connection to England, so I called Betty. She swears she is related to the royal family and will do some research too. I plan to check the missing persons list, but we do not know where he comes from. What do you think, Stella?"

"My guess would be London. Don't ask me why, it's just a feeling. The team wants to meet with me in about a week. Can I come over and read more emails?"

"Do you want to do that now?" asked Irene.

"If I can bring Blizzard, and if you don't mind," replied Stella.

"Sure thing! Can I take Blizzard for a walk? And you can have my laptop. It is connected to the printer in the office/bedroom down the hallway that leads out of the kitchen if you want to print something. What time are you thinking?"

"In about ninety minutes," replied Stella.

"Perfect, I will see you and Blizzard then," remarked Irene.

Irene chuckled to herself. She knew that when Stella said ninety minutes, it would be ninety minutes. She plugged in her laptop to ensure it would be fully charged. Next, she checked the printer to make sure it was on and refilled the paper tray. The apartment was not super clean, but it was presentable. She picked up some shoes, put the dirty dishes in the dishwasher, and checked the fridge for wine and snacks. "This will not do. I have plenty of time to run down to the corner store and get a few things," she said to herself. "That corner grocer has saved my life more than once or twice!"

She wrapped herself in a shawl, slid into her sneakers, and headed down to the main door.

"I will be back soon, Harry," Irene called out as she passed him.

"Ms. Irene, you have been busy lately, coming, going, and having visitors. Is everything all right?" he asked.

"Yes, it is fine. We are working on a project together, Betty, Stella, and me and it is taking more time than we realized. Stella is coming over today. Keep your eyeballs in their sockets, Harry!" she laughed, knowing how smitten Harry was with Stella.

"I will try, ma'am!" he said, releasing a hearty laugh.

**Irene and Stella sat by the** kitchen island as Irene poured two cups of coffee. Stella opened the laptop and saw they had a new message from Ricco.

"Hey, Irene! Get over here. You have a message from Ricco!" she exclaimed excitedly.

"Oh my gosh! It has been a week! I was beginning to think he was dead."

"Dead! Irene, you think in strange ways! Come on, hurry, hurry, hurry!" urged Stella.

Irene rushed to the laptop, handing off the coffee. "Here's a cup for you." She handed a cup to Stella and kept one in her hand. "Move over, Stella," she said as she slid a stool over to the island and in front of the laptop. She sat down and immediately clicked on the new message; sure enough, it was from Ricco. She let out a sigh of relief and began to read the message aloud.

Dear Irene,

It has been a while since we have connected. My injuries required more healing than I realized, but I am feeling much better now!

Attached, you will find the final cover. I hope you like it. Please look it over carefully and let me know if it is a green light. Do I have a copy of your bio paragraph? If not, please send that to me also. You do want a picture of yourself with your bio, don't you? If so, I will need that too. I can make it as small or large as you desire.

The interior is complete. Your editor did a fantastic job! That will save us about two months' time to printing. I am excited to see this through! I never know when they will release me from my apprenticeship, but hopefully, not until you and I have a finished product.

I miss my mom and everything about her. She is from London; and her homemade scones, served with English tea, is heavenly. Those years seem like a distant dream, and now it feels as though this is the only life I have ever known. I wish I could let her know I am alive. We haven't been able to communicate since I have no cell phone of my own. I know she will never stop worrying about me.

Lastly, we need to discuss the book fair. The registration cutoff date is only a week away. I will need your payment to secure our special early bird pricing. The cost is $7,000. That is for three days at the festival and two hours each day for book signing. It also includes one night at a four-star hotel and the pitch for your book on all four days. It is a good deal. Book signings usually run about $9,000 and up.

I hope to hear back from you soon, so we can set your name in stone for the book show.

Take care,
Harris Smith

"I must read it again. What do you think, Stella?"

"Agree! I need to hear it again too. Let's read it silently this time. I want to really concentrate on the written word and the words between the lines."

The room was soundless as Irene and Stella focused on the laptop.

Irene sat back first, then Stella.

"He's from London where his mother lives!" Irene danced with excitement.

"And his first name is Harris. Harris Smythe. That is *huge*! I must call Gaffer. They will go crazy with this info! We will be able to find just about anything regarding him!" Stella reached for her phone.

"Wait!" Irene said, stopping Stella from dialing. "Let's look at the other clues too. Then you can call. Shouldn't we include all the recent info?"

Stella placed her phone on the island. "You're right. When I call Gaffer, you can call Betty. That way we will all be on the same page. Other clues—his head. He said he was sickly, now he mentions his head, as if he had a head injury, which explains why he needed more healing time," explained Stella.

"Exactly! I agree! He says 'injuries,' not an illness. Oh, dear Lord, he must have received a wicked blow. He is lucky to be alive!" Irene's face showed worry and sadness. "These poor kids!"

"Irene, is there anything else in the letter that you picked up?" asked Stella.

"Only that he seemed pressured to hurry me up about spending that $7,000 and I believe he wants us to let his mother know that he is alive. Let's open the attachment."

"Good idea!"

When the attachment was opened, they were both surprised. Displayed was the most eye-catching cover ever! The title "Quiet. Fear." shouted at them. Then their eyes moved along the gold chain of the necklace, right down to the ash tray and smoking cigar until you reached the author's name: IRENE WATKINS.

"Holy shit! He did one hell of a job!" exclaimed Stella.

"I would say so! It is intriguing! Do you see any errors?" asked Irene.

"Not one! Like you said, 'perfect,' and he does this by himself!" added Stella.

"He must have worked on it for months, but will I ever see it to fruition?" Irene sadly realized that all this work was a front to making money.

"Of course you will! It is yours. You paid for it. We can download the cover and save it. When this is over, you will publish your book using Ricco's cover, and you can give him credit for it—using his *real* name," Stella offered consoling words. "You will share the joy of success together!"

But Irene remained to be troubled. "What is it?" inquired a concerned Stella.

"I need to make that payment. It will keep Ricco, at least for a time, alive. I understand that I am paying a militia, but the alternative puts Ricco, I mean Harris, in grave trouble. The cost will put me further in depth, but I can handle that. I have my job, and I can ask for more hours."

"If feels wrong to become a part of their act, but if we pay, we also receive an invoice, which will beef up our investigation. Irene…if you need cash, let me know. I have no kids, no husband, just Blizzard, and she does not need much. Money for spa days and the vet, that is about it! Also, we can work with the bank on reversing the charges. With a hired team helping you, I do not think there will be a problem!" added Stella.

Just then, Irene's gaze landed upon Blizzard. "Oh my gosh, Stella, I did not take her for her walk. Look, she is sitting in her carrying case looking forlorn." Irene rushed over to Blizzard and gently picked her up. Blizzard began to lick her cheek.

"She is giving you lovin.'" Stella smiled. "Do you want to walk her while I call Gaffer? I will ask him about making that payment too."

Irene put Blizzard's pink sparkled leash on and her matching tummy warmer. "What a sight!" chuckled Irene.

Blizzard gave a low deep growl.

"She doesn't like people laughing at her!" warned Stella.
"You must be kidding! Is she kidding?" Irene asked Blizzard. Only to receive another low-throated growl. "Dogs bring me so much joy. I think when this is all over I'm going to get me a small poodle. If only Ricco had another human or a pet to console him. I can't imagine not being with people. That is a cruel punishment. Come on Blizzard. Ms. Irene is going to take you for a walk."

She led Blizzard to the elevator.

## Chapter 11

# RICCO AND MAYA

**Going back to his bleak,** dreary cell wasn't as bad this evening. Ricco knew that tonight he would see Amber again, possibly for the last time. That was difficult to accept. He wanted to see her every morning and night. The hell he endured day after day would be less painful if she were there with him. Instead of thinking about the deadly situation he was in, he thought of her hands—her light healing touch. The way her thick black hair fell over her shoulders. Her eyes that looked deeply into one's soul.

She was beautiful, intelligent, and street-smart. She had plans of how to get out if he could get Irene to help too. Tonight, she was going to bring him something he would never dream of getting. He wondered what it could be. And how were they going to see each other again? How could he make time stand still, and the night last forever?

At 2:00 a.m., he awakened to the sound of the lock opening his door. She was as quiet as a mouse. She put her finger up to her lips, a sign to be quiet. Behind her entered a soldier.

Ricco sat up straight, saying nothing.

"Show me his wound!" the soldier ordered.

Maya quickly walked over to Ricco. "I must unwrap the bandage carefully. It may be stuck to the wound," she explained to the soldier and began the process. The soldier said nothing but watched her every move as he stood, looking over her shoulder. She carefully pulled back the cloth, exposing the partially healed slash. The soldier pulled back in disgust of the smell and sight.

"Is that normal?" he asked Maya.

"Yes, sir. It is healing slowly, but the infection is still there. That is what you smell."

"All right, I have seen enough. I will report to the boss. He makes the final decision. Lock the door behind me." He began to leave.

Maya did not move fast enough for him; he grabbed her hair. "I said to lock the door behind me, bitch!"

"Yes, sir, yes, sir. I understand." Maya took her keys from her pocket and, with trembling hands, locked the door. She stood perfectly still until she heard the soldier's footsteps disappear. Turning around, she looked at Ricco; tears had filled her eyes. Ricco came to her and held her with arms of safety.

"That man is always mean to me. He embarrasses me. Makes me feel ashamed," Maya explained to Ricco with her head bowed.

"He is gone, and you are now safe with me. I will never shame you. Ever!" He lifted her head up gently, and they kissed.

"How much time do you have?" Ricco asked, wanting to hear her answer of "forever."

"No more than thirty."

"Why did he come with you tonight?"

"He had to check my work and declare you healed or are needing more medical attention."

"Are you saying you may be able to come back next week?"

Maya beamed with a big smile. "Yes, but it is only a maybe."

"I do not think he liked the way my gash looked. Is it infected?"

"He knows nothing about medicine. What he smelled is the tincture I put on. There is no more infection, but the scabbing is not complete, so it does look nasty."

Ricco smiled slyly. "You little trickster! I love it!"

Maya returned the smile and added, "We must get busy. First, you get your antibiotic shot. This one will help you with your energy. Then I need to clean and rewrap the wound. We can talk while I work. Any new communications with Irene?"

"I sent an email to her. I hinted that I was from England and that I was not sick but wounded. The worse part was begging her for a payment. I really need that payment to go through. It will get the Bossman off my back for a while. They must be planning something that requires large amounts of money as we are all getting threatened to produce more income."

"A friend, who works in the kitchen, overheard Bossman talking about a new load of laborers, and the price of human trafficking has increased," informed Maya.

"That's where the pressure is," noted Ricco.

"It is also a suitable time to make plans for an escape, as they are often distracted in their disagreements, and we can use the commotion with new laborers to help cover our escape!"

"Smart thinking."

Maya began dabbing her tincture into the wound.

"That doesn't sting or hurt as badly as it did!" Ricco informed Maya.

"That is because you are healing! There, I'm done!" She put her medical supplies back in her bag and returned to Ricco, sitting as close to him as she could get.

Their hands touched one another, their kissing grew more passionate, and then she pulled away. "Ricco, we can't go any further. You understand why, don't you?"

"I do, Maya, but it is hard not wanting to wake up with you by my side."

"I understand that feeling too, but not here, it's too risky. If anyone reported our relationship to the Bossman, one of us would be put down for good."

Ricco lowered his head. "Sadly, that is true."

"I brought you something that may cheer you up!"

"What could that possibly be other than bringing yourself to me?" he asked lovingly.

"You are a romantic. Seriously, close your eyes and no peeking!" She pulled a cell phone from her front pocket.

"Okay, you can open them now!"

Ricco was shocked. "A cell phone! Does it work?"

"It is an older model, but it works and has a full charge! We can contact our parents and tell them where we are!" Maya spoke faster with excitement in her voice.

"I'm speechless! Where did you find it? How long have you had it? Do they know?" he questioned Maya. "Aren't you in danger carrying this around?" He shot questions at her rapidly as he studied the phone.

"It has been laying in the medical closet for as long as I have been here. I covered it with a big pile of rags for bandages. No one has said anything. Then I took it into my room. No one was asking for a lost phone. I believe the owner is long gone. I am terrified to have it among my belongings, but where can we safely hide it?" she asked.

Ricco did a scan of his room in four seconds. "Definitely not here! Under the desk drawer would be a possibility, but they do random room checks. With only that desk and the bed, they check them thoroughly. They even pull out the stuffing of the mattress! That is why there is so little left."

Maya was thinking equally as hard. "I hit a dead end with everything I think of. It all carries a risk."

"What about the inside of my jumpsuit? It never gets washed. We wear it when they hose us down for our 'showers.' We live in these. Sometimes I think my skin is going to start attaching to the fabric! We could tape it to the inside of my lower thigh. I do not think they will ever know. And we could use your white bandages to wrap over the tape just in case. I can tell them that I pulled a muscle, and the nurse wrapped it."

"Are you sure?" Maya was excited but also worried and scared. "I do not want to lose you, Ricco. It is not worth that! I would never forgive myself."

Ricco held her hands in his and looked desperately into her eyes, "Maya, do not allow yourself to think that way! This is a risk. Falling in love is a risk. Waking up in this hellhole every day is a risk. If I get caught with the phone, it is a risk I have agreed to take for us. Sending code words to Irene is becoming more dangerous, as I am trying to give pertinent information on our whereabouts. This phone is worth every risk. With this phone, Irene could find our location. But first, we both need to find out where we are in Thailand!"

Maya held his face in her hands. "Ricco, we are going to get out of here. Trust me! And keep your head low. Don't be a hero quite yet!" Her kiss was exciting as well as cautious.

"Since the blow to my head I have been overly obedient and haven't done anything out of routine except sending hints to Irene. With them pushing me to get more income from her, I may need to pull back as they could start doing daily readings of my email again. If she sends the seven thousand dollars, they'll back off me and put the pressure on someone else."

"Ricco"—Maya concerningly looked at him—"what if Irene doesn't make the payment?"

Ricco stood up and walked to his window wall. Leaning against it, he replied, "I don't know, Maya, and it scares me too. I could be sold and moved to a scam camp in Myanmar. I have heard they are much worse than here and five times bigger. Or Bossman could dispose of me."

"I will pray for Ms. Irene!" Maya walked over to Ricco, and they held one another tightly, taking in the energy that love has to offer.

"I want to call my mother more than anything. I worry about her health not knowing what happened to me. And the same with your parents. But we need to be careful. I will try to find out if they trace *all* outgoing calls or only the calls we make to our clients. Until then we need to only worry about keeping it safely hidden."

## Chapter 12
# BACK IN THE STATES

"**Hey, Gaffer, this is Stella**. Irene received another email from Ricco. It has information that you are going to love! Call me back as soon as you can!" Stella slid her phone into her back pocket, walked to the couch, and plopped down. *I need a nap and then a strong cup of coffee so I can keep going*, she thought to *herself.*

Sleep came instantly, only to be awakened by the vibration and ring tone of her phone. "Crap, Gaffer, I was into one of my naps!" she scolded.

"You said ASAP. That's what this is, Stella! Sorry about the nap. Fill me in with the latest info, as we don't have enough at the moment for any direct information."

"Got it! His name is Harris Smythe. His mother lives in London. He was not sick. He had an injury, and it seems like a severe head gash. Irene wants to pay the requested amount of seven thousand for the marketing of her book. She will receive an invoice, and maybe we can trace that. Any thoughts?" asked a yawning Stella.

"Yes! Irene should send a return email to Ricco, notifying him that we he has been heard and are working on an escape plan. Irene is right about making the payment. Most likely, she will lose the money, and we cannot guarantee her reverse charges. Harris Smythe from London—that is exactly the break we needed. Take care. Talk soon."

Before Stella could respond to Gaffer, the call ended, and Irene returned from her walk with a tired Blizzard.

"Did I wake you up?" Irene asked Stella, who was looking grumpy as she sat on the couch.

"No, but Gaffer did! He is concerned that Ricco, or Harris, is taking too big of a risk writing clues in his emails to you. With the information that we have, he feels that Ricco does not need to provide more. We are to compose a return email, telling him that we have put the pieces of the puzzle together. Also, he liked the idea of making the payment. You may or may not get your money back." Stella walked into the kitchen and poured herself another large cup of coffee. "Here, I'll take my little muffin." She reached out for Blizzard and cuddled her as she listened to Irene.

"I will call the bank and do a transfer to my bank credit card. It is empty, so all they will get is what I put in. Then I will block it again and we can begin working on the email to Ricco," agreed Irene.

"I will begin a draft while you are working with the bank. Do you want to call Betty? We may need her help." Stella reminded Irene of Betty's absence. As friends, they didn't want to leave anyone out.

"I forgot all about Betty! I was so wrapped up with Blizzard and our new clues that I drifted away from the moment! I will call her right now!" Irene quickly pressed Betty's number on her favorites list.

Meanwhile Stella began a draft:

Greetings, Ricco,

It has been a while since your last email. I was happy to hear from you!

You had mentioned that you were ill, and I grew concerned. However, I am delighted you are back at work, so you must be feeling well again.

I have been comparing marketing packages, and your offer is the best. I decided to move forward with the payment. My bank has advised me not to send the credit card numbers in an email. By doing so, it could fall into the wrong hands. Does your company's central office have the means to call me? I will be home this afternoon and tomorrow morning to give them the card information.

The cover is remarkable! I love it! Thank you for all your hard work. It is the best cover I have ever seen. Let us get this published soon so it can be shared with the world!

I hope to meet your mother soon and have scones and tea together. I will let her know we are in communication with one another. She will be proud of your work! After the book is printed, you might have time for a vacation.

Make sure you get me a number to call or tell me when they will be calling me to make the payment. Take care of yourself. It will not be long before you can work freely! As in freelancing! Maybe in London!

Best,
Irene

"Hello, Betty, did I catch you at a good time?" Irene inquired.

"Actually, it is a good time. I have been a bit off all day. I can't seem to focus on any one chore. Do you ever feel that way?" Betty asked. "Flitting all over the apartment and getting nothing accomplished?"

"Most certainly! I have weeks where I feel like that. I always blame it on the weather."

Betty chuckled. "Weather takes the blame for so many of our problems! What did you want to talk about? I am sure it is not the forecast!"

"Right! That is true! Stella came over this morning, and when I opened my email, I had a new one from Ricco. He gave us his first name, which is Harris, and where he was from, which is London. Stella feels that her team has enough information now to find him!" Irene shared the info, allowing Betty to catch up with them.

"London! I wonder if his mother has reported him missing?"

"We do not know yet, but I am sure we will find out! Do you want to come over and help us write a letter back to him, with clues to let him know we have it from here? He should not be taking any more risks!"

"I would love to! Take a fifteen-minute break, and I will be there! Bye!" Betty hung up before Irene could reply.

Irene shared the conversation with Stella. "She wants to help! In fact, she hung up before I could say goodbye. She will be here in fifteen minutes. How did your draft go?"

Stella was sitting at the laptop in deep concentration. "This is not easy to do. Let's take a break while waiting for Betty. Do you have any iced tea?"

"No, but I can run across the street to the corner market and pick some up. It sounds good to me too. What snack would you like?"

"Let's see." Stella sat back into chair. "Do they have a deli in the market?"

"A small one. They make the basic sandwich subs using their fresh bread," Irene informed.

"That sounds perfect! I am not picky. Any popular sub and a bag of chips." She reached into her pocket and pulled out a twenty. "Here, take this." She handed it to Irene.

"Thank you, Stella. I will get another to share with Betty. It does sound good. See you in a few minutes. Do you need something for Blizzard?"

"She will be good with water. Thanks. I am getting a headache from thinking so hard! How do people never eat in movies?" Stella smiled, waving Irene off.

Irene remarked, "Maybe we spend too much time planning and living around food!"

## Chapter 13

# LIES

**Ricco paused at his work station, his fingers** hovering over the keyboard. He muttered under his breath in a low rhythmic tone to circumvent isolation. Many workers murmured to themselves in-between their calls. Those that didn't mutter seemed hollow, their faces vacant, all hope of life growing faint. The trauma had taken over their mental and physical bodies. They no longer cared of what could or would happen to them. Ricco wasn't there yet, thanks to Maya.

"I can pretend that someone is here to talk to. They can't keep me from doing that unless they take away my voice and cut my tongue out. I don't believe they would go that far. They need me. I'm their expert on literature, the one they rely on to decode books and answer endless lists of questions for the militia's so-called education programs. Since my capture and being trafficked, talking to myself has become a daily habit. If I stopped; I would lose the sanity that remains in me."

"Journaling would be more helpful, but we are not allowed paper and pencil. We are not allowed a life; life has become a distant dream. We only have the moment. If only I could see Maya every day or every other day, I might start piecing my emotions back together. The few times we have been together, have stirred something in me. Something I thought was buried for good. My dream of finding love."

"If it is impossible to escape, maybe I can earn my way out of here, but others say that's a lie the militia use to get us to work harder. Another false promise. Still, having this cell phone strapped to my leg is my quiet rebellion, my secret edge for getting out of here. It's my reminder of hope and that I am not entirely under their thumb. I like that!"

Ricco was quickly taken out of his muttering daze when he felt a strong kick to his chair, nearly knocking him out of his seat.

A soldier's harsh loud voice filled the room with greater fear. "Okay pretty boy, enough day dreaming. Get to work or lose lunch. Understood?" He commanded angrily, making sure the others around Ricco would also hear and fear his words.

The soldier addressed the room, "Did everyone hear that? You're a bunch of pathetic freaks. If work doesn't increase within the hour, no lunch for any of you!"

The sounds of the keyboards grew louder and the clicking faster. Ricco moved on with his next customer. She was fresh out of college, lonely for friends, especially a boyfriend, and wanting to publish her book of poetry. She worked as a waitress but was interviewing for a project manager position. He began his email:

Hello Crystine,

I hope your day has been delightful! Did you take your dog for a walk this morning? You're so lucky to have such a loyal and loving companion. I haven't had the chance to own a pet yet, but I just might get one soon, after hearing your persuasive reasoning of why it is healthy for the owner.

Last night I finished reading the remaining of your poetry book, and I must say, your writing is truly soulful and your vocabulary impressive. At what age did you begin your art of writing? It reads like you have been writing forever! And the themes are contemporary issues that will relate deeply amongst teens and adults.

Are you still interested in having me design a cover for your book? It would be my honor, and I can offer up to five revisions free of charge to ensure your complete satisfaction. Currently the package is priced at $999.00, and it includes everything: a synopsis, author bio, reviews (we should discuss this in detail), ISBN numbers and your professional cover design. Five corrections is a rare find. Companies usually allow two or three changes, and then they begin charging again, as if it was a new cover. Be careful on whom you choose to do the design as there are many scams out there!

Let me know as soon as possible, so I can personally work on it with you. Ideas are already swimming in my mind.

I look forward collaborating with you.
Take care, be safe, and seize the day!

Respectfully,
Ricco Smith

As soon as he pushed the send arrow, his guts felt like they were going to strangle his insides. Every day he spent selling false goods to decent people who will eventually think of him as a monster was mentally infuriating and physically destructive.

"Mom said I should never ever lie and here I am, not only lying to strangers, but actually convincing them to choose me, a crook, over others who may be honest sales people trying to make a living. And for the grand finale, I also take their money to fund a terrorist militia. Their loss, our gain, and that's the truth of my forced labor."

Ricco flushed with an anger that bubbled just beneath the surface of his skin. "Irene must help us escape, and it has to be soon," he muttered to himself, his words flowing with urgency. "If this doesn't work, I don't know how long I can hold on. At this moment I am close to the edge of a cliff. It wouldn't take much to send me down that rabbit hole of detachment. I'll become just like them," he thought grimly. "Hateful to everyone. Relishing the act of ripping people off. Existing with only two emotions: fear and hate."

He looked up at the clock, watching the minute hand move like a toy soldier from one dot to the other. It was time to prepare for his next client — a vulnerable elderly couple searching for a reliable life insurance policy and he had a big special for today only that he hoped would seal the deal. Ricco drew a deep breath. A few simple deals like this, each day, would get Bossman off his back. That would make it easier for him to communicate with Irene.

Dear Mr. and Mrs. Barness,

This is Ricco Smith, following up on the life insurance policy we have been discussing over the past several weeks.

As I recall, your main concern was failing a health evaluation and facing denial or excessive charges. You can rest assured that this will not happen through our company. No medical exam is required for either of you. The process is straightforward: complete the form and submit your first payment of $233. From there you can opt to send us monthly checks or set up an automatic withdrawal from your bank account.

The policy will begin immediately upon receipt of your payment, without any waiting period of three months to a year. The rate is fixed for life, and the policy guarantees coverage of $250,000 for each of you. It is rare to meet such caring and devoted parents as yourselves. Your legacy will undoubtedly echo in your children and grandchildren.

Should you wish to proceed and get your protection going as soon as possible, please let me know at your earliest convenience.

It is always a pleasure to work with you.

Sincerely,
Ricco Smith

Again, Ricco pressed the send arrow, closed his eyes, and tried to get his mind off of what he had just done. He took a sip of water and wiped the sweat from his brow. As he glanced he couldn't help but notice the collective tension of the midday grind—everyone was doing exactly what he was: focusing on their screen and their typing using mechanical movements. It was a hell hole of laborers bustling to save their lives with no air-conditioning or fans, little water, and stale, humid, hot air.

At exactly noon the guard in the room blew his whistle, a signal that lunch had begun.

"Line up! You will be eating outside," the guard commanded.

The workers lined up quickly. It was a well-rehearsed action because the only way they could move—was in a line.

Again, the muttering could be heard. Ricco amongst them. They were not happy about being in the hundred-degree humid weather at high noon. The room was an oven, and now they had to eat in another oven that was even hotter! They would be exhausted and out of water before the day's end. Workers passing out and be dragged to who knows where and possibly starved until the next day.

Ricco straightened his posture and fixed his gaze firmly on the guard. He had promised Maya that he would avoid any added disciplinary consequences and her advice was wise, and following it was even wiser.

In the courtyard, the workers sat in two orderly rows under the blazing sun, with not a hint of shade to offer relief. However, an occasional breeze brushed over Ricco's skin, leaving the faint smell and touch of salty air. Ricco's thoughts were brought back to better days when he was walking barefoot in the cool damp sand of a beach, while the waves heaved back and forth. He could hear the ocean's thunder offering him a hint of freedom among imprisonment.

Two elderly women, dressed in clothing that was no longer sewn together, but wrapped and twisted around their thin frame, handed out a bowl to each worker.

It was the usual breakfast, lunch, and dinner: cooked rice, that was dry, most likely old and leftover from a militia's meal. Amongst the rice were vegetables and sources of protein. Ricco believed the protein was chicken and on some days, dried fish. Vegetables appeared to be from the fields or after market. They were bruised, overly ripened, sometimes poorly washed. Vegetables such as zucchini, eggplant and tiny chili peppers were used most frequently. If fruit was offered, it was a treat, even though they were overly ripened and bruised or not ripe at all, releasing a strong bitter taste and not the sweetness we longed for, it was deeply appreciated.

The food was not fresh or tasty. It was not prepared in a clean facility. It made many sick, but it served its purpose: to keep him alive to make money for the Bossman and his militia. If he wanted out, he could easily quit eating and drinking. But not now. Now he had to focus on continuing to heal and gain strength. He and Maya were going to escape.

## Chapter 14
# MORE INFORMATION

"**Let's see what you both** pulled up on Harris Smythe of London." An interested Gaffer waved Dog and Edge over to their round thinking table where everything was laid out before a mission. "Dog, you first."

"Harris Smythe was born in in the United States in 2000. That makes him twenty-five years old. His father was an orthopedic surgeon, served in the Medical Corps until 1992, and then joined Doctors Without Borders. He worked in the Middle East and Southeast Asia. He married his wife, who is from the Philippines, in 1995. They moved to Chicago, bought a home on Lake Michigan, and continued his work as an orthopedic surgeon. His wife had a Master of Library Science and worked part-time at the Harold Washington Library Center in Chicago. In 2000, Harris was born. In 2015, his father was killed in a random terrorist bombing of a café while attending a medical convention in London. Soon after, his wife sold their home in Chicago and moved to London, with Harris, buying a flat near the café where the father died."

"That's good for background. It sounds clean. What a tragedy for Harris and his mother." Gaffer began to take notes. The room was quiet. Gaffer looked up. "Dog, do you have a current location of his mother?"

"I do, sir."

"Good. You can pass that around. Okay, Edge, you are on! What did Harris do in London?"

"He is a good kid. No arrests or violations, not even a parking ticket. High school honor student. Worked on the school newspaper, went to college at UCL—University College London, and majored in computer science with a minor in literature. Ranked in the top ten of his class and then he disappears. The last thing he did was to check in for a flight to Bangkok on May 22 shortly after his graduation."

"And that's where he was taken, Bangkok." Gaffer stood up and walked over to the map. "Our next assignment is looking into these scam compounds or cyber labor camps in Southeast Asia. That is most likely where he is. Let us look at the map. What countries do you think we are dealing with?" asked Gaffer.

"According to info on the net, we are looking at Cambodia, Laos, Vietnam, Thailand, and the Mekong Delta," answered Dog. "Not my choice for a vacation!"

"The jungles are tough, I agree, but we have managed to get through them several times. How do these compounds work?" Gaffer asked, looking at Edge for the information.

Edge jumped in, "It is remarkably interesting. During the COVID-19 pandemic, the borders of Southeast Asia were harder to cross. The Chinese elicited online gambling operations were failing and so they adapted by building large camps for cybercrime fraud. These camps rely on human trafficking and forced labor. Scammers build trust with victims before stealing their funds through cryptocurrency transactions, a practice known as 'pig butchering.' In the past three years, these operations have generated approximately $64 billion. That's roughly $21 billion a year."

Gaffer whistled. "How is it that we don't know about these camps or this type of human trafficking?"

"It's just now starting to break out in offbeat papers and some big colleges because of its use with cryptocurrency. The scamming market has become global. Which means it's here in America. It costs the United States economy around ten billion a year, and that's old data," finished Edge.

"Man, that pisses me off. Let's shut them down." Dog was ready for combat.

Edge continued explaining, "Not that easy, Dog. Most camps are huge. They hold hundreds, even thousands, of forced laborers. If we want to get Ricco out, he will have to escape the compound. Then we can complete the extraction. That's how I see it."

"Good point, Edge. Do any of our key words from Ricco's correspond more with one of the Southeast Asia countries we mentioned?" Gaffer asked while looking at the map.

Dog and Edge reviewed the countries, both not liking the idea of going back into that region of the world for a rescue, but the cause had purpose and reason.

The ring of Gaffer's cell phone distracted their thoughts. "What's up on your end, Stella?" Gaffer asked.

"I am sending you the response to Ricco's letter. Irene is going to make a payment. Tell us what you think. How about you? Did you find anything out?" she asked.

"It's coming together. Probably the Mekong delta area," Gaffer replied.

"Oh man, that sucks! We are talking about a large area and several countries. How are we going to narrow it down?" Stella was disappointed that it was not going to be an easy in and out.

"That is going to be up to Ricco. He is going to have to give us destination information. You girls can work on that.

Start with specific words that would describe each country and move from there. We are going to call it quits for now to get something to eat, grab some shut-eye, and then get back to work. How about you?"

"I think we will start the word game and then finish it tomorrow. When should we meet? Like, all of us."

Gaffer thought then replied, "Not until we hear back from Ricco and the payment is made. That may be our airplane ticket."

"Got it. I will let the girls know. Hey, Gaffer? Is Irene safe to be doing this?"

"These labor camps are cruel and corrupt. She may lose her money. There is no guarantee. I will do what I can, at my end, but no promises. Make sure she has her card blocked to the amount she is paying." Gaffer added, "Online criminal actors are tricky, well-trained, and good at what they do. It's difficult to be ahead of them. We're stepping into a ruthless game where the stakes are high, and rules don't exist."

**Betty and Stella arrived at Irene's apartment.**

Stella saw the glass of iced tea in Irene's hand. "Here, I'll take that!" She grabbed it as if it were hers. "I need a drink stronger than this! Just finished talking with Gaffer."

"Stella," a worried Irene addressed her, "why are you so jumpy? What did Gaffer say to you? He wants to drop this entire issue, right?" asked Irene, fearing the response.

"No," Stella said with abrupt finality as she refilled her glass with ice and more tea. "I'm tired. Last night I believe I had insomnia. I started creating situations on how we could extract Ricco, and it would not stop. After some caffeine, I should be more balanced."

"Stella darling, you do know that drinking caffeine—"

Betty did not get a chance from either Irene or Stella to complete her thought. The looks on their faces clearly told

Betty to stop with the health comments. Wearing a doubtful smile, she continued, "Okay then, move on to what you wrote!"

"First," piped in Irene, "what would you like to drink, Betty? Hot tea, cold iced tea, coffee, or lemonade?"

"I would love a hot tea. Thank you!"

"That sounds good to me too!" replied Irene. "Stella, do you need a shot of vodka in that iced tea?"

"Now you are speaking my language! Yes! Where do I find such a treasure?"

Irene chuckled. "In the cabinet above the fridge. For what other purpose do people use that cabinet for?"

Naturally, Betty had an answer. "Well, I use it for my large pasta kettle and the roaster. They take up so much space!"

Stella added her two cents. "I do not use it for kettles, roasters, or alcohol. That is where I keep an extra gun and my ammunition. The liquor is right next to the glasses—fridge, glasses, alcohol. All conveniently placed close together."

Irene and Betty laughed with Stella. It felt good to add in a little humor.

Stella carried the laptop to the kitchen island to show the letter she drafted. Betty leaned in toward the screen and silently read it. When she finished, she leaned back in her chair with her eyes still on the screen.

"What's the verdict?" asked Stella.

Betty looked at Stella. "Good work! I think we should add more to the paragraph about meeting his mother. Just a sentence or two that would clearly state we have put together his clues."

"How?" asked Stella.

"Beats me!" answered Betty.

"That is a tough one," added Irene. "How about 'Meanwhile, the pieces of the puzzle have been put together.

All I need to do is glue it.'"

Stella responded, "Oh! I like that, Irene! How do we tie it into the letter?" She began to madly type and then read her writing out loud. "How about 'putting a book together is a lot like a puzzle. It has many pieces that go together. On my end, all the pieces have been put together. Now I only need to glue it together, and my friends will help me with that.'"

Stella looked up, checking out Irene's and Betty's facial reactions. Irene was in her deep-thinking pose. While Betty was busy writing and erasing. Stella waited, drinking her coffee and petting Blizzard. The five minutes that passed had tested her patience. "Thoughts please!"

"Honestly, I don't have anything better," Irene sadly admitted.

"I'm with Irene," added Betty. "We can think on it tonight and maybe come up with one alternative by tomorrow."

"That is a good idea, Betty. However, there is an urgent need to send a reply today. Especially since I want to make a payment to the company. The information they send me could be helpful for finding a location," Irene explained.

"True," answered Betty.

"I am going to add it as it was written," stated Stella. "Beginning with 'Putting a book together....' I believe Ricco will pick up the metaphor, and if anyone else is reading the email, they would think it is a clever analogy. Puzzles and books go together nicely! Besides, Gaffer will read it and give us a final thumbs-up. Then we can send it today."

**Two hours later, Gaffer contacted them.** The long wait wound Betty's nerves too tight. "What did he say? Can we send it?"

"It's a go, but, Irene, are you sure you limited your card to the exact amount of payment?" questioned Stella.

"Yes, I spoke with my banker and told him I was going to make a large purchase of seven thousand dollars to my publishing company. Prior approval will ensure that the amount will easily go through. Otherwise, I send the money then wait for the bank to refuse payment, requesting a call back. I call the bank and tell them I approve and so on."

"After this, I think all three of us will need a quiet beach for a long weekend," added Betty.

"I like the way you think, Betty. Blizzard could come too. She loves the waves and even has a swimsuit and sun goggles!"

Irene began to laugh. "I can see that image, and it's hysterical!"

"Okay! That was enough screwing around, back to the serious situation we have on hand." Stella moved from the living room to the kitchen. "Irene, are you ready to push send?"

"I am! Right…now!" Irene sat quietly with Betty, looking over her left shoulder and Stella looking over her right. All three glued to the computer's screen. Minutes passed. They were sure Ricco would answer immediately.

An hour later Ricco had not responded. Stella broke silence, "We need to give him time. He must get permission to send the number, then they have to set their people up on the phones. Once the number is given, they move quickly changing it into cryptocurrency."

"How do you know that?" asked Betty with curiosity. Sometimes she felt Stella was much more involved with espionage than she and Irene believed.

"I learned from Gaffer. He was explaining how these compounds or camps move their money. I do not know a lot about cryptocurrencies, but Asia is one of the leading countries to learn from."

"Hmm, I think I am going to read up on that subject. How about you Irene?" inquired Betty.

"No, thank you! When this is over, I am going to get a new credit and debit card. And I am going to go back to the idea of 'cash is king!'"

"Good luck with that!" piped in Stella. "Many businesses don't accept cash anymore."

Irene pulled further away from the screen. "For real? People actually refuse cash?"

"I know, it's crazy, but it's more cost-efficient. The business doesn't have to pay a worker to balance the register to the receipts, nor do they need an armor truck to pick up and deliver cash to the bank."

"I still believe that cash is king!" argued Irene. "Anyone hungry for a snack? I eat when I am nervous, and right now, I am starving!"

Betty and Stella were not interested. They kept both eyes on the screen, anticipating a prompt reply from Ricco.

Irene grabbed a small bag of dark chocolate peanuts, along with her ice water, and returned to her seat in front of the laptop on the kitchen island. In a short time, more than her own hands were reaching into the candy bag. She smiled thinking she was not the only one with eating anxiety.

Ten minutes passed. "Girls, I don't think he's going to answer today," suggested Irene. "Why don't we call it a night, and check in the morning?"

"Hell no!" It was not a surprising response from Stella.

Competitive Betty agreed. "I'm with Stella."

"What about a game of cards while we wait! Or we can watch a movie!" Irene found that waiting too long was unproductive for her mental and emotional health.

"Irene?" Stella commanded. "If you need to do something, go ahead and do it. Betty and I will sit here in case the email comes through. At least for the rest of this hour."

"Then I am going to clean out some kitchen drawers." Irene stood up and walked over to the silverware drawer, emptying everything that was in it. Silverware, plastic spoons and forks, rubber bands, and other miscellaneous items were dumped out on the kitchen counter, and at that exact moment Stella, loudly and excitedly, shouted out, "He replied!"

"Wouldn't you know," Irene growled to herself and moved quickly to her seat. She paused. "What do we do now?" she asked, looking at Stella. "Should I open it right away?"

They stared at the screen as if it were a ticking bomb.

"No!" shouted Stella, making Irene and Betty jump. "Call Gaffer first! He may need to link up with one of our computers."

"Wow, that was close! Good question, Irene. Well done, Stella," said Betty.

Stella was already on the phone. "Yes, he replied. No, we have not opened it. Why? Because I thought you may need to link our computers or another techie thing first. Yes, I will. Thanks." Stella faced Irene. "It's showtime!"

Irene clicked on the email, and all three heads leaned inward, anticipating what they were about to see.

Hello Irene,

> Thank you for getting back to me about the marketing package. We make an effective team, and I am going to set you up for success. Your life is about to get exciting!
> To make a payment, you will need to call our finance team. They will take your

information and send you an invoice. Their number is 1-800-023-7777. You will be speaking to Raymond. He is a good guy. I worked with him before.

Thank you, Irene. This is a major step forward in seeing your book off to success!

I know you will enjoy a visit with my mother. You two are alike. I have met a friend here. She is in the same facility as me. We are making plans for when we both complete our training.

Let me know if you have any questions about the payment. I will be talking to you soon regarding ideas for the festival. If I have time, I will draw several advertising ideas. Pay close attention to the background details.

Take care. Spring is bringing us new hope for our tomorrows!

Ricco Smith

**The room was silent until Blizzard's unique** throaty growl brought them all back to the present.

"What do you think?" Irene asked Betty and Stella.

Stella was hushing Blizzard, so Betty took the opportunity to answer first. "I think he is telling us about a girl he has fallen in love with and that they are planning to escape together. Also, we will receive pictures, and their location is going to be revealed in the art. That's what I think! And you?" Betty asked Stella.

Betty, you should work in espionage! I agree with everything you said," commented Stella. "Irene?"

Irene was still thinking, as usual. Stella touched her shoulder and asked again, "What do you think, Irene?"

"I am not sure. Now I think he is one of the scammers, and he's using me. I feel stupid. I was sucked in with his kindness, his knowledge of literature, always being there for me. Now, I do not know if I want to make that payment."

Stella could not believe what she was hearing. "Irene, why are you doubting yourself? You feel strongly about Ricco and his captivity."

"It is the first two paragraphs. He sounds like a fraud. All business," Irene replied.

"Did you read the rest of the letter? Are you jealous that he met a girl?" Betty asked.

"What?" Irene asked with insult. "No, I am not in love with him, but he has filled my days with conversation. He and I are friends. But are we? I do not know. Now that all my thoughts are being heard, I hear them differently. I do not expect either of you to understand. *I* don't understand."

"Irene, what you are feeling is normal. You are second-guessing yourself. What is important are your first thoughts. And this letter supports it. They are looking for a way out. And he is going to send us clues in his drawings, which is quite clever. Irene, you are doing a good thing here. You are a brave woman!" Stella put her hand on top of Irene's.

"She is right, Irene. He is still reaching out to you, and it's normal to have thoughts of doubt but don't forget, even Gaffer, Edge, and Dog believe you are right."

"Do you really think Gaffer believes all this about slave laborers and human trafficking?" Irene asked Stella.

"He and the boys have been working around the clock gathering information, and so far, it is adding up to be on target. We will have a meeting after your call, and you will be surprised by what one thought created! Trust me," comforted Stella.

"I'm sorry for doubting myself, which is not new for me! Let me pull myself together, and then we will make the call."

"I will call Gaffer while you and Betty take a break. He definitely wants to follow this call."

"He can do that?"

"Gaffer and his team can do anything. Never doubt *them*, Irene. That would be a huge mistake!" added Stella.

**"Hey, Gaffer, we have a number**, do want to hook into Irene's phone now?" asked Stella.

"Yes, give us a few minutes, starting now, then make the call." Gaffer hung up.

Stella hit the timer on her watch for three minutes and then addressed Betty and Irene, "It is showtime, girls! Irene, do you have your phone and is it fully charged?"

"It is right here, and I have an 80 percent charge. Is that good enough?"

"Yes, that will be fine. Are you ready, or do you need more time to gather yourself?" asked Stella as she scanned Irene's body language.

"I'm ready," Irene answered.

"Follow their directions," Stella began to slowly direct Irene. "Betty and I will be close but try to avoid us and focus on the conversation. Listen to every word and its tone. Here is a pen and some paper. Write anything that you feel is important to remember. Do you have your card?"

"Yes but, Stella, can't I put it on speaker, so you and Betty can hear too? That would make me feel more comfortable. Please?"

Stella looked at her watch. "We have one minute. Think, Stella, think!" she scolded herself and then looked at Irene. "Yes, put it on speaker. Betty, get paper and a pen off the table. Are you both ready? I am going to record the call with my phone. On a count of three, make the call, Irene. One...two...three!"

With trembling hands, Irene dialed the numbers to the finance center. The phone began to ring. On the third ring, a woman with an Asian accent answered, "Hello, North Winds Publishing. How can I help you?"

Irene was quiet. Stella gently nudged her shoulder, "Sorry, excuse me," answered Irene, continuing, "I am calling to make a payment for a marketing package through Ricco Smith."

"Wonderful! What is the title of your book?"

"*Quiet. Fear.* is the title. Short but to the point."

"Clever. I am going to transfer you now to Raymond, who is working in financing today. Just a moment."

Irene panicked. "But shouldn't you have my number in case we get disconnected?"

Stella and Betty were hand-signaling, shaking their heads, trying to tell Irene not to give her number to the woman.

"No, that's not necessary."

"Oh, good!" Irene accidentally verbalized her thoughts, but Raymond's deep voice snapped her right back into the conversation.

"Hello, this is Raymond. Am I speaking with Irene Watkins?"

"Yes, hello, Raymond. I am calling to make a payment for the marketing package for the book fair. My representative is Ricco Smith."

"How has it been working with Ricco?" Raymond inquired.

"How could anyone not enjoy working with Ricco? He is clever and well-read."

"That he is! Is this a full or partial payment?"

"It's a full payment."

"I have the amount of seven thousand US dollars. Is that correct?"

"Yes, that is correct. Will you be sending me an invoice?"

"Yes, Irene, an invoice and receipt should show up in minutes after we finish. Also, there is a contract for you to sign. You have three days to return it. After that, we terminate this marketing agreement. Do you understand?"

"Yes, I do."

"Okay, I'm ready for that number."

Irene looked at Betty. Betty nodded her head yes, slowly, and methodically.

Irene read the numbers. When completed, she asked, "Raymond, did you get the numbers you needed?"

"Yes, and now can you give me the expiration date?"

"09/28."

"Thank you, and now the security code."

Again, Irene paused to look at Betty and again Betty nodded her head yes.

"The security code is 323."

"Let me read this back to you…." Raymond read the card numbers, date, and code back to Irene. "Is that correct?"

"Yes, it is correct."

"We are done on this end. Thank you, Ms. Irene. The card went through, all is good, and I will let Ricco know it is paid for, and he can begin work."

"Thank you, Raymond. Take care of yourself and be safe."

The call ended.

"I cannot breathe! There is no air in here!" exclaimed Irene.

Stella quickly put her strong arms around Irene and walked with her to the deck while Betty was sliding the door open. "Irene, slow your breathing down, focus on your breath. Breathe in… one, two, three, and now breathe out …one, two, three. There you go! Let us try to make it to four. Breath in…one…two…three….four. Slowly breathe out…one…two…three…four. You did great! Betty, is there a lemon in the fridge? If so, can you bring it out and a glass of water?"

"Sure thing." Betty quickly found the lemon they had cut for the iced tea and grabbed a fresh glass of water. "Here, Irene. Take a good whiff of the lemon. It is centering. Take as many whiffs as you like! You did good, and you are so brave!"

Feeling like the present was coming back to her, Irene replied, "I do not feel brave. I feel angry!"

"That's okay," confirmed Stella. "So do I! Those—"

"Okay Stella, I think we can finish the rest of that phrase on our own," said Betty in a teacher's tone.

They all shared a chuckle. Stella added, "Now we wait to hear from Gaffer. For sure, the call was long enough. I do think we got their location. Excellent job, Irene. How are you doing now?"

"That would have been impossible if you were not here! I knew I was talking to a fraud. I wanted to strangle him, but instead I gave him seven thousand dollars. But if it helps us get Ricco and his girl out of that camp, I will never look back with regret." Irene stood up and walked over to the railing to look at the Great Lake.

"That is a healthy way to look at it. I think I am going to add a shot of vodka into my coffee cup. A totally non-healthy reaction!" Stella walked back into the kitchen, relieved that there were no hiccups. It went smoothly, and Irene was shaking off her nerves, being herself out on the deck, refusing to give up the half of a lemon. While Betty laid down on a lounge chair, looking up into the clouds. "Boy! I am glad this part is over!" implied Betty.

"It was hard trying to talk civil to a known fraudster. Or what did Gaffer call them?" asked Irene.

"A criminal actor," replied Betty.

## Chapter 15

# PLOTTING A PLAN

**Gaffer sat confident as he took note of everyone sitting at the table.** "I called you together to get us all on the same page. Edge has been looking into Ricco's life in London while Dog investigated Ricco's parents. I have been studying maps, and Stella's group has been working on communications. We have all completed our part and now we are going to put it together. You will find everything we know in these folders." Gaffer handed each a tan folder. "Dog, give us a briefing of your work."

Dog, holding Blizzard under his arm and near his chest, began. "Harris was born in 2000. He is twenty-five years old. His father was born in 1960 in Chicago. He was raised in an upper-class family. He went to premed, continued school to become a surgeon, and joined the Medical Corps. After serving, he became a part of the Doctors without Borders. While in the Philippines, he met Harris's mother. They married in 1995 and returned to the US, settling in the Chicago area where his father worked as an orthopedic surgeon. When Harris was fifteen, his father was killed in a single terrorist attack at a small café in London where he was attending a medical convention. Afterward, his mother sold their home in Chicago and moved to London, buying a flat near the café where his father passed. That's what I have!" Dog finished.

"That is such a sad story! Poor Harris and his mother! And to think that terrorists have him now! Unbelievable!" Betty often needed a reminder that few people have a Cinderella, happy ever after, life. Her divorce was her first big hardship and the last…so far.

Gaffer thanked Betty for her response and moved quickly to Edge, who was constantly rubbing his five o'clock shadow. "You're on, Edge."

"Thanks! I investigated Harris's life in London. He was a good kid with no arrests or citations. He worked at a publishing company after high school and entered college at age 20. He attended UCL where he majored in computer science and minored in literature. After graduation, he received a robust offer from a giant tech company in Bangkok. He was last seen on the day he flew out and was reported missing to the Missing People Unit in the UK by his mother. We have her address, which you will find in the folder. I also dug up information about the compounds, which we will get to later." Edge sat back.

Gaffer took the floor. "Moving forward, I want to cover what information we discovered during the transaction and phone conversation. When you called the number for North Winds, the call was routed to Washington. We used nearby cell towers to trace the call's location. By measuring the signal strength from multiple towers, we could triangulate the exact location, which was their storefront, North Winds Publishing. When we mapped it out on the computer, we found an old, unkept, brick building, with a window advertisement for 'cell phone repairs.' We believe this is their US contact point or storefront. There was no sign of a publishing company existing on that building."

Irene politely raised her hand. "Do you know what town and state?"

"Sure," Gaffer confirmed. "It is in Seattle, Washington."

"That is what Ricco told me! But how does it work being only a desk, a phone, and a person?" Irene inquired.

"That is all you need. Clearly, one can see that it is rundown and infrequently used. We watched people entering and leaving. There was only one in forty-eight hours. An Asian female, well covered in clothing, her identity could not be completed."

"After identifying the call's location in Washington, we traced its transfer to an overseas finance department. International calls can be routed through submarine communication cables which run along the ocean's bottom."

"So where did my money go? How do they get it from my charge card?" Irene clearly wanted to know all that she could about how the scam works.

"Good question! Some scammers set up fake businesses that accept charge card payments. Once the payment is made, they convert the money into cryptocurrency or digital money. Eventually, the business is closed, making it difficult to trace the funds. Then they create a new name for the business and continue the scam.

"ATMs also allow users to convert cash into crypto. They withdraw money from a charge card and deposit into crypto ATM. The cryptocurrency is then transferred to their digital wallets. Cryptocurrency transactions are often irreversible, and it's difficult to find the person who did it, creating anonymity and making it almost impossible to recover the stolen funds."

"Not much hope for my money to come back!" Irene felt her stomach reacting to the explanation Gaffer just gave.

It made her sick that this behavior is not hunted down like a monster.

Gaffer sighed. "I'm sorry, Irene, and I will look further into this." She gave him a thumb's up, and he continued, "Back to the signal we traced overseas. We were led to a town in southern Thailand called Ranong. It has a small population and borders Myanmar, which means we must be precise with the coordinates, mountains to the East and the Andaman Sea to the west. It is a small strip of land, about twenty-five miles wide. The Thailand Port Authority operates there. That not only could be helpful but also more dangerous. The rainy season in and near Ranong is the rainiest in all of Thailand. It is from May through October. The sooner we complete this extraction, the better."

Stella questioned Gaffer, "Where do we go, and what do we do from here? It is clear that North Winds is not a publishing company. Harris is surely a forced criminal actor. And time is closing in on us with the monsoons."

"True," Gaffer agreed. "I do believe our next step is to do some traveling. Here is a plan I am going to throw out to you. Let me know what you think. Stella will accompany Betty and Irene to London. Once there, you are to meet with Harris's mother. First, you will need to gently inform her about her son: where he is, his current name, and a general explanation of our plan. Next, gather names of his friends in college, at work, and favorite professors. We are looking for someone who may have been involved with trafficking. Harris had to be in contact with someone he trusted to apply for that specific job in Bangkok. Thoughts?"

"Oh, this will be exciting! I get to return to London!" Betty's enthusiasm was met with serious faces looking at her with concern. "But don't worry! I will be a serious Agatha Christie!" She reassured them with her smiling face.

Stella asked Gaffer, "Do you have a date for us?"

"Leaving this Sunday, returning on Thursday. I will have your travel expenses ready on Friday. As for Dog, Edge, and myself, we will be pulling out tomorrow evening for a flight to Ranong. There, we will meet our contact for a fishing adventure in the Adaman Sea, and a tour of a wildlife sanctuary nearby. We may have more information from Harris during that time, and it is pertinent. Therefore, Stella, make sure you burn this into memory… I am to be contacted as soon as possible with any new information. We are going to be checking the layout of the land, the town, weather, and ins and outs. Any questions?" No one responded. "Then this meeting is over until we all return from our travel. Stella, can you stay a little longer?"

"Always," she promptly replied.

"Betty and I will return to our apartments and begin packing. Will you call us, Stella?" asked Irene.

"Tomorrow morning. I will be your guide and security so I will be wearing a suit. Just wanted to give you a heads-up." She smiled. "No leather except for my boots and carry case. Pack light because I will be carrying your bags!"

Irene replied, "This feels unreal. Like I am coming out of a dream. Harris is real."

Gaffer addressed Irene, his tone was certain, "Harris is real. There still could be the possibility he works with and for the militia, but the records and info that we have collected, point otherwise. It is remarkable that you have been able to decode Ricco's plea for help. Your work is complete. Trust the team to get the job done. This is the work we do. Safe travel and listen to Stella. She is remarkable!"

## Chapter 16
# HARRIS AND AMBER

**The eerie sounds of the jungle** haunted Maya as she walked from her building to Ricco's. The frogs and the cicadas seemed more active, as if her presence were unwelcome. The pitch-black night sky had no moon, and the stars were imprisoned behind heavy clouds. She wondered if it was a sign from the universe to run. Her heartbeat quickened, and she picked up her pace. The winds whipped against her back, forcing her to move forward. Freedom. When it is gone, so is the soul.

Ricco could not sleep knowing Maya was about to arrive. Was she safe at night? Who was ensuring her safety? The building was unnervingly quiet except for the occasional creaks and groans. Once in a while, he would hear a cicada, but tonight, he wished for their aggravating high-pitched whine to keep him focused. The smell of the rain reminded him of an old wooden greenhouse—wet flowers, decaying leaves, and rotting wood, it all sickened him. The stench of the sewer was always stronger after a rain. He longed for the fresh crisp air of the ocean, soft green grass for his feet, a mattress for his body. Freedom. He had taken it for granted, but never again!

The rusty lock on his door began to rattle. His heart pounded in his chest. It could be Maya, but it could also be the militia. His shallow breath was caught high in his chest; his eyes were wide and alert. It was Maya. He stood up, greeting her with a hug. To feel another human's life in his arms made him feel more alive than ever. The lack of human contact was harrowing and taking it away was torture.

Maya returned the hug. It felt as if the two of them were one warm, comforting body. A feeling that she did not want to let go of. It gave her strength and confidence that she wasn't aware she had. She felt she could face anything as long as Ricco was her guiding light.

He tenderly led her to his bed, now covered with new elephant ear leaves. The fresh smell and the coolness of their wax covering was comforting to the skin. They laid down, embracing one another.

"I want to stay quiet and hold you," Ricco softly whispered in her ear.

"I feel the same. This is our last meeting." She looked away briefly with tear-filled eyes.

"I understand. One more minute?" He couldn't imagine never seeing and feeling her again.

"Of course." She leaned into him as they passionately kissed, holding each other's face in the palms of their hands.

"We will have many nights like this where we can be together without fear and without a timed visit. Ricco, hold on to this moment, as I will too. It will be our forever memory."

"A beautiful thought. And I will always hold the memory in my heart." Minutes passed, and Ricco sat up with thoughts swimming in his head. "Today, six workers were violently taken out of the workroom, and they didn't return. I am worried they will come back for me. Are you safe?"

Maya stood up, pulling Ricco up with her. "I am safe at the main building. Once we earn the Bossman's trust, he keeps us around longer than most. However, there is something going on. During breakfast I sat at a table closer to the soldiers than I should have been. I overheard them talking about a new shipment of laborers. When that happens, there is always increased movement between camps and sometimes it is chaotic. A few laborers' parents are allowed to pay large ransoms for their child's return from captivity, and with that money, the militia buys new laborers. I think that's when we should escape. The night before the arrival of the new laborers."

"Why is that?"

"Because every guard is being briefed on who is coming in. Each guard will have a dozen or so names and faces to remember. Then they celebrate their success and the influx of money, often drinking alcohol late into the evening. In the morning, it will be strict and heavily watched."

Ricco eagerly added, "And the guards would already be busy with the crowds of newcomers, which they cannot leave alone, so that would be to our advantage. By morning, we would hopefully be close to or already picked up by Irene's people."

"Exactly," confirmed Maya. "I briefly walked past the calendar in Bossman's office. I glanced and saw the last day of the month circled in red. My friend, who cleans his office, will know what that means. She could help."

"I don't think it is a good idea to let others in on our secret it is too dangerous."

Maya, deep in thought, continued to move about the room. "Let me think. After breakfast, they discuss business matters before proceeding to their respective tasks. On Monday mornings, the Bossman and his security go into town. I have no idea why, and they come back with no visually seen supplies."

"How long are they gone for? What are the other workers doing then?"

"They are gone for at least an hour, sometimes longer. The other workers, like me, do our daily chores and duties. The routine is tightly kept and highly organized, but that may be a time to make it work. Sometimes I think Bossman was a surgeon because he is so particular and detailed in organization."

Ricco chuckled lightly. "My father was a surgeon, and you described him to a tee."

"*Was?*" asked Maya.

"He lost his life in an accident. I was fifteen." Ricco rarely spoke of his father's death as it stirred up unwanted memories.

"I am sorry, Ricco, it's tough to lose a parent at any age, but especially when you are so young." Maya saw Ricco's body language slump. She knew this was a subject Ricco didn't want to take further.

"Thank you, Maya. It was difficult leaving the life I knew and moving to London. Anyway, that was then. Now, we keep planning. I do not have the opportunity to move about the compound, but you do. Have you seen any way out?"

Thinking, Maya replied, "There are two: the road that goes to town and the path that leads to the beach. The road is not traveled at night. It is dark, but less dangerous than the jungle forests. The fence around the compound is barbed wire, except for a small section near the main gate. It was damaged and repaired with regular fencing wire. No barbs. We could easily get through or under it."

"What about the path?" inquired Ricco.

"The path is always in use. The militia like to take the women down to the beach. I can hear their screams at night. Some girls come back while others, I believe, are thrown into the sea and taken out to the deep, by the tides."

"That's terrible! Maya, how can I protect you from those beasts?" asked Ricco.

"I think I am hands off because of Bossman. He has no other medical personnel on his staff. In my prayers, I never forget how grateful I am."

"Maya, can I ask you a question?"

"Of course!"

"If I can get one of their uniforms, and you could wear my jumpsuit, it would look like I was taking you there, to the beach. We would move farther away from others and blend in. Or if lucky, no militia would be there in the early morning hours, knowing a new group of laborers were coming. Would that work? And how far does the beach go?"

"That could work, and it's a clever idea! The beach goes almost to town. It stops near the port authority office, but not close enough for them to see us with the naked eye."

Ricco's heart was racing. Escaping and thinking of the dangers for Maya were difficult. "Has a militia taken you down there?"

"No, Ricco, like I said, Bossman must have threatened the soldiers to not even look at me and Ammara, who's a friend and the cook's niece. We go to the beach, not often but occasionally. The beach goes far both ways. To the south, it becomes rocky. The rocks are hard to walk on. We tried and slipped, and eventually, we turned around, and went back. To the north is the border of Myanmar, which is extremely dangerous, and the jungle lines the beaches. We can always hide in there, but there are mangrove trees, and their root system is massive! The same with the road. The mangrove roots make it difficult to move safely and swiftly."

"I hope Irene and her team have some ideas! They may know more about what is beyond these walls than us," Ricco said hopefully.

"Good thinking," Maya replied and then added, "*We* are amazing. *We* are going to do this! *We* are going to be free!"

"I can send a message to Irene and make it disappear within minutes. Tomorrow I will do that. I will tell her I am going to call. There is a fifteen-hour difference between here and Chicago."

"Have you worked on the drawings?"

"I have, and I am not happy with them sneaking through inspection. The clues are too obvious. I wonder if they can pick up our coordinates with tracing the cell?" Ricco asked.

"Ricco, that worries me! Can the militia pick up calls coming out and in to this area?" The thought terrified Maya. The phone would be useless.

"I didn't think of that! Of course they could! Are they doing it? We don't know." Ricco returned to the mattress on the floor and sat down. He buried his face in his hands. He wanted to scream and pull out his hair, but all he did was a muffled growl showing frustration.

Maya sat down next to him. She gently pulled back his hair and put her arm over his shoulder. "How?" she asked him. "How did you not think about that? You are recovering from brain trauma. Your body is starving and most likely dehydrated. No one thinks clearly in that state of being. I talked the Bossman into allowing you another antibiotic shot. Infections in this hole runs high and takes lives. That cannot happen to you. I also have an extra water bottle for you and two protein bars." She walked over to her medical bag and began preparing the shot.

"Thank you for the food and water and for looking over me. Infection in my wound still concerns me even though it is healing nicely. I don't know why, but they have cut our water down to two bottles a day, and our food has been only rice and mangos. Maybe they plan to sell us to a larger camp to make room for the new laborers. That is a daily worry for me. I think it could be any hour, and without warning. How can we stay in communication?"

"The same way you are going to be communication with Irene." Maya smiled. "Once I read your email, it will disappear. What you send her, and what she sends you, forward to me. Don't worry. I will be extra cautious." Maya paused. "It also concerns me that they are cutting down your food and water. There is plenty of protein powders and vegetables in the stock room. Water too!"

"Say nothing," warned Ricco. "We both have to be careful so as not to draw attention. The computer messaging will work." Ricco walked over to Maya and held her hands firmly, "We are getting out of here, right?"

"We are, do not doubt it. Only positive affirmations from here on out. We wait for Irene and her friends. Do your best work. Act as you normally do, but without any backtalk. If asked a question, answer it immediately. They hate waiting. They will be convinced that your beating took care of disrespectful behaviors."

Momentarily, she lingered for one last embrace and its tender promise, before slipping away as softly and delicately as the first sight of the morning's sun.

**The following day, Ricco immediately** began to draft a letter to Irene. She would have one minutes to read it and snap a photo. He would then forward it to Maya. Communicating to the outside world while in the compound was risky—maybe even deadly.

Ricco was sweating before he even entered his workroom, partially from the humidity and heat, but also from what he was about to do. As usual, two soldiers stood outside the double doors. He walked past them with his head bowed and hands behind his back, as expected.

No greetings or names, just head down and arms still. He walked through the doors and then lifted his head. The room, usually filled with fifty desks and computers surprisingly, had only a dozen. A few of his colleagues looked up at Ricco with expressions of confusion and curiosity. He shrugged, signaling that he didn't know what was happening either. Maya was right—something was brewing.

Ricco hurriedly took his position at his computer and turned it on. Moments later, one of the guards entered the room. He stood at attention in front of the door, moving his gun from over his shoulder to the front of him. His face was emotionless, his movements robotic. In a deep, loud, and unforgiving voice he yelled out an order. The laborers immediately looked up at him, fearing the worst. He was going to shoot them all, clean up the mess, and call in the next group.

"Eyes up!" he commanded. "No breaks today. Your water is next to your computer. You will have dinner tonight. Begin!"

The room instantly filled with the pounding sound of the keys on the keyboard. No one looked up or sideways; they focused only on the screen in front of them. The soldier walked around to each station and then exited to his position outside of the door.

At that moment, Ricco began typing furiously. He had to get the note out to Irene before the next check, which could come at any moment. Quickly, almost in a panic, he typed the following:

Dear Irene,

> This is a confidential email that I learned about in college. You have two minutes to read and take a picture for

reference. It will permanently disappear. Take the picture first.

We found two escape routes. One goes to the sea, the other to the small dirt road that leads to a nearby town called Ranong. Road is lined with jungle and mangrove trees. Same with beach. We found a working cell phone. Can we use it for you to trace our coordinates? Or too dangerous. New laborers are coming in. That would be the best night to escape. Date is unknown.

Ricco

He pushed the send button, and he waited. It went through. His next task was to write a thank-you letter to Irene, as expected. With each scam, the thank-you letter became harder to write. He was the bad guy thanking someone he stole from. And worse, their hard-earned money was used to help the militia grow bigger and stronger. It was like stabbing them in the back and then twisting the knife.

Dear Irene,

I want to thank you for investing with me in our marketing plan for the book fair. I will immediately begin writing the press release, bookmarks, and postcards. If you have any questions, I can help you out from this end.

You may not hear from me until later this week. I do want to work on the confirmation of the printing and ISBN numbers. Also, I haven't heard from you about your bio and picture. You do not have to do a bio, but I highly suggest that you do. The picture you can opt out of.

Also, please give thought to the width and length that you want your book to be. Six-by-nine is extremely popular, but it's your choice. And the size of the font as well. We use only one font, which is Aptos. I like it and we have not had complaints, but the size of the font and line spacing is up to you. Lastly, the color of the paper: White is more expensive; we have a soft vanilla that I think works well. I understand that this is a lot to work with, but if I can have the information by Friday, it will be appreciated.

Again, thank you for marketing with us. Exciting days are ahead!

Ricco Smith

**He sat back and reread his letter.** He was self-destructing doing this work. The letter was a lie. Her book would never be published. And if by chance they did, which had happened, they would take all her royalties. She would be feeding them for as long as they could milk sells out of it. They change their name and use cryptocurrency to cover who they were and where they are.

Today he was selling time shares that did not exist, except for the picture he was holding. Pictures the Bossman had made with artificial intelligence. If he did escape, he would not hesitate to help bring down the Bossman and make him eat the letters they had to write, until it killed him.

## Chapter 17

# PACKING

**Stella met Betty and Irene** the following morning at Betty's spacious and contemporary apartment. She wanted to be on the plane with the guys as missing out on the action and collaborating was tough. Their extraction plans always involved working as a whole team, not splitting up at the planning stage. However, she understood Gaffer's reasoning: putting Edge or Dog with Betty and Irene would have been as bad as mixing oil and water. Their unpredictable nature would clash horribly with the calm and collected approach needed for this part of the mission. The chaos they could potentially bring was a risk Gaffer couldn't afford to take. Stella knew this, though it didn't make staying behind any easier. Her time would come to be with them as a group, and when it did, she'd be ready.

Stella addressed her friends with a determined tone: "All right, girls, we are going to London! There are a few directives I need to talk about with both of you."

Betty quickly interjected, "Can I get my writing pad and pen? It will only take a minute. My memory is unreliable when I am anxious."

Stella replied, "Sure, Betty, go grab it. I'm a notetaker too. Irene, do you want to grab a notebook or piece of paper also?"

"No, I can use Betty's notes if I need to." She chuckled. "I'll be a phenomenal listener. I haven't been to London, and I am pumped!"

Betty returned with a purple leather planner and a dark purple ink pen. Stella was momentarily fixated on the combination, thinking of how a piece of paper and a normal pen or pencil would also have worked. But that was Betty, all about presentation! Irene was the only one, out of the three, who was practical. Her life was consistent, which made Stella believe the fraudsters that took Irene for granted must have been well-trained professionals.

"First, we will be leaving Friday morning at 6:05. I will be picking you up with an Uber at 4:30. I know that is even before the early bird gets up, but we can dose on the plane. We arrive in London around noon, and we have the rest of the day to tour, shop, and eat. Any questions?" asked Stella.

Betty raised her hand eagerly.

"Yes, Betty?" replied Stella.

"Have you been to London before?" she inquired.

"I have spent months in London. I know it well. The smell of baked goods, especially scones, the black cabs, the cool air and hot tea, the earthy smell after a rain, the red buses—London is full of sights, smells, and experiences."

"What do we need to pack?" asked down-to-earth Irene.

"We are returning late on Monday, so keep it light. Make sure your walking shoes are of high quality. Pack a small umbrella or a good raincoat. Several sweaters, in fact, spring in London can be chilly. And whatever you feel the most comfortable in. Also, bring medications you are taking, over-the-counter vitamins, and first-aid articles included."

Betty grew overly excited hearing 'first aid.' "Do you think we will be in danger? Or subject to a kidnapping? I don't think I would be much help in a labor camp!"

"No, Betty. Calm down. I mentioned first aid because if we get a blister from walking or a cut, we will have to spend double or triple the money for Band-Aids. That's all. It's convenient to have those simple items with you," explained Stella.

"Let's move on. Any other questions about packing?" asked Stella.

Betty looked at Irene, Irene looked at Betty, and they both agreed that subject was over. Betty was excited to bring some of her new spring outfits while Irene worried about where to find quality walking shoes in one day.

"First, we will meet Maureen Smythe, Harris's mother. I have her address and have located her on the map. Gaffer wants us to show up rather than call ahead. We do not know whether she has found someone to stay with her while Harris is missing or not, and it's better to be cautious. That 'someone' could be part of the scam. We have three days to talk to her. However, the sooner we do, the better it is to explore his college activities," explained Stella.

"We should stop and pick up chocolates and/or flowers before the visit. I remember my mother, and I always did that when going to visit," Betty exclaimed, overthinking as usual.

Stella glanced at Irene who was beaming. Stella mirrored her smile. "That is a thoughtful idea. We will definitely do that. Now, I want to go over a few rules, and I will add more as we go. Always follow protocol. Keep your phones fully charged and with you at all times, even when you sleep. Make a copy of your passport and hide it in your suitcase or toiletries. I have a money belt for each of you to wear, and that is where your passport, charge cards, and even your cell phone can be kept at all times, even to bed. Do not bring cash—I will have that. And most importantly, *do not* let anything slip out as to why we are in London. The only response you use is 'We are visiting as tourists.' I will start conversations, but if I am not around, remember, *you are tourists.*"

"Stella, do we say we are from America?" asked Betty.

"No one needs to know we are Americans. They will figure it out on their own. If someone asks, just say 'a different country,' and change the subject. We aren't in any danger. No one will be following us. Gathering information and getting to know Harris's mother are our goals. Oh! One more thing, have fun while getting to know London."

"Where will Blizzard be?" asked a concerned Irene, petting Blizzard as she spoke. All these meetings had brought the two together. Stella noticed and thought that when this was over, she would take Irene to some shelters to find her own little four-legged fur friend. It would be healthy for Irene. Betty, involved with many committees and social events, had no time for puppy behavior; boredom or loneliness was not on her calendar.

"Irene, I appreciate your new found love for Blizzard. It appears she feels the same about you." All six pounds of Blizzard was curled up on Irene's lap. "Our precious Blizzard will stay with my neighbor while we are gone. Remember? That's her 'better' second home. Anything else? We are going to have a blast, and it may be our last one until after the rescue."

"I am so excited. Is there no way I can bring my tiny gun?" inquired Betty.

Stella looked long and hard at Betty. She could not imagine Betty at a shooting range. "You have a gun? A licensed gun?"

"I sure do!" replied Betty. "I have been shooting since I was sixteen. Isn't that right, Irene?"

Irene laughed. "She's right, Stella. Betty is a good shot. She hit her target nine out of ten times. And that one miss can be blamed on taking her eyes off the target to check out a guy."

"A little Annie Oakley! Well, I'll be damned! However, Slinger, you cannot bring any size gun into the airport. You know that!" Stella sternly reminded Betty.

"I know that!" Betty responded with sarcasm. "I thought with you being ex-military and whatever, that we could have an exclusion to the rule. That's all!"

"Slinger, that special rule is only for Gaffer. Even I cannot bring a gun!"

Irene piped in. "But, Stella, I have noticed that every time you go out you wear a weapon."

Stella stood back, a little surprised. "What are you saying, Irene?"

"You know what I am saying. Hair pins, necklaces, heels, rings, and bracelets. Some of them look pretty lethal."

"Wise, watchful Irene! You know me better than I thought," Stella answered slyly.

"Oh my goodness!" added Betty. "Now I can be known as 'Slinger.' Imagine that! A real spy, like on television!"

"Betty, my love, I am not a spy, but I do get involved in missions of a different nature. Now, Blizzard and I are going home to start packing. I suggest both of you do the same. Do you need a ride home, Irene?"

"Thank you, Stella, but I think I will walk today."

They began to gather their belongings when Irene heard the *ding* notice for her email.

"I feel like I should see who that is. It could be Ricco." She pulled out her phone. "It is from Ricco. Come here! Hurry!" Excitedly, she waved them over and opened the email.

Stella read the first line, grabbed her camera, and took three photos of the screen. Irene was reading out loud, with Betty mouthing every word; and then, poof, it was gone.

"Oh...my...Gosh!" Irene sat back, flushed, and nervous. "Did you get the photo, Stella?"

"I did. That was unexpected! I will send it to Gaffer. He's in flight now, but he will see the message when he lands. I'll mark it with our special code." Stella turned away and immediately did what she said.

Betty was quietly thinking, *I've never seen that before!* She asked, "How did he make it disappear?"

"With a self-destruct timer. He's clever! Gaffer will be impressed. Guess Harris is learning a few tricks with privacy and computers," Stella responded.

"What should I do?" asked Irene.

"We need to respond discreetly. Let me think." Stella walked around the apartment repeating various beginnings aloud.

"Why don't we chat about the book and weave the conversation into a sentence that states, 'One minute can seem like a long time, but it can also go by quickly!'" suggested Betty.

"I like that! It doesn't have to be long," added Stella.

"Wait, I have another email that popped up from Harris. It's a normal message thanking me for the purchase. We can tie the sentence into my response."

"Great!" Stella agreed. "Now for the beginning...Dear Harris, it was a surprise to hear from you so promptly. I hope all is well on your end and that you have time to rest this weekend. If I had your address, I would send you cookies and candy bars!"

Betty added, "Our time working on Quiet. Fear. is moving swiftly. One minute can seem like a long time, but with you, it goes by fast! Faster than a flashing camera!" Betty sat down grinning like a Cheshire cat. "What do you think?"

"I can work with that!" Irene called out. "Got it! I added a little about my bio and…sent." She pressed the arrow with satisfaction. "He'll know we received his message!"

"Looks like we did our work! Now girls, I have to run. Talk tomorrow!" Stella left like a flash with Blizzard in arm.

"You know what I'm thinking, Irene?" asked Betty.

"I sure do. Let's look at that map! Where is Ranong?" replied Irene.

The apartment door closed and locked automatically behind them. They rushed to the elevator, ready for their mission back at Irene's condo. They had a map and a country to study.

## Chapter 18

# THAILAND AND LONDON

**Gaffer, Edge, and Dog grabbed** as much sleep as they could on the twelve-hour flight to Thailand. They would land in Bangkok and then hop on a small private plane to get to Ranong. There they were to meet up with their contact and fishing guide, Direk.

Direk was born in Thailand and served in the Royal Thai Armed Forces for two years. Upon completing his two-year obligation, he learned to fluently read and write English in preparation of joining the US Army, eventually working with people like Gaffer.

Derek met the guys on the tarmac of Ranong's small, remote airport. Gaffer, Dog, and Edge were dressed in expensive casual wear. As they walked from the tarmac to Direk's jeep. They looked like wealthy American businessmen coming to visit for vacation.

"Hey, it's good to see you again!" Direk gave each a strong handshake. "The first thing to do when we get into town is change your clothes. Those threads are great for a round of golf, but for fishing, you need to wear the gear I left in your rooms. It's a good thing you all look the same as you did three years ago, because that is how I sized you!"

"Gaffer keeps us on a controlled diet," Dog joked around while Edge was already committing information to memory. His brain was like the black box of an aircraft.

"Follow me!" Direk led them to an older Toyota Tundra, opening the front passenger door for Gaffer while Edge and Dog jumped into the back. Direk threw their bags in the flatbed and jumped into the driver's seat to begin the short journey into Ranong.

"You wouldn't have packed any bottled water by chance?" Gaffer asked Direk. "I forgot how hot and humid it is here!" He wiped the beaded sweat from his forehead.

"Sure did! See the cooler on the floor, Dog. Cold waters are in there."

Dog handed everyone a bottle and thanked Direk.

"How have the rains been?" asked Gaffer.

"Not as often as they should be. We get a good six hours of sunshine, then it clouds up, and if it rains, they are short but strong for about thirty minutes, and then we have more sun," answered Direk. "Need to always be ready! We have a full moon tonight. The fishing will be great! Moonlight brings the fish up to the surface. There will be many boats out in the water, which will help us blend in. If you can't fish tonight, early morning is my other pick."

"Full moon, that's helpful for all of us," answered Gaffer.

"Are you leaning to an extraction on the sea or inland?" asked Direk.

"Not sure, that's what we are here for. What is the distance from the airport to our hotel in Ranong?" Gaffer asked, trusting Direk as he had helped them on several other missions.

"About fourteen miles," Direk replied. Do you want to visit the port first or the hotel? I ask because the way you are dressed now, they are going to treat you like royalty. Rich Americans spending American money!"

"Then let's do the port!" agreed Gaffer.

As they drove down the narrow, bumpy road, they appreciated Direk's defensive driving. The sides of the road were lined with tropical evergreens and mangrove trees in the wet areas. The contrasting aqua water and white sand beaches grabbed their attention. The aqua water led their eyes out to the sea where a brilliant dark blue water blended into the skyline.

Edge was in awe. "Damn, I want to get out, take a swim and dry off on that beach! How about it, Gaffer?"

"Another day, Edge, that's a promise!" replied Gaffer and added, "Hey, Dog, how are you doing? You're awfully quiet back there."

"Thinking about those kids, and how in heaven are they going to get to the beach?" responded Dog. "And how are we going to get to the compound?"

"No worries yet, Dog," Direk assured him. "I have been watching deliveries to the compound come and go. They also have a back room in one of the stores in the market. There are holes in their business."

"Is that right?" asked Gaffer.

"Not kidding you! Our street and road lights are dimly lit, if lit at all. That's to our advantage," offered Direk.

"Tomorrow we will do sightseeing on land. Any way to rent motorcycles?" asked Gaffer.

"Maybe I could round up a couple old scooters. Be careful on these roads!" Direk reminded the guys. "People die every day. Keep your speed down. Always remember you are dumb American tourists."

Gaffer turned up the air-conditioning. "By the way, where are we staying?"

"The only place here that has air-conditioning. The Sino Mansion. It looks like a Southern plantation home with three floors, all white exterior, and columns. The market is across the street. You can get fresh fruit daily with only a few steps. Big crowds, but few steps. I reserved three rooms with private baths."

"Great work!" praised Gaffer. "It sounds accommodating, and I hope to walk the market before we leave."

"We're coming up to the port," announced Direk

Edge was impressed. "It's bigger than it looked on the internet. Check out those old fishing boats! And over there are the new power boats. Interesting. Where do the ships come in."

Direk pointed out a large L-shaped dock. "In that direction. This port is Ranong's lifeline. It employs many men and keeps us connected with the world. Sometimes we get big yachts stopping in. The whole town talks about it."

"Hmm, interesting! Is the port authority friendly to that?" inquired Gaffer.

"Yes, especially when someone famous is on the yacht," answered Direk. "But the port authorities are tough. All papers and documents must be accurate. I see people being arrested every day. Typically, fisher men without licenses. Okay, now I take you to your rooms."

Once in the room, Gaffer took out his phone to check his messages. He saw that Stella had sent him four. He quickly opened the oldest first.

**Gaffer read the message Stella sent to him** from Ricco—sent via as a self-destructing email to Irene.

Immediately after reading it, Gaffer replied to Stella: "Sorry I didn't check earlier. Having trouble with the cells.

Arrived safely. Checked out the port authority. It's tight. We were right on the location. It is Ranong. Harris was smart to send in self-destruct. Reply cautiously. I know you three can do better than me. Heading out with Direk. He says hello.

Will send a message to you tomorrow. Stay connected and safe travel. PS: It feels strange without you."

Gaffer knew that if he didn't sent the "PS," she would be pissed off and probably forever.

The team gathered in the lobby, waiting for Direk. "Hey, guys, while we are waiting, I sent each of you the message I received from Stella. Have you read it?" Both agreed that they had.

Gaffer continued, "It is a relief to know that our tracing is right. He's not far from us. How are going to find this camp?"

"I don't know, Gaff. The locals have eyes like flies." Edge was feeling anxious being watched by everyone. "There's no blending in, that's for sure!"

Dog added, "When we get out into the countryside you'll feel differently. And today is our first day. They're watching and waiting for us to begin using our money. Just wait and see."

"That's exactly what we need to do now while we're waiting! The market is right across the street. Let's check it out and make a few purchases. I hope that will take some curiosity off our shoulders," Gaffer agreed.

The market was congested. People were moving from shoulder to shoulder. The late morning sun was hot, and the air smelled pungent from all the perspiring bodies. Gaffer, Edge, and Dog moved closer to the covered stands on the sidewalk. Here they could feel a slight breeze and more smells of fresh fruit and sticky rice. Each bought a T-shirt representing Ranong and added a few dollars extra for the purchase. The seller was happy and wanted to sell them belts, but they moved on to a stand of fresh mangoes. They picked up a bag, paid extra for it, and returned to their hotel.

"Man, this market is too crowded for me," complained Edge.

"Nah," said Dog, "you don't like crowds. Admit it, Edge!"

"You're right, I don't like concerts, sporting events, malls. I prefer small shops, with personal shopping. Not fighting for your life over a banana!" replied Edge.

The guys were sharing laughs and short stories when Direk pulled up in the truck. "The fishing gear outfits suit you all much better! I see you bought some local T-shirts. Good idea. Keep them with you. You may need to do the tourist act in the near future. The dirt road that most likely goes to the camp isn't the safest. I am not familiar with it, and the locals appear to have amnesia, but I know *they* know about it. Darn frustrating."

"What about dirt bikes? A bunch of reckless Americans tearing up the road. It would be a good cover," Gaffer thought aloud. "We could have a few drinks and go crazy. What do you think, Direk?"

"I can get four dirt bikes. They are not going to be new. How good are all of you at riding? As I mentioned before, the roads are deadly," Direk reminded them.

"Edge and I take ours out a few times a month. I'd say we are experienced, but I can't speak for old Gaffer here!" Dog said with a smart short chuckle.

"All right, Dog! I am going to kick your ass. And what are you snickering about, Edge? I'll kick yours too! I've been riding dirt bikes since I was seven," Gaffer said, turning to address Direk. "Does the gear come with it? Helmets and gloves at least? We have our own goggles and boots, and we can wear our new T-shirts. These military-grade kakis are tough."

"Helmets and gloves should be easy, then let's get going. The rain is coming this afternoon," Gaffer announced.

They grabbed extra bottles of water and jumped into the truck. Direk led them out of town, down a country road where they stopped at an old garage that looked like a century-old junkyard. "This family has been fixing anything with a motor for as long as my father and mother have lived here. If it has a motor, you bring it to Chai Son. We are good friends," Direk said proudly.

"Man," said Dog, "I would love to have a day to walk over his land and look at these artifacts! What do you say, Edge?"

Edge whistled, "Absolutely!"

"Let's get going, the day is slipping away from us," urged Gaffer.

Direk, speaking in Thai asks Chai Son about the dirt bikes, helmets, and gloves. Chai Son and Direk negotiate a price. "That's done. One hundred American dollars for the four bikes and gear. Fair?" he asked Gaffer.

"More than fair," Gaffer replied. "But where are they? I've been looking around and cannot find any."

"They would not be here long if they were outside-thieves. He keeps them in here." Direk pointed to the makings of a house, attached to the garage, and had been added onto several times. "His family keeps growing. He owns the land, a lot of land, and the family stays on it."

"I get it." Gaffer confirms. "Let's help him move them out." He looked at Edge and Dog. "Hey, you monkeys, move ass and help Chai Son and Direk get the bikes."

They gathered together and went inside. The air was thick with the smell of oil and gas. They came out pulling four Honda CR500 bikes, about twenty years old. Their jaws dropped as they beheld the pristine condition the bikes were in.

"Can you believe this?" whispered Edge to Gaffer.

Gaffer and Dog whispered back, "We can't find these back home! Chai Son has a gold mine here!"

"He threw in two extra gas cans. He said the road we are looking for is only a mile or so from here. We can leave the truck and use the bikes."

Gaffer looked at Chai Son and then Direk. "How do we know it's going to be here when we get back?"

Direk chuckled. "In town, I worry about that more, but here, Chai Son and his family will sit in it and pretend they are Americans. No one is going to hot-wire it and drive off the property unless they have a death wish!"

"Okay, grab the waters, gear up, and let's see where that dirt path, or road, leads us."

Dog and Edge took off like fourteen-year-old kids, racing down the narrow road. Gaffer and Direk followed behind at a steady pace. They reached the "road" that led inward, through the mangrove trees toward the foothills. The road was nothing more than two parallel dirt paths for tires, with some greenery in between.

"Whoever made this 'road' sure didn't want visitors!" commented Dog as all four stood studying what they were about to enter.

"The massive root systems of these mangrove trees is a treacherous maze," Gaffer pointed out.

"And beware of the potholes. They are filled with water from the rains, but we have no idea how deep those puddles are," added Edge. "The wet sand and peat can be problematic too."

"Look at those roots in the forest, how could anyone get through those at night?" inquired Direk.

The four kept looking down the road. "What do you think? Go in a mile or forget this option and go fishing to check out the coastline?" asked Gaffer.

Dog and Edge were sharing thoughts. Dog spoke up, "Let's go as slow as the dirt will allow us to. It may improve as we travel inward, or we may meet some militia."

"Direk, what are you thinking?" asked Gaffer.

"I've seen worse, but we can't have a race or be smart asses. It's serious biking."

All nodded in agreement. They jumped on their bikes and began moving forward. After ten minutes, Gaffer pulled over to the edge and stopped, signaling the others to pull up and stop also.

"How is everyone doing so far?" he asked.

Direk was quick to respond. "So far, it's doable. We want to watch the sky because there is no way we would make it out of here in the rain. It comes down like tiny hammers, beating your body and the earth."

Gaffer checked the weather on his watch. We have about two hours. Let's go a little deeper, then we'll turn around and come back."

No one could take time to study possible places to hide or run; they had to keep their eyes focused on the pits and roots of the road. The hideous loud buzz of the bikes drowned out all sounds of life. They hadn't traveled far before everyone saw Gaffer try to stop quickly and wipe out. He pulled himself up and immediately held his hand out to inform the others to stop. All four bikes went silent. No one spoke. They looked ahead with Gaffer. An old jeep was coming toward them. It was the militia.

"Everyone, stay quiet. Let me talk," Direk firmly ordered.

The jeep stopped a few feet away from Gaffer. Direk was alongside him. The four militia soldiers drew down their guns and walked toward the bikes, stopping to have a solid look at each man and each bike.

"Americans?" the leader asked.

"Yes, Americans," Direk answered.

"Nice bikes! Where did you get them?"

"We rented them, sir," Direk answered without looking him straight in the eye, as that would be disrespectful.

"From Mr. Chai Son," one soldier firmly stated.

Direk was being set up. If he said no, they would know he was lying. If he said yes, he could get Chai Son and his family in trouble. Direk said nothing.

Gaffer answered. That way Direk would keep his respect in the community. "Yes, Mr. Chai Son! What a gift he has with motors. A good man and family."

"What's your purpose here?" the head militia spoke directly to Gaffer.

"To have a vacation, go fishing, relax, that's about it!"

"You military in America. You look military except him." He pointed to Direk.

Gaffer smiled. "He's our bookkeeper at our gym. He's smart but not big."

The militia leader returned a smile. "Turn around now and go back. Tell Chai Son he has nice bikes. We won't see you again."

They jumped in the jeep, waited for Gaffer and the guys to move their bikes to the side, and drove forward to town.

When they were far away, Gaffer asked Direk, "Where do you think they are going?"

"First, they will stop at Chai's shop. Our stories will match, so no problem there, but Chai may need to pay them something. Then they will go into town," he replied.

Gaffer stood thinking for a minute. "We'll give Chai Son a nice tip, so he makes something from our business. That's it for dirt bike riding. We're heading back. I don't think this road is a possibility for extraction. Let's get out of here and back to town. Maybe we can find where they stopped. That could be their main office."

**Stella, Betty, and Irene** were brimming with excitement as they stepped into the bustling chaos of London's Heathrow Airport. Their laughter and chatter filled the air as they rolled their suitcases behind them. Stella waved down a black cab, and they adventurously hopped in, heading to The Waldorf Hilton.

London was foreign to Irene, and immediately the black cabs and iconic red buses amused her as they whizzed by. Their journey had just begun when Stella pointed out the London Eye in the distance.

"I never thought I would see that!" exclaimed Irene. "Do you think our driver will take us to Picadilly Circus? I heard it is comparable to New York's Time Square."

"Hold your horses, Irene! We have so much to see in the next three days, you are going to erupt with excitement! I will ask the driver to take us to Picadilly first. Do you want to get out and walk around?" asked Stella.

"Oh no, that's not necessary! Riding around to sightsee is fine. We can walk when we get to the Waldorf." The chatting paused, and Irene asked Stella, "How did Gaffer pull off a stay at the Waldorf? I have heard it's expensive!"

"I have no freaking idea! I have known Gaffer since I was twenty-three, and I still don't *really* know him. He rarely talks about himself, his childhood, young adulthood, or even his family! I don't even know his real name. I guess the military is his family. And us course, me, Edge, and Dog."

"I bet he's in a witness protection program! Maybe his parents were foreign spies, and they were killed. Then the military raised him!" Betty was stirred with the secrecy of his life.

"No, Gaffer is not in a witness protection program. He's too visible. I have painstakingly stayed awake trying to figure him out, with no success. I suggest you see Gaffer as Gaffer is, and don't look any further."

Betty remarked, "Maybe we should investigate him! Irene! This is material for your next novel! He had to be born somewhere and given a real name."

Both Stella and Irene shook their heads no. It was not going to happen.

"Oh well, I do have good ideas!" Betty mumbled as she returned to watching the hustle and bustle of London, remembering the many good times she and her husband shared while on their honeymoon in London.

"After we settle and check in with Gaffer, do you mind going for a walk to Covent Garden? It's right by the Waldorf and is full of shops, pubs, restaurants. You can see the Royal Opera. The Apple Market is fun if you enjoy art. There's always street music. It's pleasurable and also relaxing. And wear your walking shoes because the cobblestone is hard on the feet and a bit offsetting with one's balance. We can split up for now and meet up later." Stella calmed her tone. "To be honest, I didn't pack many clothes to wear. So now I need to pick up a few outfits."

"For heaven's sake, why didn't you pack any clothes? You have such interesting and creative pieces. Some have a hard look, almost gothic. Then you mix it with a soft feminine flare using fabrics and accessories," Irene admired Stella.

"Thanks for the compliment. I didn't pack because I was in a bad mood." Stella spoke with a tone that told Irene and Betty not to pursue this line of questioning any further.

They drove around Picadilly Circle and the surrounding area, pointing out various lit signs and the cinematic characters in Leicester Square. "One night, I would love to take you both to the Piccadilly Circus Underground station," suggested Stella.

"What is it?" inquired Irene.

"It is the heart of London. Basically, it's a bomb shelter where people went during air raids in the Second World War. The tour is outstanding!" remarked Stella.

"That would be fun to see! They use it in movies!" added Betty.

"That is true! Now are you both ready to check in at the Waldorf?" asked Stella.

"I am!" stated Irene. "Please tell me what it looks like inside, so I am not shell shocked."

Betty shot Stella a smile as she could see Stella wasn't born to be a patient tour guide.

"It was built in the early 1900s," Betty began. "It has a simple but elegant art deco–inspired décor. I think that's why Gaffer chose it. Simple and elegant. Clean and comfortable. It was closed for a long time and reopened in the 1930s. At one time, it was the tallest hotel in the world, becoming a hangout for the rich and famous. You will love it! We each have a shopping break one-bedroom suite with a king bed."

Stella broke in, "After we are checked in, how about an hour to unpack and shower and then meet in the lobby? Remember the rules! Do not tell anyone why we are really here. Instead, tell them we are visiting a friend and sightseeing. Tonight we enjoy London! Tomorrow we investigate! Cheers!" Stella raised her water bottle. Betty and Irene followed suit.

In the lobby, all three girls chatted at one time approving their rooms, as they began walking to the garden. When they entered the square, Irene's eyes grew wide! "This is beautiful! And look over there! Those are the old-time red phone booths! I need a picture of that! Where do we start? It's overwhelming!" she asked Betty and Stella.

Stella, smiling a Cheshire grin, answered, "I am going inside the mall to a few quaint clothing stores. Betty, is there anything you want to see first? I know Irene wants to see everything!"

Betty grew quiet and then replied, "I would like to go to The Apple Market, and from there, we can get a tourist map and go on adventures. That is if you think it is a good plan, Irene."

"Yes! It's a great plan and of course I would like to stay together. It would be fun to hear what you remember and how it is different or the same today. Should we meet somewhere in a few hours?" Irene turned to Stella.

"In three hours, we'll be tired and hungry. Let's meet at the Ave Mario. It's the best Italian restaurant. Or we could do Flat Iron, which is a steak house. And if you would rather eat a lighter meal, we can meet at Chequers, which is a popular sandwich pub. Your pick. I'm good with any of them."

"We're not dressed fancy, and we'll be tired. I vote for the sandwich pub," suggested Betty.

"That good with me. Maybe tomorrow we can try the Italian!" Irene commented as she continued to be immersed in her surroundings.

"Look at your watches, set a timer for three hours, and I will meet both of you at Chequers." Stella watched her friends take off giggling like they were young teens. They didn't look like they were in their fifties. They were spry, in good shape, clever, and funny. Now she wished she had packed so they could experience the Garden with them! She took out her phone and called Gaffer.

Gaffer answered immediately, "Hi, Stella, how was your trip?"

"It has been well-planned so far! Thank you for that! What is happening on your end?" she asked. "It feels strange not being there, like my right arm is missing!"

"Yeah, the guys and I have the same feeling. Direk said hello. He hasn't changed one bit. The same Direk we worked with a few years ago in Africa."

Stella smiled to herself. Direk had a difficult time when they first met because he insisted on treating her like a helpless female, which she certainly wasn't. "Tell him hello from me, and I will see him soon. I do believe he owes me a drink."

"I will do that. As far as we have experienced, I believe a land extraction is not going to work unless we make a unique, never-seen-before, creative plan. The road leading to the camp isn't really a road. It's a rough path through the mangrove forest. The roots are everywhere, and they're sometimes difficult to see. And there are potholes filled with water, which we don't know their depth. We didn't get far before the militia were onto us. At night, it would be *more* difficult to navigate. On foot would be easier, but the chances of a broken or sprained ankle are high because of those darn trees and their root systems. We took dirt bikes and had to be on guard all the time."

"What about the sea?" asked Stella.

"Tonight we are going night fishing to check that out. We think their headquarters may be in town. We will be looking at that too. I forgot how humid and hot this part of the world is. How's London?"

"London is gorgeous and busy as usual. We are going to hang out and relax tonight and begin our work tomorrow morning. We will start with Harris's mother."

"Sounds like a plan. I will call you when we have news. Right now, I want to see if we can locate the militia's jeep here in Ranong. Have to run, Stella."

"Talk soon, Gaffer. Say hi to the guys for me! Have a cold beer tonight!" With that, the call ended, and Stella strolled to the upper level of shops, beginning to put together a comfortable outfit, and another that was in between. She loved shopping, but it still could not keep her mind off the guys. Direk was her replacement, she thought to herself, and he was a better choice for this particular scouting. He speaks so many languages, knows the sea and boats, and has fly eyes too. I need to relax and enjoy this opportunity. It's wonderful to be with Betty and Irene!

## Chapter 19
# CHANGE OF PLANS

**Maya woke up to th**e blazing morning sun, her skin already shining with sweat. She squinted out the small open window, seeing dark thunderous clouds inching across the horizon. Yesterday, the Bossman had ordered her and the other workers to secure everything they could as the approaching rains could be merciless.

She hurriedly dressed, washed her face, brushed her teeth, and tied back her hair. She hurried down the hallway to a small mess room where she and others like her ate. Next to it was where the militia ate. The two were never to mix, but occasionally, they would. Maya believed they were snitches, spying and waiting for one of the workers to say or do something wrong. Even direct eye contact was forbidden.

Today, there were no strangers or militias—just a couple of Maya's friends sitting casually at the roughly made rubber wood tables and benches. The ever-present pot of overly sweet Thai red tea steamed on the counter, a mockery of normalcy. Maya longed for a spicier tea blend or a hot coffee, but the overly sweet tea was all they had, and all they would have for years to come. With a disappointing sigh, she poured herself a cup.

Breakfast was a meager bowl of sticky rice and fresh mangoes. She sat next to Ammara, who worked in the kitchen under the orders of camp's cook. She was from Thailand and was also scammed into believing this would be a progressive addition to a hospitality career.

"Good morning, Ammara. It's like a ghost town here! Where is everyone?" she inquired.

"I'm not sure," answered Ammara equally as inquisitive. "The air feels...off, eerie. And tense! I was up at four to help cook. We served an early breakfast, and then most of the soldiers left in jeeps. They didn't head toward town, instead, they headed toward Myanmar. We were all scared! Why Myanmar?"

"Hmm, that is strange and scary. Just like the air. Did they take any laborers with them?" Maya's mind raced.

"No, it was just militia. No covered trucks. Only jeeps," replied Ammara.

Maya's fear was changing into curiosity. "You're saying no one is here but a few soldiers?"

"Yes, and they are keeping an eye on the laborers. Do you think they are avoiding the storm? Floods can be deadly here, especially this close to the sea. I wonder if the townspeople are moving to higher ground?" Ammara looked and sounded concerned.

"I wish we could get to town to see what's happening. We've had severe rains before but no floods. Moving water is powerful. I've seen videos of entire houses swept away from the power of moving water. And in college, three students were killed by storm waves. The water snapped their necks. We're done if the water gets that high here and the field workers... no chance with those flimsy huts. What are we to do?" Maya's nerves and anxiety pulsed through her entire body.

"I have no idea. Like I said, my family always took off toward the mountains," answered Ammara as her face paled.

"The barracks where the laborers are is four stories high. We could take refuge on the roof if it's strong enough," Maya pondered out loud.

"Maya, we do not even know if a flood is coming. We can only tie down what we can and wait!" Ammara explained, trying to remain calm. "And that roof is as old as the hills. I doubt it could hold."

"Why don't we leave and move quickly inland?" Maya wasn't one to wait passively for disaster. "Stay here! I'll be back!" She dashed out of the room.

"Where are you going?" Ammara called out to her.

Maya turned briefly. "Please, stay right here. Have another cup of tea. I'll be back soon. I need to check on something." And with that, Maya was out of sight. She couldn't tell Ammara she was heading to Bossman's office. If Ammara ever let it slip out, it would be over for both of them.

Cautiously and attentively, Maya walked down the narrow hallway to Bossman's office. She examined the thin bamboo walls and dried grasses. She knew it would never withstand the hurricane-like winds and pelting rain. She listened carefully for any noise, a creak, a door, voices, even sounds from outside. It was unusually quiet. It was far from normal, and it frightened her.

The door to the Bossman's office was ajar, another unsettling sight. She knocked softly. No answer. Then louder—still no answer. Slowly, she opened the door, just enough to fit her body through and swiftly moved to the large map on the wall. She did everything methodically. If she was on camera, she did not want to appear suspicious. She was simply looking at a map using her fingers to trace various routes while actually looking at where they were.

The faded map was worn, crisscrossed with many lines connecting cities, towns, and villages. She zeroed in where it said "Home." They were in southern Thailand, near the town Ranong. The foothills were to the east. She turned her attention to the Bossman's desk; and behind his desk, on the wall, was a large calendar marked with notes.

As she backed away from the map, she tried to read the notes on the calendar, specifically looking for "new laborers." There it was, written inside a large red star on June 20: new laborers.

Suddenly, the sound of breaking glass shattered the silence. Her heartbeat rocketed to her throat. She paused, breathless, and then moved cautiously past the open door and into the hallway. There, she exhaled slowly, placed her hands over her stomach, as she took in a deep breath and closed her eyes. In minutes she felt centered, straightened her posture, and returned to Ammara.

Ammara was exactly where Maya had left her, with cold rice, mangoes, and tea. "Hi! That wasn't long! But your breakfast is cold as well as your tea," Ammara wore an untrusting look.

"That's all right. I'll eat it cold. We can't waste food here! Hey, when I was gone, did you hear glass breaking?" Maya asked.

"I did! It sounded like it came from the kitchen. The person who broke something is lucky no one is around. They'd get a beating!"

Maya finished her cold breakfast. "We have it good here. Not like the laborers. They break them down to a low level of being human. Anyway, that sound of breaking glass, was different than a heavy dish being broken. It was a finer glass. We should take a walk around the grounds before we begin to tie things down." Maya's thoughts drifted to Ricco. Did someone break a window in their building? Did the laborers notice the small number of soldiers and begin a takeover? Her mind was racing.

Maya grabbed her medical bag just in case she was needed and the two of them walked over to where the laborers were held. Normally, she would make this walk during the night, when the darkness hid the grime and decay. Now, in the harsh daylight, every detail was revealed—the roots breaking out of the earth like thick skeletal fingers wanting to grab you. And the intense heat slowly simmering her skin. The smells of sewage and swamp were stronger than the smell of the sea. She mentally prepared herself for anything that laid ahead.

Ammara spoke up. "I am going back to our building. We are not to be here during the day. Maya, please come back with me. Don't take a risk over the sound of breaking glass. It's not worth it. Like you said, we have it so much better than these people. Come on!" She tugged at Maya's arm.

Maya pulled away. "There's something I must do."

"Do it tonight when you make your rounds. Keep everything the same. It's safer that way."

"Are we to let all these people not have a chance to save their own lives if a flood happens? Are we, Ammara? Are we to think only of ourselves?" Maya's voice trembled with anger and passion.

"Maya, in this hell hole, everyone focuses only on one life: their own. Now, come back with me."

"No," Maya remained firm. "I'll move ahead on my own. You go back, and if you see the Bossman returning, do the bird call we learned to warn others."

"I will." Ammara turned and began to run back to their building.

Maya took another deep breath, contemplating an excuse to get into the computer room. They had to leave a soldier behind to watch them—maybe several. She could ask the soldiers if they had heard of any flood warnings for the afternoon and evening and then check to see if Ricco was there. If so, she could ask his presence for a wound check, claiming she wouldn't be able to do rounds tonight due to the weather. It was a solid plan.

Nervously, she approached the old rotten wooden door of the once popular hostel. It had several locks, some new, some old. The rusty hinges seemed ready to give way. The entire compound appeared as though it could collapse with the slightest nudge from Mother Nature. Perhaps escaping wouldn't be as difficult as she and Ricco feared.

Slowly, she pushed the door open and immediately, the stench of sewer, sweat, and heat hit her in the face. There was no air circulation. The barred windows offered no relief. She followed the sound of clicking keyboards up to the second floor, a familiar route from her night rounds. Ricco was on this floor.

With steady, confident steps, she navigated the corner and down the long hallway. At the end was the computer room, guarded by two soldiers. As she approached, their relaxed stance turned defensive.

"State your name!" the tallest burliest soldier sternly shouted.

"I am Maya from medical." She extended her lanyard, displaying her photo and the keys she used for rounds.

"What is your business?" he sternly demanded.

"I heard there is a strong storm approaching and I am doing my rounds now instead of tonight. Did you hear anything about the storm?" she asked innocently.

The burly soldier replied, "At early breakfast, there was a little noise about such a storm, but nothing since."

"Well, I am here to do a final wound check on Ricco Smith." Maya couldn't believe how calm she felt while lying to their faces.

The two soldiers conferred with one another as the burly one kept an eye on Maya. After their talk, he approached her. "Give me your medical bag." He searched through it recklessly, zipped it up, and put it on the floor. "Put your hands in the air," he ordered and began patting her down, pausing at her slim waistline. She restrained from hitting him, holding her emotions at bay and feeling the throbbing warning from her heart to stay calm. She knew any reaction would cause a more harmful response. He stopped, then handed back her medical bag.

"We will bring him out. He can sit on the floor while you check his head wound."

When the soldiers left, Maya shook off her nerves and focused on her shallow breathing. She needed to stay calm and collected.

When the double doors opened, she saw Ricco, looking pale and fragile. The life in his soul was gone. Her heart sank.

They helped him walk to the corner and ordered him to sit. He did exactly that, not letting on how much he wanted to grab Maya and run. If he only had the strength. But lately, they wanted all the laborers to be weak, restricting food, water, sleep, exercise, and even outdoor time.

Maya had him slide forward as she crawled behind him. She moved his hair gently toward the side to expose the wound. Ricco's shoulders relaxed feeling her soft healing touch again.

While she was moistening a cloth to clean the healing gash, she whispered into his ear, "Are they feeding you? Head down for no."

Ricco dropped his head down.

"Are you getting three bottles of water every day?"

Once again, his head dropped downward.

"Has Irene contacted you?" Ricco's head stayed steady.

"Do they know where we are?" Ricco's head stayed steady.

"The twentieth of June are replacements. There are hardly any guards today. Bossman is gone. Headed toward Myanmar early morning with most soldiers. There's a big storm coming. I am afraid of flooding. Love you. Check your pockets."

"That's enough time!" one of the soldiers yelled.

"I am done. Would you like to see the dirt and dried blood I removed?" Maya wanted to scream at them, poke their eyes out and push them down the stairs, but instead, she taunted them. It was stupid and dangerous.

"You're done!" The soldier walked over to Maya and poked her with the barrel of the gun.

"So sorry! I forgot to put this ointment on. It will only take a minute, then I am done. Thank you. Thank you." The soldier's rank of authority was much higher than hers. She bowed to his feet several times, pulling her anger inward.

Swiftly, she applied the ointment and zipped up her medical bag. She mouthed to Ricco, "I love you!."

As soon as she turned the corner, she began to run down the steps, barging out the door, and into air that she could breathe and enough safety that she could let her tears fall. When she reached her room, she began to pack what she thought they would need into a pair of soccer socks.

The soldiers grabbed Ricco under his arms, pulled him up, and pushed him forward, back into the computer room. "Work!" one soldier commanded. Ricco kept his head down and walked to his station. Once he was sure no eyes were watching, he checked his pocket. He felt two protein bars and a key... Maya slipped him the key to his cell.

Ricco began to sweat more than usual. *My god! She has put a death sentence on her head. She can't stay. She has to leave tonight. But where can we meet? Think Ricco, think? By the gate where the fencing is broken? Or on the beach where the women were raped? Which one would Maya choose?*

His hands trembled as his mind raced. He couldn't think of anything but Maya. He closed his eyes, trying to remember their time together. Had she given him a clue?

His eyes widened. *The beach! She spoke more about the beach.* He would leave as soon as they brought him back to his cell.

*Now, I must send a note to Irene.*

Dear Irene,

We are preparing for a strong monsoon rain. There could be flooding, and I have no idea if our camp will survive. Maya and I have a plan. We will head to the beach by the sea. There are only a few militia, maybe a dozen at most. I hope your friends have our location. We have the cell phone, and the battery is at 80 percent. I will turn it on when we leave for the beach. Hopefully, they can locate us.

I am sorry for scamming you out of your money. It is not who I am, but what they forced me to be. It is almost impossible not to be scammed these days. They have worked through the problems. Don't blame yourself or feel ashamed. I was scammed too! If I do not make it, hunt these animals down.

Self-destruct in five...four...three...two...one.

**Ammara came running into Maya's room.** "Where have you been?" she asked Maya, who was frantically stuffing medical supplies into a sock.

Maya had reached her breaking point. Prisoner no more. Life and death were indistinguishable. She was desperate for freedom—for herself and Ricco. "What does it *look* like

I'm doing?" Maya rudely answered. She had no patience for anyone who wasn't on the same page as her.

"I have no idea! You're behaving like a wild animal!" replied Ammara.

"I'm getting out of here. The timing is perfect, and there are few guards. When the rains come, everyone will want to move to the upper floors or the roof. It will be a disaster. Remember, Ammara, when we arrived, and the rain belted down so fiercely we couldn't stand, and the soldiers had to carry us? That's the kind of rain we are facing! The laborers haven't had much food or water for at least a week. They are frail. This is a death trap, and the Bossman left us to die."

"Then I am coming with you and Ricco. I can be helpful. I know this country, the language, and the land. You need me." Ammara stood firm. Maya stood firm. They stared each other down, words hanging in the air.

Maya broke the silence. "You're right! We do need you. Now tell me, is running to the sea safer than taking the road into town?"

Ammara gave the question thought. "We always left to higher ground. Neither of those choices are good."

"Can we climb the mangrove trees or the pines?" Maya's voice was desperate.

"The mangroves are treacherous. Their roots are like Medusa's hair. They are not safe. The pines are stronger. But my advice…is to stay away from a tree to save your life."

"Then what? How?" Maya's voice cracked as she screamed through tears of fear and frustration.

Ammara paced, racking her brain. "Maya, what about the rocks?"

"What rocks? I don't understand!" shrieked Maya who was now in an intense form of panic.

Ammara closed her eyes, trying to maintain her composure. Maya kept unraveling. "Stop yelling!" Ammara directed in a low, slow voice. "Calm down and listen!"

Maya sank onto her bed, dried her eyes, and focused on Ammara's words. "The beach. We have been there together. Remember, to the south, we could not get to town because of the rocky ledge?"

Maya sat up straighter. Her eyes widened. "Yes, I remember! We found a path carved by people, but we had to return to camp and didn't finish the exploration."

"Exactly! During heavy rain and high winds, those rocks will shield us from being swept out to sea. It's dangerous, but it's the best chance to survive. The forest is mostly mangroves, and the road will become a swift moving river."

"Then the rocks it is! We have to reach them before the sun sets. Ammara, do you think we have a chance?"

"Today, yes. It's like the powers of nature are giving us a sign. A good omen. When do you think Ricco can meet us?" Ammara asked Maya.

"Nothing is predictable today. I have no idea, but he will come. I know it." Maya's face stained with tears and her eyes filled with fear.

"Okay, breathe, relax your shoulders, and focus on preparing the camp," Ammara placed her hands on Maya's shoulders. " Like you said, we need to do all that we can for those who are left behind. What if Bossman returns and nothing is done? We would have no choice but to jump into the sea."

Ammara and Maya faced each another again. Both understanding that their lives would either end in the camp or during the escape from it. The latter had more honor.

Together, they began to secure large items down with rope and tarps. Frequently, they glanced at the once-distant thunderous sky, which continued to creep ominously closer. Maya began to swear, as a pain shot up from the bottom of her foot. She collapsed onto the ground; Ammara quickly ran over to help. A large fragment of glass was lodged in Maya's foot.

"Ammara, go to my room and bring me my medical bag. Hurry!"

Ammara swiftly dashed to Maya's room, picked up her bag, and returned.

"Do you want me to pull it out?" Ammara asked, her voice trembling.

"Use my scissors. I think it's deep. On the count of three. One…two…three!"

Ammara pulled hard and fast. The sharp glass slid out easily as Maya winced in pain.

"Damn!" Maya was visibly upset. "This is going to make climbing rocks and running so much harder. I am angry at myself. Why am I barefoot? I can't think straight!" She scolded herself as she applied pressure, her herbal wash, an ointment, and then a wrapping.

Ammara tried to comfort her. "Maya, it is a clean cut. If you put a sock over the wrapping and wear my boots instead of those stupid slip-ons they give us you'll be fine."

"I can't take your rubber boots. You will need them."

"Remember, I grew up in Thailand. I was barefoot most of my life! I will feel like a kid again! If I can't make it, we'll share them…each of us will have one good gripping foot!" Ammara laughed until she noticed Maya studying the sharp fragment of clear glass.

"We don't have glass like this on camp. It must have come from the main building. We heard it shattering earlier. Whoever dropped it must be planning to escape also. This broken glass could be a good weapon against the militia. It's a good four inches long. And look at the pattern. I haven't seen anything similar to this on the camp's grounds."

Maya handed Ammara the glass. Ammara held it up to the sky. "You're right. This glass didn't come from the camp. Someone was here. Who and where did they go?"

## Chapter 20

# PLANS HAVE CHANGED

**Not knowing about the monsoon,** Betty, Stella, and Irene blindly continued to enjoy their time together. They met at the sandwich shop and ordered the daily special ciabatta bread, which came with a free cup of the popular, renowned tomato basil soup. Since it was a take-and-go restaurant, they agreed to take it back to the hotel.

"Are you sure this is all you want to eat?" questioned Stella.

"Irene and I have been sampling an array of food and drinks at the mall! The Humble Apple crumbles were out of this world! And we *had* to share a scone with dark chocolate bits scattered in it! Heaven for me! Soup, fresh bread, and wine sounds perfect for now!" answered a tired Betty.

Stella grinned as she looked at the collection of bag sizes each held in their hands. "I guess you two did pretty well on your own…plenty of tastings and shopping bags!"

"Oh, we did, Stella! How about you? Did you find the clothing you were looking for?" asked Betty.

"I did! And I know you'll both approve." Stella held up several bags as well.

They walked up the steps and into Waldorf's Good Godfrey's Bar. The bar was charming with dark wood on the walls, floor-to-ceiling glass windows to watch shoppers, and quaint tables with comfortable chairs just waiting to be sat in. They chose a table in a quiet corner and began to take out their food.

A waiter approached, bringing them water, napkins, and silverware. They ordered a fine red wine and began to chat about their day and the sights they had seen while they ate. A valet asked if they would like him to carry their shopping bags to their rooms. Stella had everything gathered for him in a split second.

"Why are you two looking at me like I committed a sin?" she asked.

"Stella, we can carry our own shopping bags!" Irene bluntly replied.

"Nonsense! You are at the Waldorf. You are queens for the night. Enjoy! Give our feet a rest! And this soup is award winning!" Stella paused her eager soup slurping, while looking up at her friends. "That's the truth! The bread is amazing, too! I wish we would have bought a small loaf to finish the wine with! Here's to us!" She raised her glass, the others following suit.

They toasted to the safe trip and for a successful day tomorrow. Then the conversation shifted to Ricco and his predicament with scammers, fraudsters, and impersonators.

After finishing the second bottle of wine, they agreed to return to their rooms for a pleasant night of restful sleep. The day had been exciting and lively, but now exhaustion had set in.

**Irene was taken aback by the room's** simple beauty. The various shades of blues in the bedding and curtains against the white walls created a crisp and clean atmosphere. She couldn't wait to crawl into bed and watch television until she fell asleep, something she only did in hotel rooms. Then she glanced at her laptop.

"I should check my emails before I settle in." She opened it up and there was a note from Ricco.

All of her exhaustion evaporated. She now sat straight and tall, anxious to see what he had to say. She quickly skimmed through the letter. Oddly, it appeared to have no ending. She wasn't going to take a chance.

Irene ran to her phone, grabbed it, and ran back to the laptop. She snapped a picture of the email with only a millisecond to spare. Relieved, she sat down to read.

Dear Irene,

> We are preparing for a strong monsoon. There could be flooding. I have no idea if our camp will survive. Maya and I have plans. We will get to the beach on the sea tonight. There are few militia, maybe a dozen, no more. I hope your friends know our location. We have the cell phone. The battery is at 80 percent. I will turn it on when we get to the beach. Hopefully, they can locate us.
> 
> I am sorry for scamming you out of your money. It is not who I am, but who—

At this point, the note vanished.

She reread the note. "Tonight? No, this can't be! No, no. no! They must wait! Wait? What am I thinking? Gaffer is there. They can help Ricco and Maya to safety. Oh my, this is happening too fast! I have to tell Stella and Betty. Then we must call Gaffer immediately!"

Irene flew out of her room and down the hall to Betty's. She stopped at her door and knocked as loudly as she could. The door opened as far as the chain lock would allow. Betty peeked out. "For heaven's sake, Irene, what is the matter?"

"Ricco sent a letter. Gaffer needs to know what is happening, like…right this very moment!" Irene couldn't stand still; her body pulsed with tension; her legs were running as her body stood still.

"Stay calm, Irene! I'll be right out." The door shut, and seconds later, Betty was in the hallway wearing her coordinated pajamas and robe. Irene couldn't help but give her a look.

"What is *that* look for?" Betty demanded an answer from Irene.

"Nothing! Betty, please forget about it." Irene pleaded.

"Well okay, but it wasn't a friendly look. We're all tired. Let's get to Stella's room."

They both knocked on her door, with no response. "I bet she's wearing ear plugs or headphones. Let's go back to my room and call her," suggested Irene.

"No, you go to your room and call, while I stay here and keep knocking!"

"Good idea Betty!" Irene ran back to her room, grabbed her cell and dialed Stella. She let it ring at least a dozen times. She hung up and redialed. This time, Stella answered.

"Who is this?" Stella growled into the phone.

"Stella, it's me, Irene. Ricco sent a note. Everything is changing as we speak. We need to act quickly!"

"Damn! Someone's knocking on my door!" Stella's voice was raspy and frustrated.

"Oh! That's Betty. She's been trying to wake you up," informed Irene.

"I'm coming right down with Betty." Stella hung up, wrapped herself in the hotel robe, and opened the door.

"Betty, let's get going!" Stella let the door shut behind her and listened for the auto lock. "For crying out loud, I just locked myself out of the room!"

"You have your phone, don't you?" asked Betty.

"Yes, but I don't have the room key."

"We don't need to worry about that. You have to call Gaffer!"

They both entered Irene's room like a whirlwind. "Where's your phone?" Stella asked. "You did take a picture of it, right?" she asked Irene with a tense and worried look on her face.

"My phone is right here. The email is on the screen. I took a picture of it." She handed it over to Stella and Betty.

They read the email from the phone. The room was quiet. Eerie quiet. No one knew what to say.

Irene whispered loudly, "We need to call Gaffer."

"Right. We do. However, they are twelve hours ahead of us. So it would be around noon there. They were going out on the fishing vessel. Fingers crossed that they have service." With that, Stella pressed his speed dialing number. She was on speaker; Betty and Irene were counting the rings. Gaffer was not answering.

Stella wasn't wasting a moment. "I'm going to try Edge." Again, the phone rang and rang with no answer. "Our last try is Dog." Again, only the sound of ringing filled the room.

"I have no choice but to keep trying. We have an emergency number we agreed to use only in dire situations. This is one of them!" Stella pushed the numbers. There was a strange squealing sound, then a ring, followed by Gaffer's voice.

"Gaffer here. Is this you, Stella?" He was speaking in a hushed tone.

"Yes, it's me. Can you talk? We have an emergency." Stella also spoke softly. "It's about Ricco."

"I'll call you back from this number. Too many ears here." The call ended.

Irene, under heavy psychological distress, shakily began talking. "What if he can't reconnect? Ask him if it is raining. What do I tell Ricco? And what if he's not by his computer anymore?"

Stella carefully laid her hands on Irene's shoulders. "Irene, relax your shoulders. We can adjust quickly for changes in plans. It happens more than we like. We'll work this out!"

"Are you sure?" Irene asked Stella.

"Yes, I'm sure! What's that smell?" Stella looked around the room and then into the bathroom where she saw Betty sitting by the cracked window, in her charming, matching robe and pajamas, taking deep drags from a cigarette. "Betty!" Stella scolded. "When did you start smoking?"

Startled, Betty replied, "About three minutes ago. I always carry a pack with me for seriously last moments."

"Put that disgusting thing out, now! And I mean *immediately*!" Stella went back into the room. "Irene, do *you* have any strange things you do in a crisis?"

"I bite my nails! Why isn't he calling?" Irene was sitting, standing, walking, and repeating the steps which also included nail biting.

"He must not be able to find the quiet that he needs. Oh shit, Betty, give me one of those cigarettes," Stella demanded.

Betty started to reply, "You just scolded me for…." but didn't finish as Stella looked ready to kill. "Here, have the whole pack! I'll get another." Betty handed her the pack and the lighter.

Stella pulled one out of the pack and put it in the corner of her mouth, biting down on it. Neither Irene nor Betty dared to ask her if she wanted it lit, so they watched as Stella rolled it from side to side, took it out, and put it back in.

Then the phone rang.

"Gaffer?"

"Yeah, it's me."

"Is there a storm moving in?"

"There is. They are predicting flooding and high winds. We've been helping the port authorities securing the boats to the docks with more ropes. No way can Ricco and Maya take the road. It's deadly in dry times, and with rain, it would be a river."

"So you received my message, and you know the kids are escaping tonight and going to the beach!" Stella's voice spilled with the urgency she felt inside.

"The beach is a good idea if they have rocks to get behind. Tell him that! And make sure Ricco puts his cell on. We have the number to trace. Edge is working on communications as we speak. If they have pieces of bamboo tied together, it will help them float in the rough waters, should they be swept out from shore. We will do everything we can to get them on Direk's fishing vessel. It's heavy and has ridden out storms like this before. We are already planning. The militia is usually tight in Ranong, but I didn't see any today. They must have gone north to higher grounds. We can't save the camp. At least not at the moment. Check in at 0100."

The call went dead.

"When is 0100?" asked Betty.

Irene answered, "That's one o'clock."

"An hour from now," responded Stella. "Let's send Ricco a note and hope he gets it. The girls began collaborating sentences and words.

Dear Ricco,

> No apologies needed. We will print and use the cover. Trust me, I know this!
> You and Maya's safety is of utmost importance. Bamboo floats, if there is

any at the camp, grab it! A grouping of boulders on the beach will give you shelter until help comes! The sea will be wild and unforgiving. I heard that fishing vessels are powerful and heavy enough to withstand these storms. If you have a cell phone, keep it on for its signal. They will find you.

"I am too nervous to write. My thoughts are fragmented. What do you think?" Irene turned to look at them and what she saw was a sorry sight. They appeared as helpless as she felt.

"This will be his last note from you, Irene. I believe it shows a close friendship with genuine worry. Can you believe the militia would leave them there to die? Why weren't *they* moved to higher ground too? Even if they had to walk for a day, they would have a better chance of survival than being right by the sea. I will find out who that leader is, and I will bring him down." Stella was steaming mad.

"Stella, let's work on a strategy to help the guys get them out of Ranong!" encouraged Irene. "We can be angry later."

"Right!" Stella shook her entire body, refocusing herself.

Betty, laying on her stomach, on the bed, with a pillow over her head mumbled, "Leave me out of this! I am too stressed right now. All I want to do is jump on a plane and fly there." Her muffled voice was heard.

"That's it!" Stella lit up! "We go to Ranong. The storm will be over tomorrow. We make reservations tonight. We will create a distraction for Gaffer and the guys."

"A distraction?" asked Irene hesitantly.

Betty removed the pillow, sat up, and said, "A distraction? That could be fun!"

Irene interrupted Betty. "Betty! You and I are exhausted from the trip to London and now you want to fly another twelve hours to Thailand? That's not a good idea. However, Stella, you should go. Flying from here to there and back has been your life. You are edgy and anxious not being there. And Gaffer appears to be off too. Something is going on between the two of you. I can feel it in my gut."

"You're right about that, Irene," added Betty. "Gaffer likes his team together, and that means you too."

"You are both right. I am miserable not being part of the plan. I see things in a different light, and it worries me that because of my absence, something will go wrong, and I will never be able to forgive myself. You both can meet Harris's mother. I'll send you a list of questions. You could also gather more info on his time in college and even his father."

"That sounds like a better plan. Betty and I will be safe here and getting around won't be that difficult, just keep your phone with you, Stella," Irene calmly insisted.

"To be honest, I would love to go to Thailand, but during a more relaxing time," Betty explained her true feelings.

"If I understand correctly, you are asking me to go to Ranong to assist the team while you stay here in London to further our research. Do I have that right?" Stella asked eagerly.

Betty agreed with a nod and Irene replied, "That is correct."

"Which means I better call the airport and pack a small bag to take along. Can either of you think of anything they may need but cannot get in Thailand?"

"Give Gaffer a call. He may have a list in his head ready to unload for you," suggested Irene.

Stella held her arms out. "You two get over here for a group hug."

After the hug, Stella went to her room to call Gaffer on the change of plans.

"Gaffer, are you comfortable with the new plan?" asked Stella.

"I am, and can you fly out tonight at midnight? I'll have Frank pick you up at Heathrow. You know the routine. The storm will be over. It should be a boring flight, so grab some shut-eye. When you land you will be busy," Gaffer spoke quickly with excitement in his voice. Stella was relieved to hear the change in his tone.

"I know the routine. Midnight at Heathrow. Do you or the guys need me to bring anything?"

"Yes! Two plain light blue or white blouses, size small, and two plain colored skirts, size small also, and yourself, fit for a mission."

Gaffer placed his order as if he were going through a drive-through eatery. "Orders taken. See you tomorrow. Ready and fit."

Stella disconnected the call. She was already in mission mode. It was who she was. Now she needed to tell Irene and Betty and ask if they could return to the mall to buy the blouses and skirts. Then pack, grab a few hours of sleep, leave at ten thirty for Heathrow Airport. From there, it was business as usual.

## Chapter 21

# THE STORM

**The wind's gusts grew fiercer,** lashing through the afternoon with a relentless fury. Ominous clouds gathered overhead, threatening their every move. Maya and Ammara fought against the weather, completing their task of securing whatever they could. Exhausted, they collapsed onto the ground, watching the swift movement of racing clouds. For a moment, they felt the freedom of leisure. A simple but freeing feeling that was never allowed.

"Except for the wind, it's too quiet. What's missing, Ammara?" Maya asked.

"The birds have flown to the mountains. Animals and birds can teach humans a lot about the weather if we take time to watch them!" answered Ammara.

"True! It's creepy without the birds. Will they return after the storm?" asked Maya.

"Yes, they return. This tropical marsh and wetland offers them a plentiful amount of food." Ammara sat up. For a brief moment, the two friends sat silently, lost in their own thoughts—one dwelling on the storm, the other on their escape.

"I've been looking at the laborer's building. It's extremely old. I don't think it will withstand the storm. What will Bossman do? Do you think he will build a new one?" Ammara's curiosity paralleled Maya's thoughts.

"I have been thinking about that too. He may have to disappear if there is a huge loss of life. Like karma catching up with him. I think he will leave and rebuild another cyber camp in a safer location, further from town and the sea. What about the other prisoners? I can't leave without a plan for them too!" Ammara was now serious about being the ambassador.

Maya thought out loud, "We can't take everyone with us, but we can send help after we are rescued! We can tell them that help is coming and not to be afraid of them when they arrive. They will be police and port authorities in uniforms. I do not believe any of us are trustworthy at the moment."

Ammara was quiet, trying to concentrate on other plans, but none came to mind. "Okay, we will do that. And we will pray that no life is lost."

Maya was anxious to keep moving for their own safety. "We secured a lot of equipment while fighting with the wind. I'm wiped out, but we should be preparing. Ricco has nothing to bring but himself. We need to think for him."

"What are the chances that the remaining militia will send the laborers back to their cells early? They know about the storm. They will want to get out of here too. Some have families in town," Ammara stated.

"A point well made," replied Maya. "Perhaps they are waiting for it to get closer. They only need to get to town."

"They say, 'The quiet before the storm.'" Maya stood still, listening.

"Like animals, I instinctively feel the need to do something! Let's go up to our rooms and make sure we have what we need. There's no one else there. We can go to the kitchen and take a few knives!"

Maya stood up. "Come on! Let's do that." She turned to look at the hostel thinking, *how can I get Harris out?*

Walking freely back into to her building felt exciting but also frightening. They entered on a different level that they were never allowed to use. It was for the officers. This was forbidden territory. Following one another closely, they slowly and carefully moved down the steps, keeping their eyes and ears on high alert. The air was thick with a sense of dread and the long hallway stretched ahead like the throat of a monster.

When they came to the first closed door, Ammara placed her ear against it. She heard nothing and signaled Maya to join her.

Maya slowly pushed the door open. Quickly scanning the area, she concluded, "There's no one in there. What a filthy mess! Who could sleep there? The smell is nauseating. What *is* that smell?" she looked at Ammara, who was near the closet door.

The door groaned as Ammara opened it. Her breath jerked. A lifeless form slumped against the closet's wall. Her glassy eyes stared into nothingness. Ammara's stomach churned as the stench of decay hit her like a brick wall. She slammed the door shut. "She's definitely dead! Let's get out of here! This place reeks with evil."

Both girls flew up the steps, returning to their floor.

Maya caught her breath and asked, "I wonder who she is or was? And how long has she been down there?"

Ammara replied, "Sadly, those are questions we will never have an answer to. Shake it off, Maya. We need to stay focused. We're here to look for raincoats, boots, rope, money."

"Money?" asked Maya in surprise. "Why money?"

"What if no one comes? If we are on our own, we will need it to survive! We need money!" Ammara reaffirmed.

Maya never thought about not having Irene's people there, but then again, they were escaping earlier and without much given time for them to respond. It could happen. "If we are going to look for money, then let's start in Bossman's office."

They quickly walked to his office. The door was exactly as Maya had left it, which gave her a sense of security that no one else was in the building. She and Ammara shuffled through the desk drawers. There were many keys, pencils and pens, and several tubes of an ointment for burns. *That's unusual*, Maya thought. *Did he burn laborers with cigarettes for torture? Why would he have so many tubes?* She dismissed the curiosity and continued to search for items they would need.

She moved to the bottom drawer where she found a small patina finished metal box engraved with various flowers. She was about to open it when Ammara called her over. She looked up at her friend, seeing her holding an envelope filled with money.

"I would think they are returning if they left this behind! They are banknotes with a denomination of fifty thousand each."

Maya's eyes opened wide. "How much is that in American money?" she inquired.

"About 1,500 dollars for each bill," answered Ammara.

"Oh my gosh! Can I hold it?" Maya asked.

Ammara tossed it over to her. Maya's fingers trembled as she held the envelope. It's weight much heavier than mere paper. "There must be at least twenty thousand dollars in this envelope!" Maya calculated. "Is it enough to buy our freedom?"

"It would be close. This paper money could save our lives."

"I wish Ricco was here." Maya's chest tightened. They were so close, yet every "if" screamed in her head. What if the guards capture them? What if no one comes to their rescue? What if the storm swallows them whole? "Look outside!" Maya's attention was pulled to the sky when she glanced out the window. "We have to move faster! Is there anything else we can use? What about this leather shoulder bag?" asked Maya, holding it up in the air.

"Grab it! We can pack your stuffed socks in there. Perfect! Now let's go to the kitchen for knives. That's where I work, and they have several sharp dangerous knives!"

They swiftly moved to the kitchen, grabbed two knives, one large and one smaller. They wrapped them each in a towel as they were dangerously sharp and put them in the leather shoulder bag.

"I think we have enough. We did good, but no raincoats. I have never seen Bossman wearing one. Have you?" Ammara asked Maya.

"No, not ever. They do not have plastic bags either, just a burn pit for the garbage." Maya begin to overthink. *Hmm*, she wondered, *were the burn ointments for the workers who did the garbage burning?*

"Focus Maya!" Ammara yelled. "Let's get back to our room, finish packing, and go to the beach to search the area out in daylight. We need to see how far the rock cliff is."

Maya stalled. "Flashlights! They have flashlights! I use one when I go on my rounds. Bossman or his guard hand one to me. Did you see any in the office?"

Ammara answered, "No, I haven't. We can go back and check in his closet. It's big enough to store a box of them."

Feeling frenzied, they rushed back to the office zeroing in on the closet, pulled the door open, and their gift of light was there. Maya grabbed three.

"That's it. The clouds are ready to burst! Ricco knows we'll be down there. And I have been praying that he'll be there before sunset."

They both wore the only clothes they owned: camouflaged pants and heavy button-down shirt. Maya wore the shoes while Ammara wore the boots.

"How did you get those boots?" Asked Maya, checking them out.

"When I came here, they had no shoes, so Bossman threw a pair of boots at me. I put them on. Thanked him. And he never came to take them away."

"He's an odd man. He wears that black ski mask all the time. I have no idea what he looks like. He turns or stands right behind you so you can't really see his eyes. And sometimes he reminds me of a father, one that was gentle and kind. Then he turns into a monster, respecting no human life. His voice can cut like a knife. Not being able to figure anything out about him makes him scarier."

"I agree! He's psycho. A 'Dr. Jeckel and Mr. Hyde' kind of guy. I'm ready! How about you?"

Maya replied, "As ready as I'll ever be. The next six hours with the storm and us being by the sea will be dangerous. Oh no! I nearly forgot!" Maya walked over to her room's window and pulled off the bamboo shade. "Ammara, get yours. I'll find another for Ricco. They may come in handy to keep the wind and rain out of our faces."

Outside, Maya took a long look at Ricco's building. She wanted to run inside and pull him out stabbing the two militia guards with their knives and setting the prisoners free. While Ammara was pulling her arm, coaxing her to move faster.

"Ammara, give me the knives!" Maya ordered.

"Oh no, Maya, I know what you're thinking! You can't go in there like Rambo. You're not him. It won't work. Ricco won't get out. And that knife will be inside of you!"

"The knives, Ammara. Now! There are only two guards. One for you and one for me. We can act terrified of the storm, begging them for help. You can speak their language, right?"

"Yes, I can, but I cannot kill another human being." Ammara's answer was finite.

"To be free? To be able to give everyone in that room a fair chance. To cause pure chaos. To destroy this camp. We can do it. We can. The knives, Ammara. Which one do you want?" Maya gave no choice.

"Maya, if I freeze and it all goes wrong, don't say I didn't warn you. This is a crazy, unrealistic idea. Ricco does not want you to put yourself or me in danger! Let's go to the beach as planned."

"The knives, or I go alone," finalized Maya.

"No!" Ammara stayed true to her feelings.

"The knives, Ammara!" Maya's voice was deep and threatening.

"Here!" Ammara threw the shoulder bag at Maya. "And you better come back to this exact spot in ten minutes. After that, I go without you and make my own way."

Maya grinned slyly. "But now I have the money!" She took off running to Ricco.

**As Maya approached the door**, she took out the two knives. The larger one disappeared into the deep pocket of her pants while the smaller blade slid up her sleeve. The door was exactly as she had left it—another reassuring sign. Perhaps the militia were not taking their duties seriously.

The winds howled with a strength that echoed through the long-abandoned hallways. Occasionally, an open door slammed shut, jolting Maya and making her pause. She slowly ascended the stairs to Ricco's workroom floor. She took one step and paused. Another, pause. Doubt gnawed at her conscious. Could she truly go through with this? Her nursing classes had given her some confidence. She had seen blood before but never caused it with her bare hands.

Step by step, she crept upward, pressing herself against the wall. She moved with the lightness of a mouse, and the deliberate pace of a sloth. Suddenly, a tug on her shoulder sent her instincts into overdrive. In a flash, the small knife was in her hand, ready to strike.

It was Ammara.

"I could have stabbed you!" Maya hissed in fright as her heart pounded high in her throat. She closed her eyes, drawing in a shaky breath.

"And yet here I am! Hand me the knife—quickly!" Ammara whispered, her tone sharp and low.

Maya handed her the blade and whispered, "Copy me."

With their backs pressed to the wall, they inched upward, step-by-step, avoiding the treacherous center of the staircase, where the floorboards creaked under pressure.

At the top of the landing, Maya leaned close to Ammara and murmured, "Stay behind me. Look scared and afraid. Worried."

They rounded the corner, and Maya's face crumbled into tears. She moved at a measured pace toward the guards, Ammara following close behind, amplifying the scene's drama.

"We're so scared! Please can you help us? We're begging you!" Maya's voice cracked as she pleaded. "Bossman always takes care of us, but we cannot find him! He's left with the others, and the storm…it's going to sweep us out to sea! What do we do?"

She was a mere three feet away from the towering, menacing guard. Her tear-filled eyes locked into his. "You are scared too! We all are! Help us, please!" Her voice softened, trembling with emotion. "Do you have family waiting for you? A wife? Children?"

Ammara collapsed to the floor, crying at the other guard's feet. He glanced down at her in disgust and over to his partner. "How do we handle this? That one," he muttered, pointing to Maya, "is the big man's nurse."

The tall guard's hand hovered near his weapon, a flicker of doubt and fear crossing his features before he barked his orders. "Tell your friend to stand up!"

"Please, Ammara, stand up." Maya sobbed.

The tall guard watched Maya for what appeared to be eternity. "We don't know what to do." His voice was uncertain. "Boss did not leave instructions." He kept his hand on the gun in his holster.

Maya's sobbing slowed as she wiped her eyes. "If he didn't leave instructions, then why are you still here? Run! Save yourselves and your families!"

Maya observed him for several minutes. There was a wedding band on his finger. "Is your wife safe? Your children? Are these prisoners, half-dead already, worth more than your family? Go! We will take over guard duty. Bossman will honor us for such a risk. There is one jeep left. You can make it to town before the storm hits. Go!"

He turned his back to Maya and signaled for his partner to join him. He whispered in his ear, "Why did he leave us here to die? He knows we have families. If we leave now, we can reach town before the skies open and drown this place. What do you think?"

His partner nodded eagerly. "I want nothing more than to get out of here. We escape with our families... far from the sea."

Then he turned and walked closer to Maya. He reached for the keys on his belt. "Here." He held out a larger and heavier key than the others. "This opens the door to the roof at the end of the hallway on the fourth level. This key with the snake on it unlocks the third and fourth floors. Take the prisoners up there. If they try anything, use this." He handed her his gun. "The worst of the storm should pass by midnight. Boss said they would be back by early morning if the roads aren't flooded. Good luck."

Without another word, the guards sprinted down the hallway and out of the building toward the jeep.

Ammara stared at Maya, whose face was a mix of shock and disbelief. Maya spoke, "Can you believe it was this easy? We didn't have to kill anyone! He even gave me his loaded gun and the keys. I doubt they will come back... They will pack up their families and run from here and the storm. Are you ready?"

"Ready! Hot-wired ready!"

Bursting through the double doors, Maya's gun and knife were ready as she scanned the room for threats. "Everyone!" she shouted. "Shut down your computers. Stay seated! I am the nurse here at camp. We come in peace to help you escape before the storm."

The scene before her was frightening and pitiful. Thirty terrified young men looked up at her in horrific fear. Their gaunt faces and bony frames were swallowed by the same hideous orange jumpsuits. Maya felt a pang of fear—not for herself, but for them. She and Ammara froze, overwhelmed by the sight.

Ricco stood and approached cautiously, making no sudden movements. "Both of you, lower your weapons. Let them know you mean no harm."

Ammara set down her knife, and Maya set down the gun. Next she reached into her shirt pocket pulling out a key, her voice steady but urgent. "We are here to set you free!" She held the key up in the air.

But the men remained seated, unmoving.

"Ricco, why aren't they moving? What did they do to them?" Maya's voice wavered with frustration.

"They've been traumatized," Ricco replied, his tone somber. "We fear the rules. And abandoning our station is one, moving without permission is another."

Ammara, equally confused, asked, "Can you talk to them, Ricco? Will they listen to you?"

"I can try." Ricco looked over his colleagues. Their jumpsuits, like his own, hung loosely on their skeletal frames, their hollow eyes enlarged with fear. "Some of you will understand me, and please help those that do not." He began, steady but firm, while Ammara translated. "Bossman is out of the camp. No Bossman." Again, Ammara translated. "There are no guards that we know of. A strong storm is coming our way." Another translation.

The laborers were now moving in their seats, murmuring to one another. "Quiet!" Ricco raised his voice. "Listen carefully!"

They stopped talking, and the atmosphere grew tense. "You can leave and walk the road to Ranong. Or, take the beach to the port. Tell them who you really are and ask for help. Through the gates or at the beach, turn right! Do not go left." Ammara continued with translation in Thai. The left will take you to Myanmar…and Bossman!" Ricco's confident tone, and Ammara's translations appeared to have some success as a few workers begin to smile. "Or you can stay here, but only on the highest floor. You will be safe there during the storm."

Maya whispered in his ear, "Tell them we will send help."

"Listen! We will send help," Ricco spoke loudly and clearly.

The laborers began to move in their seats. They all knew of Myanmar and its dangers.

A young man stood up and threw his chair at the wall. He shouted, "Free! Run!"

A chain reaction began. Others followed, flinging chairs, smashing computers, and exiting in chaos.

"Ricco, we have to stop them!" cried Maya. "They don't know where they are going! They will drown!"

"It's too late," Ricco replied grimly. "They will come to their senses once the fear lessens."

Ricco shook his head in uncertainty and turned to Maya. "What do those keys unlock?"

Maya held up them up. "They unlock the third and fourth floors. This big one unlocks the door to the roof."

"Got it," Ricco replied with a sharp nod, his eyes alert with determination. "I can't wait to hear how you two managed this! First, we're unlocking the doors for those still trapped inside—and if we have to, we'll rip them off their hinges. Those who have already fled might come back, and if the building is still standing, they'll find shelter upstairs."

Ricco and the girls rushed, opening each floor up to all the workers. Finishing it off with tearing the door down that led to the roof.

Feeling a sense of accomplishment, they returned to the workstation. Ricco's computer was the only one that remained in working condition. "The past half hour completely caught me off guard! Maya, when I saw you bust through the doors with weapons, I only heard the word *nurse*. And then I thought the men would rush you and Ammara. I stood up, walking like a zombie toward you, to help you and save them. There was no us! But now my head has cleared, and we definitely need Irene's help!" He hastily sat down and sent a short note to Irene.

Dear Irene,

I am with Maya and her friend Ammara. We are headed for the beach to escape. The storm is nearly upon us. I will turn on my phone. We will get to the rocks.

Harris

He pushed send and without hesitation he smashed his screen and laptop. Stomping on them and striking them with his metal chair. He ended his days of being a criminal actor.

"Done! Let's go! Hurry!" Despite his fragility, Ricco found escaping the camp to be invigorating. He ran across the field to the headquarters, keeping up with the girls until they reached the darkly shaded trail that led to the sea.

He plopped down on the cool ground as he struggled for a full breath of air. The wind picked up and rain pelted against their bodies.

"I will run up and get our supplies and the bamboo. Anything else?" Ammara shouted through the pounding rain.

"Bottles of water and food. Any food," Ricco yelled as loud as he could.

Ricco and Maya entwined one another. "There's so much I need to tell you!" Maya spoke, seeing his worry. "We are going to be fine. We have weapons, even a gun, food, and money."

"Money?" Ricco asked in surprise.

"Yes, I'll tell you later. We must get to the beach and find a place to protect us. Ammara and I found large boulders, nearer to the town. They will give us shelter. Here comes Ammara. I am glad she is part of our team!"

Ammara held out a pair of soldier boots for Ricco. "They were under the desk in Bossman's office." Then she handed him a large cloth napkin. "Here is chicken, bread, and water. Now let's go! Night isn't waiting. And neither is the storm!"

Maya led the way, Ricco was last, hastily eating as he moved. He heard men yelling and screaming. If it weren't for Maya, he would be one of them, not knowing where he was or where to go! He wondered: How many would escape? How many would take refuge on the higher floors? And how many would perish, desperately trying to find life again?

## Chapter 22
# FINAL PLANS

"**Where did you sneak off to?**" Edge asked as Gaffer returned to the boat.

"It was Stella's check-in call. We have a new development," Gaffer replied. "Direk, is there a place we can have a private discussion?"

"Not here," Direk said, his voice low. "Too many hired ears on these docks. The boat is almost ready. Once we are out on the water, it will be safe."

"We need to talk before we set out," Gaffer insisted in a business-like tone. "How about our hotel room?"

Direk shook his head no. "Too many paid ears there too. But I know a nearby beach. It is a secluded lagoon. From there, we can keep an eye on any approaching boats. We can call it our test run!"

"That will work! About how much longer?" Gaffer asked, his impatience surfacing.

"Give me ten minutes," answered Direk without looking up from his work.

"Anything I can help with?" Waiting during a mission was one thing. But waiting in leisure time was not one of Gaffer's gifts.

"Nope, go grab a cup of coffee," Direk answered dismissively.

Gaffer made his way to the boat's cabin where he found Edge and Dog busily studying a map of the sea's coastline. "Hi, guys," he said, curious. "Anything interesting?"

"Not really!" Edge replied. "It's pretty much what we discussed earlier. A beach extraction seems like the best option. I've been looking at this lagoon." Edge pointed to its position on the map. "It could work for the pickup."

"How so?" inquired a curious Gaffer, leaning in.

"The lagoon is shaped like a reversed peninsula. It is surrounded by land on three sides with only one opening to the sea. The waters will be calmer and shallower than the open sea," Dog brainstormed various situations and added, "Open sea or enclosed? What's your thoughts, Gaffer?"

Gaffer considered both using scuba gear. "A shallow sea would make it easier for us, especially if we are pulling bodies."

"Good point!" Dog added, returning to the map.

"Direk's ready to take us for a test run," Gaffer announced, straightening up. "I think he might take us to that lagoon. Let's move!"

Once on deck, Gaffer barked orders, "Untie those ropes for Direk and shove off! The storm is not going to stand still for us. Direk, you ready?"

"Yes, sir! Shove off!" Direk shouted back, standing at the wheel.

Dog, Edge, and Gaffer pushed the fishing vessel away from the dock, steering it clear from other boats. Direk spun the wheel sharply, guiding the boat toward open water.

As they sailed further out, the calm aqua waters of the morning, darkened to a chilling royal blue. The waves grew larger and more powerful, but Direk's vessel cut through them with ease. The lagoon was not far from the port—a perfect test run. Direk dropped anchor, allowing the boat to drift with the ocean's rhythm.

Gaffer shouted out his orders, "We're secure! Get below to finish planning!"

"Big news first," Gaffer began addressing the group. "Ricco and Maya are escaping from the camp today, in fact, as we speak…during the storm…with a friend, Ammara. The head of the camp took his best men and left for higher grounds, leaving a skeleton crew behind. The kids are making their way to the sea as we speak. I told Stella to warn them to hide behind rocks if the winds and rain become too rough." Gaffer turned to Direk. "What do you think? Can we be out here in the storm? Will the boat hold up?"

"The boat will, but that's not the problem," Direk replied grimly. "It's the shoreline. The waves will be brutal and with the pelting rain…it's going to be tough. Can those kids fight through that until we find them? And then what?"

Dog jumped in. "We have our diving gear. Could we swim to shore? We can locate them using the phone they have—if it still has power. Or we can split up and search the beach. The coastline to Ranong isn't that long, but there are jagged cliffs that block it off. The real danger for us is visibility… and lightning."

"Damn that lightning! What about the mangrove trees? Those roots travel wide and far. Direk, could we get tangled in those?" Gaffer asked.

Direk replied calmly, "If we stay clear from the little islands, you'll be fine. There are no mangroves around or in the lagoon. The bigger question is, once we find them, how do we get them back here? To the boat. They are going to be weak and may not have the strength or be able to swim."

"Damn!" Gaffer slammed his hand down on the table, "We were to have another month to plan and prepare. I'm coming up blank—no ideas on how to bring them back. Come on! Think!"

Hesitantly, Edge leaned in. "Hey, I'm just throwing out words here: boat, tubes, life jackets—"

Gaffer sharply interrupted. "That's it! Life jackets! They're deflated, so they'll be easy to carry in the supply pack. Once we reach the kids, we can put one on each of them, pull the cord to inflate, have them on their backs, head up, and pull them back to the boat. It won't be easy, and it will take every ounce of our energy, but it's better than a deep-sea rescue."

"Agreed!" Edge said, and Dog affirmed with a nod.

The shrill ring of Gaffer's phone shattered the moment. "Hey, Stella, we are working on an emergency plan now. Any updates?" he asked.

"Yes, they have already left for the beach. Maya broke Ricco out. And I don't know whether I told you or not, there's one more person. Ammara. She's been helping them, and her only request was to go with. Is that bad?" Stella asked in a worried tone.

"No," answered Gaffer. "Three of them and three of us. Thinking about using our diving gear and using floats coming back. Each of us will take responsibility for one. What's your status?"

"I will be in Ranong in thirteen hours. I have the clothing you requested, and Frank has notified me about the flight. If your team can lay low until then, the airport extraction will go smoothly."

"Thanks, Stella. Can you arrange flight plans and—"

Stella interrupted Gaffer. "Gaffer, I have arranged so many flights that I could do it in my sleep. Yes. I will contact you at the exact time and location after the storm, and when everyone is safe. Just promise me you'll be careful!"

"We'll do our best, Goldie," Gaffer replied in a rare soft voice. "Talk more after we succeed with the extraction tonight." Gaffer disconnected the call and returned to the table.

"Stella will be here tomorrow to help with the airport. The kids are on the move. Three of them. We can head back to the port to prepare, but—"

Direk broke in. "Gaffer, we are already on the shoreline. Why waste time going back? All your gear is here on the boat. The port knows we're out here, and no one is looking for us. This lagoon is as good a spot as any. The waves will be high, but the rocks will break their force. And the water's shallow enough for them to wade partway to the boat."

Gaffer was slowly nodding his head in agreement. "I see what you're saying, Direk. Staying put will also give us more time—maybe take a practice dive. Everyone take a fifteen. Look for gaps, anything we might have missed or ideas for a safer approach. Edge, work on locating their signal. Direk, keep monitoring the storm."

As Edge began working with his tracking equipment, Direk turned his attention to the weather radio. Dog paced the main deck. He went over every minute of the plan in his head, paying close attention to the details.

## Chapter 23

# PELTING RAIN

**Walking single file along the unfamiliar path** awakened all of Ricco's fears. Were soldiers watching them from the shadows of the woods? Would they have heard his whispered conversation with Maya and Ammara? Would they be waiting at the beach? Lined up, guns cocked, ready to kill?

Ricco strained his eyes, looking deeper into the woods. The slightest movement became a phantom threat, every shadow a soldier. Maya watched him carefully, her own imagination feeding her fear. At any moment, a militia could jump out of the woods, slitting her throat, and shooting Ricco. Ammara, the strongest and the fastest would get away to the rocks and hide. At least, Maya hoped she would.

The rain hardened into sleet, stinging Ammara's skin as the wind lashed against her. She raised her bamboo curtain in front of her face, weaving her fingers between the reeds, making two slits to see through. She paused, turning around to face her friends. "Sheilds up!" she yelled over the storm's fury. "Like this—it helps! You both okay?"

Maya and Ricco gave a thumbs-up. Ammara nodded and turned around, pressing into the storm's rage. Her one boot gave her more grip than the flimsy shoes from the camp. But every step was a battle forward. Behind her and Maya,

Ricco moved like a man on the verge of collapse, pulling strength from reserves he didn't even know he had. He stumbled and fell repeatedly, but each time, he forced his way back up to his feet.

The words of Maya echoed in his mind: "Pull yourself up and keep moving! You can rest tomorrow." But for Ricco, tomorrow was unthinkable. Only the next step mattered.

Ammara stopped abruptly, yelling over the storm's chaos, "We're getting close to the beach. I can smell the salty air and hear the waves crashing. Five-minute rest!"

They huddled together in a tight circle, curled up like wounded animals. They rain had soaked trough every layer of clothing, filling the chill of the storm's temperature drop. Maya and Ammara both nursed the one foot that was not protected. They were raw and badly scratched from the tangled roots. They exchanged the single pair of boots, unsure if it would help or worsen their injuries.

Ammara passed out protein bars and water, dividing them equally. They ate in silence; the storm's roar their only company. Maya put her arm around Ricco and pulled him closer. His skin felt warmer and clammy against her own.

"You're burning up!" she whispered, panic pounding in her chest. He was pushing himself too hard, and she knew this was the easy part of their journey. How would he survive the rocks ahead? Her stomach sickened. If it came to it, she and Ammara would carry him.

"Amber," he uttered, barely audible. "You're strong. So beautiful. If I don't make it—just know that you are my first and only love."

Tears blurred Maya's vision. She tightened her grip around Harris and whispered fiercely, "Harris Smythe, don't you dare talk like that! You are going to make it! We all are!"

She voiced loudly and sternly, "Up we go, and forward to the beach." She held her hand out to Ricco, giving him a strong yank upward. They all smiled. It was the first smile they shared in freedom.

Jokingly, Ricco added, "I guess this means that leaving me here to die is not an option."

"No way, Ricco Smith. Get those feet moving!" Maya and Ammara shouted in unison, their voices cutting through the storm.

The path opened to the beach, but the sight stopped them cold. The sea was a raging beast, roaring with each turn of the wave, clawing at the shore, and taking the sand with it. Then came the sound of distant gunfire from the direction of the camp. Maya screamed, "Run!"

They ran. Waves knocked them down, driftwood tripped their feet, but each time they fell, they helped one another up. Maya and Ammara supported Ricco. One on each side, gripping his arms tightly to steady him as his legs buckled. Together they pushed forward, one agonizing step at a time.

Finally, they stumbled upon a patch of sand. Collapsing in a heap. Ricco sat up, gasping for air, when his eyes locked on a figure in the distance. A soldier sprinting toward them with a rifle in hand. The man's shouts were lost in the storm, but his intent appeared clear.

Without hesitation, Maya reached for her gun. Ammara held the knife. They stepped in front of Ricco as his shields.

The militia was closing in fast.

Outnumbered…outgunned…this was the end.

But Ricco had other plans. With a death-cry roar, he surged to his feet, shoving Maya and Ammara aside. He charged full speed right at the soldier. The man raised his rifle, but Ricco was faster. He slammed into him with all the force one human can have, sending them both crashing to the ground.

They wrestled in the sand, the storm turning the beach into a battlefield.

Waves crashed over them, sleet stung their skin, but Ricco fought like a man possessed. Maya sprinted toward them, her gun trembling in her hands. She circled, searching for a clear shot. The yelling, the screaming…drowned by the storm. Then the moment came—a split second of opportunity. She fired.

The soldier jerked then slumped forward, his weight pinning Ricco beneath him.

"Ricco!" Maya screamed sliding her knees beside him. She shoved the lifeless body off. Her hands painted red with blood. "Ricco, wake up!" She slapped his face, her voice trembling. "Don't you dare leave us!"

Ammara knelt on the other side of Ricco, frantically searching for a wound. "Maya, this isn't his blood," she shouted over the storm. "There is no wound. I think he passed out!"

Relief flooded Maya, but there was no time for a celebration. "Help me drag him up to the sand," shouted Ammara.

Each girl grabbed a leg, hauling Ricco out of the surf and onto drier sand. Maya dropped to her knees beside him, her hands trembling as she cupped his face. "Damn you, Harris! Wake up. You're not dead."

Ricco's eyes fluttered open, a weak smile upon his lips. "Did I tackle him?"

Ammara let out a choked laugh, tears streaming down her face. "You sure did!" Ammara was crying with happy tears.

Ricco's gaze shifted to Maya. "Maya, did you shoot me?"

"No, I didn't shoot you, but I shot him!" Maya said, pointing to the body sprawled on the beach.

Ricco pushed himself upright, feeling the adrenaline pumping through his veins. "I think it's Bossman," he muttered with a tinge of uncertainty. He seemed to have more energy now than he did before he tackled him. She chalked it up to adrenaline. "When we were wrestling, I grabbed at his face—it was covered by a black ski mask. But there was something in his eyes…it made me freeze and shutter. Then you pulled the trigger."

Maya, still shaking from knowing she took another life, straightened up and returned to focusing on the moment. "Let's go and see."

The three trudged forward to the lifeless form. The sea was now spraying mist, mingled with rain onto their faces. Ricco used his boot to nudge the body. There was no response. Kneeling, Maya checked his pulse. No pulse. Vigilantly, she removed the ski mask revealing a face disfigured by severe burns. Ricco was breathless.

Could it be…? No, that would be impossible, thought Ricco.

Ammara noticed a puzzled look on Ricco's face. "Ricco, do you know this man?" she questioned.

He hesitated. "I don't think so," he finally replied. But his voice held a doubtful tone. "The burns make it hard to tell." After a momentary pause, Ricco slipped off one of the man's gloves. "He's white." He glanced up at the others. "Bossman isn't white."

"Okay, I hate to break up this Nancy Drew moment, but Harris, is your phone on?" Ammara spoke with urgency, still shouting over the storm's voice.

"It was. I'll check," he replied and quickly unsnapped his jumpsuit and looked at the phone taped around his thigh. The green light was visible. "It's still sending a signal. Maybe that's how he found us? Should I turn it off?"

Both girls shouted, "No!"

Ricco heard the panic in their voices. "I'll leave it on!" And hurriedly snapped his jumpsuit back up.

Maya and Ammara were evaluating the situation. Ammara, once again, began shouting out orders, "Grab his boots! The storm is worsening. We need to find rocks to hide behind. The waves coming in are monsters. Hopefully, the rocks will protect us from their force. We move south. That way." She pointed to a pitch-black nothing.

They gathered their belongings. Harris gave Ammara the dead man's boots. Ammara gave Maya hers. Now each had protection on their feet .

Ammara placed her hands on Maya's shoulders, demanding direct eye contact. "Maya, it was self-defense. You saved us all. Don't carry the guilt."

Ricco, reading the emotional struggle in Maya's face, added, "It was him or us, Maya. You made the right choice."

But Maya remained silent. No response. In her mind, she held the questions she couldn't voice. Had Bossman been coming to save them? What if it was Ricco's dad reaching out to them? And instead, she … The thoughts lodged deep within her.

The cold metal, its weight, the faint smell of gunpowder disgusted her. "Should we throw the gun in the sea?"

"No," Ammara rushed to Maya. "We're far from safety. Hand it to me." Maya hesitated then gave the gun to her.

Ammara slipped it into the leather shoulder bag.

As the rain lashed harder, Maya squinted into the swirling mist and rain mixture. "I can't see a thing! Do you think it's safe to use a flashlight?"

Ricco's eyes widened with the look of surprise. "You found flashlights?"

"Actually that was Ammara's doing. Thank her!" Maya said quietly, her thoughts flashing from now back to the beach and the lifeless body.

"We can't take the risk of being seen." Ricco's tone left no room for argument. "We stay close to each other—left hand on left shoulder of the person in front of you. Ammara takes the lead, and we move slowly ahead."

"I remember rocks by a lagoon," Ammara shouted, though her voice barely broke through the roaring storm. "But… I think fear clouded my memory that day." Her words were lost to the group.

They hugged the shoreline; the crashing waves and biting winds were their only constant companions and the sea's voice was now in command.

## Chapter 24

# UNDER PRESSURE

**Edge tapped the map with his finger to where the ping** was glowing. "Gaffer, I have a hit! It's close...look!"

Gaffer leaned over Edge's shoulder as he examined the map closer. "Good job!" he gave Edge a slap on the back. He straightened up and turned to address the others. "The storm is gaining strength. Wait an hour, and it will be ten times worse! Gear up—we hit the beach now!"

Edge, Dog, and Gaffer suited up quickly, pulling on wet suits, and strapping on their night-vision goggles. They placed their thin light packs inside their suits. They had a grueling mile underwater, followed by another mile of supposedly shallower water. But tonight, the word *shallow* could be tricky. They were prepared for the worst-case scenarios, but there was no preparation for what Mother Nature had in plan. That's where experience came in handy.

"I have you locked into the GPS and acoustic comms. Let's double-check. Are you all connected?" Direk said calmly, his voice as steady as an anchor.

Gaffer echoed the question to Edge and Dog, who both gave sharp affirmatives.

"Inflatable life jackets?"

"Yes," they both responded.

Being a wise guy, Gaffer asked, "Have you both said your 'no lightning' prayer?"

Dog smirked and patted his belt. "I have my leather strap on!" There was a light welcomed chuckle from all.

"Time!" Gaffer's one-word command cut through the moment. Without hesitation, they plunged into the churning waters.

On the boat, Direk looked down into the tumultuous water where the men went under. He shook from the relentless beating of rain and wind. Being the one left behind to man the boat wasn't an ideal job. He missed Stella. They worked well as a team; she knew what to do without being told. Monitoring the electronic equipment while battling the unruly deck was no small task. But his greatest fear was avoiding the port authority—that interference they couldn't afford!

He glanced at the horizon. The sun sank rapidly as the storm intensified. "That is not good," he muttered, gripping the rail tightly as a bolt of lightning cracked the sky, illuminating the monstrous towering waves rising from behind.

The rain struck his face like icy needles, but there was no turning back. The storm was no longer a distant threat; it was here! And it demanded everything they had…and then some.

**"I don't see rocks!" Ammara's voice was barely** heard from the thunderous storm. She raised a hand, signaling the group to stop. "Without the bamboo shields, it's impossible to see. Does anyone want to lead? My eyes are shot." Her voice cracked with exhaustion.

"I know this beach. I think we are close to the inlet. I'll take the lead," Maya offered.

Even as she shouted, the wind and pounding water shredded her words. "What did you say?" Ammara called out.

Maya strongly nodded her head "yes." She pushed to her feet, taking the lead. Ammara gripped her shoulder, and Ricco clung to Ammara, forming a human chain as they fought their way forward.

The next wave struck them without warning. Out of the sea rose a monstrous wall of water that crashed down with the force of a freight train. "Hang on!" Ricco screamed with all his might, wrapping an arm around Ammara as she scrambled to hold onto Maya. The wave threw them down like ragdolls, its retreat pulling at their legs, washing the sand out from under them as they began to sink into the unknown. They could hear one another's muffled drowning screams. But the darkness shed no light as to see.

The trio was dragged six feet away from the safety of the bank before they could claw their way upright. Gasping for air, they leaned on each other for balance, each movement a battle against the storm. Ammara coughed violently, her voice barely a whisper. "Unbelievable…" It was all she had the strength to say, seawater burning in her lungs.

Maya sat up, vomiting the salty water the sea poured down her throat. She saw Ammara and crawled to her. "Where's Ricco?" she shouted.

"I lost him! We were pulled apart!" Ammara voiced, still coughing up seawater.

"I'm going to look for him!" Maya screamed.

"We go together!" Ammara shouted back.

The two friends helped one another up. Still shaken by the monster of all waves, they plodded along the beach, looking for a body.

"We're walking in the wrong direction!" Shouting and using her hands, Ammara tried her best to communicate to Maya.

"Turn back!" Maya, tired and frustrated, struggled to keep her strength from crumbling. Feeling Ammara's determination fed hers. She held Ammara as tight as she could, as they pushed against the wind's wrath.

"There! Straight ahead!" Maya saw Ricco's motionless body lying in the shallow water pools of the waves. She released Ammara and ran. Sliding on her knees, she rolled him over. She checked his breath; he had none.

Her scream matched the scream of the storm. Ammara kneeled down next to Maya. She grabbed Maya's shoulders and shook her as hard as she could.

"Maya! Maya! Get a hold of yourself! You're a nurse! Help him!"

Maya grabbed onto Ammara's shirt; her eyes widened. "Of course! I'm a nurse! Grab his feet!" Maya pulled Ricco's limp arms back as she and Ammara dragged him further from the water.

She opened his airway, pinched his nose, and breathed two rescue breaths into Ricco's mouth. He remained unresponsive. She ripped open the front of his jumpsuit. She began the compressions counting, "One and two and three…" She pushed hard and deep, down into his chest. After thirty compressions, she pinched his nose and gave two more rescue breaths.

Ammara sat near him, shaking from exhaustion and fearing more death.

"Come on, Ricco! Wake up!" Maya shook him with the anger of a mother's loss. "I have a heartbeat! I have a heartbeat!"

He began to sputter. She rolled him onto his side and let the seawater escape back to where it came from. Then she rolled him back onto his back. She checked his pulse again. She laid her ear upon his chest and felt it rise.

Maya looked up at Ammara. "He's back!" And the tears fell.

Maya put Harris's head on her lap. He slowly awakened, coughing and spitting. "What happened?" he asked grabbing onto her shirt.

Ammara leaned over him, speaking softly but close to his ear. "You drowned! Maya saved your life."

He reached out for Maya's hand. Holding it tightly, he spoke, "I owe you many."

Maya closed up his jumpsuit and laid her wet heavy shirt over him. She nodded for Ammara to come closer.

"I don't know how he's going to do. We better find those rocks soon. He is so frail. There's not much there to fight with." Maya knew his condition was grave.

"You really think he could die?" Ammara had to ask but didn't want to know.

Maya softly expressed her sorrow, nodding yes.

"Well," an angry Ammara began, "it's not going to happen. It won't. Let's go! Those rocks better show up soon!"

They attempted to hold Ricco up in a walking position. But it was closer to dragging him along. They pressed forward, moving with cautious determination, facing the elements of the maddening storm.

It was about a half mile from the drowning when Ammara shouted, "I think I see them!"

A surge of hope pumped the adrenaline through their veins, giving them the strength they needed to cover the short distance. Black rocks, ten to twelve feet tall, jetted out of the sand, like ancient ruins unyielding to the force of nature. "There!" Ammara yelled, pointing to a cliff that overlooked the lagoon.

Breaking their chain, the three sprinted toward the largest rock, its massive form rising like a dark monolith against the night. They collapsed behind its shelter, backs pressed against its cold, steadfast surface. It felt solid. Comforting. Their breathing mirrored one another in the silence. The horrific pounding sounds of the mighty sea were muted. They found a guardian.

"Ricco, are you able to check the phone?" Maya asked, her voice still edged with urgency. "Maybe someone sent us a message."

Ricco blinked, momentarily disoriented. "I will try." He fumbled with his suit, reaching for the phone strapped to his thigh. Maya noticed his trembling fingers.

"Here, let me help, Ricco." His head fell back as her fingers worked quickly, unwrapping layers of bandages and plastic. "It's wet but not soaked! There's a good chance that if they lost our signal, it was only a half mile away!" Hope filled her voice.

Ricco softly mumbled, "Maya, you've some serious waterproofing skills."

"Enough!" Ammara felt no humor. She was wet, cold, exhausted, and afraid. Fear sharpened her voice. "Did we get a message?"

Maya tapped at the screen. "We did! It's from a man named Direk. It says that there are three divers headed to the lagoon's beach. Gaffer, Dog, and Edge." She paused, a faint smirk playing on her lips. "Strange names, huh?"

"Forget the names! What was the sent time?" Ammara struggled with patience. She had so little left.

Ammara took the phone from Maya. "An hour ago. The message says that it will take them about an hour or a little longer because of the rough sea. Guessing, I can say that we have another thirty minutes or less."

Ricco sat back, his face clouded with frustration and guilt. "I'm sorry," he muttered. "I'm not myself. My head's splitting, and sometimes I think I'm going to pass out." He felt he should be the one in charge, but he didn't have it in him.

Maya moved closer to him. She had nearly forgotten about his fever. "Ricco, close your eyes. Ammara and I will keep watch." She rolled up her jacket and slipped it behind his head and neck. "Sleep. We are safe now." She leaned forward, pressing a kiss upon his burning forehead.

"Ammara, is there any water left?" she asked.

Ammara opened the leather bag, which felt as if it weighed more than her. "The last one." She tossed it to Maya. Maya helped Ricco take a long drink, making sure he swallowed every drop.

"That should help. Now please, Ricco, rest for me!"

Ricco faintly smiled, lifting Maya's hand to his lips for a kiss. Then, folding her fingers inward, he whispered, "That's for you to keep."

"Ricco, we are almost there. Stay strong! I can feel it!" Maya reassured him.

"So can I," smiled Ricco.

**The girls took turns facing** the sea and relentless rain, scanning the waters for any sign of the three men. The storm was nearing its finale—a final act of fury. They could only imagine the damage it was doing inland.

Through the darkness of black, Ammara thought she saw three man-like silhouettes emerging in the lagoon's tumultuous waters. She ran toward Maya. "Maya, come quick!" Ammara grabbed Maya's arm, pulling her up. "I think it's them. Hurry!"

Maya grabbed a flashlight and joined Ammara running to the shore and into the waves. They stood rooted, waving their flashlights furiously. "Do you think they saw us?"

Ammara pointed out to the water. "Look! That is one creepy sight! It's like alien creatures rising from the deep, or maybe a spacecraft! Who knows? This image is going to haunt me forever!"

"Cut it out, Ammara! The night is scary enough without letting your imagination run wild! There!" Maya pointed in the direction of the silhouettes. "Did you see it? The blue blinking light? They are here for us!" Maya began jumping up and down, waving her arms frantically, and shouting "We're here!" Meanwhile, Ammara stayed cautious. Her eyes locked on the figure. She wasn't entirely convinced of what she saw.

As the shapes came closer, the girls backed away from the crashing waves. One man stepped forward. "My name is Gaffer. I am a friend of Irene's. We need move quickly to a fishing vessel about a mile out of the lagoon. Can either of you swim?"

"I'm Maya. Yes, I can swim, but not in these turbulent waters."

"I am Ammara. I can swim too. I have dealt with waves before."

Gaffer raised his voice to be heard over the roar of the sea. "What's in the bag?" He motioned to the leather shoulder bag hung over the shoulder of Ammara.

"Supplies!" Ammara shouted back.

"Leave the bag here. And, both of you, take off the boots. They'll weigh you down!"

Maya immediately began unlacing her boots while Ammara was reluctant. Instead, she began emptying the bag, tossing its contents into the sea, one by one. She slipped the shard of glass in her top pocket and reluctantly handed the envelope of money to Gaffer. "Protect this!"

Gaffer unzipped his diver's suit and tucked the envelope securely into an inside pocket. "I will return it!" He assured her and then bellowed again, "Ammara, take off the boots. They will pull you under."

Finally, Ammara nodded, kicking off her boots.

Gaffer returned to his men. "I will get Ricco. Edge, you work with Ammara. Dog, you're with Maya." He assigned each man with a pointed gesture. "Get their life jackets on!"

Without delay, Gaffer ran to the rock formation where Ricco was slumped. The young man was taller than he anticipated, with strikingly handsome features, and visibly weak. Gaffer knelt beside him, gently shaking him awake.

Ricco's eyes fluttered open, and he recoiled slightly at the sight of Gaffer. "Who are you?" he asked hoarsely.

"I'm Gaffer, a friend of Irene. We're here to bring you home. Are you okay with that?"

Ricco's gaze sharpened. "The girls?" "They're coming with us. Can you walk?" "I think so," Ricco hesitantly answered.

Gaffer held out his arm for Ricco to grab. "Can you swim?"

"I don't think so. I'm dying."

Gaffer paused then shook his head in a determined way. "Nope, not today!" He hoisted Ricco onto his shoulder and walked back to the crew who were already prepared to move.

"Ricco, we are going to help you stand. Work with us the best you can."

Ricco braced himself, mentally commanding his legs to cooperate and his feet to steady. In one quick motion, Gaffer secured the life jacket around him and yanked the inflatable cord. Dog and Edge stepped in, gently easing Ricco into the water. The flotation device cradled his head keeping him afloat. He offered a weak smile, giving everyone a thumbs-up.

Gaffer wasted no time. "Orders. Listen carefully: Keep your mouths closed as much as possible. Turn your head to dodge a wave and to avoid swallowing the seawater. If you get a mouthful of seawater, spit it out. Stay calm. Controlled breathing will keep you afloat. Fear is your enemy. The neck pillows elevate your heads. Trust the equipment and the diver pulling you. Use the cord we are pulling you with to communicate."

They advanced, wading from the sheltered lagoon toward the unforgiving sea. Ricco was towed behind Gaffer. When they reached the edge, where the lagoon met the thrashing waves, Gaffer called out, "In positions!"

Dog guided Maya onto her back, grasping her cord to pull her through the water.

Edge mirrored the action with Ammara.

Gaffer bellowed, "Go!"

It became a brutal contest: the team against the relentless sea. Waves tore at them, scattering the group, but the glowing lights on their diving gear acted as beacons, drawing them back together.

Suddenly, Ricco tugged his cord wildly. Gaffer stopped, swimming over to check on him. Ricco, choking and struggling for air, had taken in too much water. Gaffer reacted instantly, turning Ricco's head to the side and performing abdominal thrusts until Ricco coughed up the seawater. "Good job tugging the cord," Gaffer praised. "We're close now. The waves are calming. You're doing great—just hang in there!"

Dog swam over to Gaffer, calling out, "Want to switch?"

They briefly converged, exchanging cords in the midst of the waves. Dog shouted, "Fifteen minutes to the boat!" The group pressed on with renewed determination.

When they saw the fishing vessel, it was comparable to uncovering a buried treasure! New adrenaline surged into their bloodstreams. Edge, the strongest swimmer, took the lead, with Ammara kicking her feet to assist.

When they reached the boat's stern, Direk, clad in a raincoat, was there to haul them aboard. First came Edge and Ammara, followed by Gaffer and an exhausted Maya.

Finally, Dog arrived with Ricco in tow. The crew banded together to lift Ricco's limp body onto the deck. Direk moved swiftly, administering oxygen, removing Ricco's-soaked clothes, and layering him in blankets for warmth. Gaffer helped bring Ricco below deck to monitor Ricco's vitals.

The others laid sprawled upon the deck, drenched and drained. No one spoke. Each lost in their own space of relief and thankfulness.

## Chapter 25

# ON DECK AND BELOW

**Harris's vitals worried Gaffer,** they were at the lowest range of normal. "Direk, how do you feel about starting him on a round of antibiotics? He's not recovering as I thought he would."

"You're thinking up my alley—antibiotics, fluids, and nutrition via IV. Mind helping me?" Direk asked, moving around the room in practiced precision. "Okay, I'm ready to insert the needle. Can you hand me the green packet on the silver tray?"

"Sure." The room was small, and Gaffer only had to turn around and take a few steps to grab the packet. He handed it to Direk. "Where did you get your medical training?"

"Here in Thailand. I volunteer with the rescue system. I can't spend all my time fishing! My wife would never tolerate that. And my oldest son tags along sometimes. He is showing interest in medicine."

"You must be proud of him," replied Gaffer.

"We are! The other kids are all doing great in school too. Maybe old age will treat us well!" Direk lightly chuckled as he attached the antibiotic drip to the IV.

"You don't need to worry about your future. You know I am just a call away, and I'll get you what you need—whatever it is! Wherever you are. You will call, won't you? Your help has been critical in many of our extractions." Gaffer was forthright in his loyalty.

Direk paused, meeting Gaffer's gaze. "I will, Gaffer. I promise!" The room was silent, except for the annoying beeps of the vitals monitor. "He should wake up feeling better than he has for weeks!" A knock on the door broke the silence. Direk called out, "Come in!"

It was Maya. She was now dressed in dry oversized sweat pants and sweat shirt. She walked so softly she was nearly inaudible. Standing by Harris's side, she visually examined him before whispering to Direk, "How do you think he is doing?"

Direk, standing by her side, also looking at Harris, replied, "He's terribly weak and dehydrated—probably fighting an infection. He needs a hospital, but he's going to pull through."

"I have never known anyone to drown twice in one day and live to tell its tale!" Looking at Direk, she smiled. "Thank you! You are saving his life." She gave a gentle respectful bow.

"This room is too small for all of us. I'm heading up to the deck to join the others. We can debrief and then rest! Thanks, Direk." Gaffer gave him a gentle pat of approval on his back and turned toward Maya. "We'll see you later. You've had something to eat, right?"

"Thank you, Gaffer, I had coconut milk and rice. Did you make it Mr. Direk?" she asked. He nodded yes. Maya continued, "It was delicious! Much better than the rice at camp!"

"He's a master of everything—that's why we're keeping him!" Gaffer quipped and left the room, quietly closing the door behind them.

"Can I stay with him tonight?" Maya's eyes pleaded more than her words. "Before the kidnapping, I was a nurse."

"Once a nurse, always a nurse!" Direk patted her on the shoulder. "There's one more pouch to hook up, and then I'll take a break to debrief with the guys. When I return, I'll bring you hot tea, a warm blanket, and snacks."

**Up on deck, the crew, minus Maya,** and Harris, gathered in the captain's room around his table.

Gaffer began, "Direk, the mission went off without a hitch! You are the equipment guru. I didn't have a single glitch, how about you, guys?" He looked at Dog and Edge.

Dog grinned. "Not a hiccup."

Edge added. "Same here. Smooth-sailing. But, Gaffer, can we send out a mayday for the other prisoners? They will be scattered all over, and they need help too."

"Good point. Direk, can you safely send a mayday to the port authorities that we saw young men running on the beach toward town and give them a different location than ours?"

"Done. I will take care of it. No worries." Direk went to the communications controls and returned shortly. "Completed. They already have picked up two young males. Their night will be a busy one." All agreed. "Now it's time to celebrate! I snuck a little something on board before we left." Direk walked to a small cupboard and pulled out a bottle of bourbon and four shot glasses. Glancing at Ammara, who was curled up on a chair, near Edge, he smiled. "Ammara, would you like a shot?"

Ammara hesitated. She enjoyed bourbon with her brothers but hadn't touched it for over a year. And she didn't know if drinking with all men was proper. She had been imprisoned, and during that time, there was no camaraderie. And no time to consider life's pleasures—only survival.

"Ammara," Edge said warmly, flashing one of his characteristic smiles, "you're always welcome at our table. Think of us as your older brothers!"

Ammara blushed, untangled her legs, and slid her chair next to the table. "I would love a shot of bourbon!"

Direk poured each a hefty shot, and Ammara gave the first toast. "To my fearless, strong heroes!"

"'Here, here!" shouted Gaffer, raising his shot glass high. The others followed suit, their glasses clinking together in unison. In one swift motion, they tilted their heads back, sending the fiery liquor down their throats in a single, burning gulp.

An hour later, all but Direk were asleep. The waves and rain had considerably lessened. The sunrise owned the morning with its stunningly brilliant colors, which was common after a heavy rain. He would soon wake them as they neared the port.

They didn't have any fish to show for their effort, but they did have an empty bottle of bourbon to help them ride out the storm—a gesture that most port authorities would appreciate, especially since Direk had saved another bottle just for them!

**Stella was now on her flight to Ranong in a small twin engine airplane.** She gazed down at the sprawling terrain below. Thoughts of Ricco, Maya, and Ammara haunted her—three lives strapped to her own resolve. Her mind wandered to the brutal reality of scam camps: cyber laborers tricked, abducted, drugged, and auctioned off to the highest bidder. Freedom stripped away, their very existence claimed by those monstrous enough to buy them. Her worry and disbelief pressed heavily on her chest, yet beneath it, ideas began to take shape—quiet schemes to destroy the camps and free the prisoners.

Every few minutes, she glanced at the phone, resting on her lap. Gaffer hadn't called. Neither had Direk. She wrestled with her worries, reminding herself of past missions and their grueling demands. Diving and swimming in raging waters during a storm were both physically and mentally challenging—especially when you are dragging someone else through the same waters. You are saving two lives, theirs and your own. If all went according to plan, they would be back on the fishing vessel, exhausted but alive. She exhaled deeply and held on to patience, though it felt like a thin fine thread, ready to be snipped.

Landing was a welcomed sight and feeling. Finally, she could put herself back together and be part of the team. The hotel was just a short drive from the airport, but the stifling heat and humidity made the journey feel endless. She had forgotten this combination of weather and how difficult it was to adjust to. The driver offered her a bottle of water. It was cool, but not as cold as she had hoped for.

She was now among the ruins of the storm she had seen from the air. Streams and rivers had swelled, spilling over their banks and flooding the fields which drowned the crops that the farmers had worked on for months. Dirt roads turned into streams of mud. Debris, fallen branches, torn leaves, and tangled dead grasses blocked every visual passage. A few houses weathered the storm, while others laid in debris. It was a strong reminder of nature's fury. The sheer power of moving water is a force no human can match. A shudder ran through her core. Again, she thought about the rescue.

The mission wasn't over—far from it—but for the first time in a day, a sense of calm began to take hold as the vehicle approached the hotel and the sight before her left her speechless. Leave it to Gaffer to find this gem in such a remote area. It wasn't the Waldorf, but it was breathtakingly beautiful! It resembled a grand white mansion from the late

1800s. The giant towering columns stretched elegantly from the ground to the fourth floor. And the semicircle of steps curved up toward the entrance, inviting guests with an air of royalty.

"Thank you. Once again your company was stellar!" Stella thanked the driver, handed him a generous tip of American money, grabbed her bags, and ascended the pristine steps to the lobby.

Pausing at the double-doored entry she surveyed her surroundings. It was a habit from her work. She took note of the small, yet respectable lobby, which was meticulously clean with a few tables and chairs scattered around. The beauty of the curved stairway leading up to the rooms, and the smell of a busy kitchen preparing for a meal.

The serenity was slightly interrupted from the noise of the market, which began across the street from where she stood.

Before Stella reached the check-in desk, two service workers met her, one carrying a tall glass of ice water on a tray.

"Welcome, Ma'am." Bowed one of the young men. "May I help you with your bags?"

"Yes, please, that's very kind of you." Stella sighed with the relief of having both her arms and hands back.

The other young man then offered her the iced water.

"This is wonderful. It is quite hot out today," said Stella graciously, reaching into her handbag and handing each a five-dollar bill. They bowed respectfully and left.

Stella corrected her posture, now that she was free of the extra weight, drank the ice water, setting the empty glass down on the check-in counter and addressed the clerk. "Hello, I am Stella Rivers. I believe I have a room here for two nights."

"Yes, welcome, Ms. Rivers. Your room is taken care of. Do you need help with your luggage?"

"No thank you," Stella politely answered. "But I would like a pitcher of ice water delivered to the room as soon as possible. And do the rooms have air-conditioning?"

"Yes, ma'am. The rooms are comfortable for you. Is there anything else?"

"Yes, what is this delicious smell in your lobby?" Stella asked curiously.

The clerk smiled. She was young, carefree, and pleasant-looking. "It is our dinner tonight for our guests—pad Thai and pad kra pao. The first is a stir-fried noodle dish, and the second is a stir-fried meat with basil. It is served with rice."

"Basil!" Stella remarked. "That's what I am smelling. I look forward to dinner tonight!"

Stella turned and began her way up the staircase to her room. She wore black wide-legged linen pants, a white silk blouse, and a long red lacey scarf she draped loosely around her neck allowing it to flow down the front of her blouse. Her feet adorned a red pair of flats.

Up two flights of stairs and down a narrow hallway, she arrived at room 20. Stella used a key card to unlock the door.

She opened the door and noticed that her bags were already delivered and a beautiful pitcher of iced water with glasses was on the side table by the bed. The floors were newly laid cream-colored tile which gleamed under the soft lighting and the walls were painted a crisp white. The only accent color in the room were the tan pillows on the bed and the sleek black fixtures in the bathroom. The room was white-glove clean, the bed invitingly plush, and most importantly, the room was blissfully air-conditioned!

Stella walked slowly to the one long and narrow window and gazed upon a small section of green grass and unkept forest, which was much better than the alternative—the market square: overcrowded, noisy, and packed with vendors.

Relishing in the cool quiet stillness of the room, she was brought back to the present by the ring of her phone. *It must be Gaffer*, she thought to herself and quickly answered. "Hello, Gaffer?" she anxiously asked.

"Stella, it's good to hear your voice. Where are you?" Gaffer asked.

"I just arrived at this little gem of a hotel. And it is air-conditioned! No small talk now! I'm bursting with curiosity-are you and the guys safe? Did you get Ricco and Maya? Is everyone healthy? Please give me a quick rundown."

"The mission was successful, but not without its challenges. Maya and her friend Ammara are both in good health. Ricco, however, has been severely mistreated—he is battling dehydration, malnutrition, and an infection we haven't pinpointed yet. He's weak but able to stand and walk today. He is young and, with time, will be himself again! We are going to the hotel soon. Direk will stay on the boat. The hull was cracked from a wave, and the deck needs to have all the hinges checked and secured tightly, as well as the equipment. The kids will stay below where they are safe and getting rest. Did you bring the clothes for the girls?"

"Yes, and a few other items they might enjoy. The flight went well, and everything is fine here," Stella assured him. "I can't wait to see all of you! Maybe a game of poker tonight?"

"Stella, we're beat, but I'll check with the guys. I can't see Edge saying no. You keep robbing him blind! It might be good for a little downtime. See you soon." The call ended.

She had forgotten to plan mentally for the weather. She laid out the sundress she had rolled and placed in her bag.

"This will be perfect: a cooling, calm coral with silver sparkle near the hemline, backless, loose and comfortable.

First, I will take a cool shower. No need to worry and stress; everyone is alive. I'll walk the market as I wait."

**The market was growing with people as** the dinner hour approached. A mixture of tourists and locals. Flags were flying, and products were being waved in the air. It had a circus-like feeling. People bickered on prices with the owners— the buyers wanting a deal and the owners seeking a profit. She smiled as she found herself eavesdropping. Then she spotted a stand with Thailand coffee beans.

Thailand's coffee beans were breaking into the market and were in high demand. In the States, they were too expensive, but here, she might reach a bargain! She walked around smelling the roast of a few different beans and picked her choice. She had observed that most sellers could speak some English. A young man, about eighteen, addressed her. "You want coffee?"

"Yes, I like this roast." Stella walked over to a large burlap bag. "How much is five pounds?" she asked.

The young man looked confident about his product. He grinned at Stella. "For you, beautiful woman, five American dollars!"

"Then I will buy two five-pound bags. Wrap it well as I will be bringing it back through Customs."

"Yes, ma'am. I will double-bag it for you." And with that he disappeared into the back, returning with two smaller burlap bags. He filled them and handed both to Stella bowing his head slightly saying, "Thank you."

Stella nodded as she handed him a ten-dollar bill. His face lit up.

She stopped at another table to watch a local woman sewing. Her skills were amazing, and she moved at an incredible speed. Stella picked up a sundress that she had made. It was a heavy cotton, nothing like she would find back in the States, and the colors were bright reds swirled into dark greens. She felt the pattern and colors suited the surroundings of the tropical terrain. She handed the lady ten dollars, not knowing if it was too much or too little, but the young woman appeared pleased.

Eventually, the crowded and noisy environment felt like it was swallowing her up. She sought the cooler, dry air of the hotel, and its peaceful atmosphere. She made her way back through the crowded street and to the open end of the market and then moved swiftly to the lobby where she sat down for a short respite before meeting up with the men.

In the silence of a humming fan, she drifted off. A very unusual event for Stella since her life was to be on guard, see everything, and never miss a beat.

Dog entered the hotel first. Seeing Stella dozing on a chair, relaxed and unguarded was too tempting. "Hey guys, time to play a little trick?" He mouthed noiselessly stepping closer to Stella.

Gaffer pulled the back of Dog's shirt. Dog turned around, giving him a nasty look.

Gaffer shook his head "no" and lipped, "I wouldn't do that!"

But Dog was ready for some fun, and he continued moving forward. He took his pointer finger and, as slow as a sloth, moved it toward her left shoulder, making contact.

In a second, Stella was awake, and Dog was on the floor with her standing over him. "Never ever do that again!" she warned and then offered him a hand in getting up.

"Damn you, woman!" chuckled Dog. "A little on edge today?"

"Do you really want to see 'on edge' today?" asked Stella with a daring tone.

"All right, that's enough, you two. We are in the public eye," warned Gaffer as he walked over to Stella and greeted her with a short hug. "Sorry about Dog. That was not part of our planning. You good?" he asked Stella.

"I'm fine, and don't be angry with Dog. It was a good training review. I still have my fighting skills!" she smiled. "Where do you want to 'talk,' Gaffer?"

"Not here, it's not safe. How about getting some ice water and going up to my room?" Gaffer stopped to take in the scent of dinner. "What are they making that smells so damn good?"

"Dinner," replied Stella. "I will have them set up a table for four and to have four more dinners packaged to go. You can take them to the boat."

"Thanks, and while you're doing that, the guys and I will go up to our rooms. See you in a bit," said Gaffer as he motioned to the guys to join him.

Stella returned to the front desk. "Would you please send a pitcher of ice water up to Gaffer's room…" she waited to see if that was the name he used.

"I can do that for you," replied the clerk. "Anything else Ms. Rivers?"

"Oh yes! I would like to make a dinner reservation for four at 6:00 here in your lobby and then for four meals to go."

"Yes, ma'am." The clerk smiled and moved swiftly to the kitchen.

Stella walked up to Gaffer's room where the team was waiting for her.

## Chapter 26
# COME TOGETHER

"**We need to come up with an idea on how to get the girls** on the plane," stated Gaffer. "I am not worried about Ricco—he can wear my fatigues, taking on an American soldier identity. It's the girls that have me worried."

"It sounds as if you feel good about Harris. I do believe that Gaffer should be with Harris because Gaffer is more of a father figure, a teacher, and seeing him with a young man would appear natural," offered Stella.

"Good point!" responded Edge.

"The girls are beautiful and could easily be seen as escorts or dates, and the worst would be the staff at the airport seeing us guys as trafficking them. Neither have papers or a passport. Their identities were stripped from them before they were sold!"

There was a knock at the door. All four stood perfectly still and soundless. Then Stella remembered the water. "I ordered ice water to be delivered," she said, moving toward the door with her satchel. The men moved to the side of the room where the waiter would not see them.

Stella opened the door slowly; it was the waiter. "Thank you," she said, handing him a five-dollar bill and taking the tray into her hands, closing the door with her hip.

After being in silence for several minutes, they relaxed, poured themselves a class of the iced water and continued their collaboration.

"The question of the evening is how we are going to get the girls on board that plane, and we don't have much time," stressed Gaffer.

"Let's start with the Thailand government...the US Embassy. They have helped us before," suggested Edge.

"They could get the girls on that plane with a phone call and a fax. Maya and Ammara could take on the role of social workers assessing the need of more help to the Ranong area from the storm," suggested Dog.

"That's an excellent idea," agreed Gaffer.

Stella burst in, excited about the plan. "I love it! Papers from the embassy would be the safest bet. What do they call that department for people who have lost their passports... Let me think...ACS... who also works with USAID."

"Right! The American Citizen Services...it is in Bangkok. Gaffer, do you know how to work around this?" asked Dog.

"I have a contact in the US that can help us out...and Direk may know someone in the embassy in Bangkok. Time is not on our side," replied Gaffer. "I would like to bring the kids here tonight to get a good sleep. The girls can use my room, and I'll sleep on the couch. Edge, how do you feel about giving up your bed for Harris?"

"Only if I can sleep with the Dog!" Edge teased.

"I will take that as a yes, and you'll do a sofa sleep tonight too."

"And so will I," chuckled Stella.

"Guess this time I'm the one to sing 'All by Myself'!" Dog broke out in song while the others threw the decorative pillows at him.

"Let's grab a fast dinner, I'll meet you all downstairs in five or ten minutes. I need to get the dots connecting and get a hold of Direk. Good work, team!"

**The staff had set up a lovely table for them in the lobby.** They all took a seat, relieved that they had an idea that was realistic and solid. Two waiters came out with bowls of steaming pad Thai and pad okra pao, setting the bowls in the center of the round table.

"The smell is making my mouth water, but what exactly are we eating?" inquired Dog.

"When have you ever cared what you eat?" asked Stella. "This mission changed all of you!" Stella declared. "Anyway, pad Thai is a noodle stir fry with just about everything in it. Pad kra pao is a beef stir fry with basil, served with rice. Do want to order a Singha or a Chang Classic?"

"Let's see," hummed Edge. "Can we do a round of the Chang Classic? It's a smoother beer in my opinion. A cold lager sounds perfect to take my 'edge' off!"

"I knew that was coming!" Dog rolled his eyes.

The lager was ordered, and they began to eat when Gaffer showed up. "Did you order me a lager too?" he asked Stella.

She slid the glass over to him. He took a large gulp and began to fill his plate. "It's rolling. Sounds like an easy-out plan. Now, how do we all come in here tonight without attracting attention"—Gaffer scanned the room—"like we are doing now!"

"It's Stella!" whined Edge. "How can she be in a room without drawing attention?"

Gaffer looked at Stella and softly smiled. She had always had that problem! When he began training her, back when she was twenty-five, he asked the same question, but over the years, her looks had saved their lives many times. "Edge, maybe it's your stench that's attracting everyone."

"He's right, Edge," Stella complimented Gaffer's statement. "When was the last time you cleaned up?"

"Ten minutes ago, Stella!" he snapped back.

"Alright, be nice everyone. I'll take a look around after we eat," offered Dog. "If there is a kitchen, there is usually a back door where the workers enter. We could come through there to avoid the lobby."

"That's a good start. We will meet in Stella's room at eight o'clock tonight, but for now…let's eat! Cheers!" They all raised their lagers with Gaffer.

**By dusk, Stella was short of breath and sweating profusely**. "I swear we are in hell! The weather is incredibly hot and humid." She plopped onto the bed. "I went with Dog, and there is a service door to the kitchen. Here are my thoughts: Edge will sit in the lounge with a drink. Gaffer, you are going to send the girls up the steps and to my room before anyone else. Have them carry a few market bags and tell them to chit-chat. Next, you and Harris go together. Harris may need some added strength for the steps. Dog, Edge, and I will be eyes for you from the lobby. I may pick a fight with either Dog or Edge if I see a need for a distraction. Whoever I don't pick, you are to join in building attention to our fight and shifting it away from who's going up the stairs. Everyone good with this? Time is pulling its strings. Tonight and tomorrow is going to be intense trying to keep eyes off. It's the girls. They don't match with the guys. How are we doing with travel papers?"

"It's moving from the US to the embassy as we speak. I should be hearing from our connection within the hours, but from what I have been told…it sounds like a solid plan." Gaffer updated his team, as he also began wiping the sweat from his forehead. "Aren't these rooms air-conditioned?" he asked.

"They are, but when you are over heated, it takes time to get your body temp back to normal, if that is possible with you, Gaffer." Stella grinned. "Once again, are we all in on the plans? Everyone know their place?"

It was unanimous, the plan was a green light.

**"Maya and Ammara**, are you ready?" Gaffer was sincerely worried. He could see fear in Maya's eyes, while Ammara's fear presented itself in her body movements. She was hard around the edges, and her beauty was intriguing. Whereas Maya was shy, modestly beautiful, and soft around the edges.

They looked at one another, joined hands, and nodded yes.

"If anything goes wrong, get back to the boat. Direk will be here. He knows what to do, and you know you can trust him. He is from Thailand, and he's been doing this kind of work since he was fifteen. Plus, the locals trust him too. Do you understand?"

Maya answered, "Yes!"

Ammara nodded in approval.

"Harris, you ready?" asked Gaffer.

"What if I can't make it up the stairs?" questioned Harris.

"Listen!" Gaffer looked directly at Harris. "You can do it. And I am going to be right next to you if needed. Now, what are you going to do?"

"I am going to walk up the stairs, sir!"

Gaffer gave him a solid pat on his back. "You've got it, Harris!"

"Edge and Dog, where are you two at?"

"When we get close to the hotel, we start a loud conversation on whose fish was the biggest as we share our whiskey. We keep eyes in the lobby with Stella, and if a distraction is needed, she will start one."

"Girls, do you have the market bags?" restated Gaffer.

"Yes, we do!" answered Ammara.

Gaffer then said the last words, "Let's go!"

**They didn't walk the regular path to the hotel.** They walked the path the locals used. It gave them more protection and was faster. When they neared their destination, they split up with Edge and Dog using the tourist path while Gaffer walked ahead of the girls on the local path with Harris. When he reached the west side of the hotel, he waited for a time that would be safe to wave the girls over to join him.

Stella was standing outside of the lobby, right next to the large open doors. She gave a nod to Gaffer to proceed. The girls walked up the steps, past Stella, talking softly to one another. The immediately set their aim for the stairway. Maya shook her nerves and began to chat about the beauty of the hotel to Ammara. Ammara took the cue and began to respond. In minutes, they appeared to be two regular tourists going to their rooms. Stella watched them with pride. They already were actresses, faking reality, but taught to do so in the wrong manner.

Now it was Gaffer and Harris. Stella's fly eyes gave him the go.

Harris casually walked behind Gaffer through the lobby. At the landing, Gaffer held Harris's elbow, pointing to the height of the ceiling as if he were giving his student a structural analysis. When in reality, Gaffer was allowing Harris to rest before he began the next and last flight of steps.

Stella walked to the front desk. "How do I get clean towels around here?" she asked the desk clerk.

The clerk answered, "I can have them sent to your room. Please, write your number on this paper."

Stella skimmed the little slip of paper. It was a service order. She wrote her room number down and the time they were to be delivered. "Thank you," she said warmly.

Stella felt that all was safe and exactly where they wanted it to be. She departed from the lobby to Gaffer's room. She was anxious to meet Maya, Harris, and Ammara. She gave a nod to Edge and Dog to go up with her, but they appeared to have found a friend in the whiskey and waved her away.

She didn't take too kindly to that; besides, tomorrow morning they had to be alert. She walked over to them. "All right, boys." Stella picked up the whiskey bottle. "Tomorrow, Gaffer needs both of you alert and performing at your best, so drink this last shot and then head upstairs." Stella poured them each a double shot, waited, and the three left together.

"What are you going to do with the bottle?" asked Edge.

"Probably finish it off with Gaffer on the plane." She stopped dead in her tracks, turned to face Edge, and asked, "Why?"

Edge took one look at her body language and decided a half of bottle of whiskey wasn't a good-enough reason to set her off. "No reason," and he took the lead heading up to Gaff's room.

**They scattered about**, finding or creating comfortable seats. Just as they settled, a soft knock was heard at the door. Instinctively, the group and Stella went into their prepared-for-anything mode. One stood behind the door, another hid in the bathroom, Stella concealed herself in the closet, and one crouched beside the bed away from the door.

They moved as one without uttering a word.

Gaffer asked, "Who is it?"

"Service from downstairs. I have extra towels for you."

Gaffer released a sigh and lowered his shoulders. He opened the door, exchanging a tip for the towels. The door closed quietly, and the room remained quiet. Everyone let time pass.

"Clear. You all can come out of hiding!" Gaffer directed with a chuckle. "I do believe we are being a bit overwhelmed with safety at this point."

"But you have said over and over, 'The mission isn't over until we are home,' right, Gaffer?" corrected Edge.

"Yes, you are correct, and I am proud that each of you acted accordingly. Putting that aside, I do believe that Stella is patiently waiting for a few introductions," added Gaffer. "Stella, the floor is yours."

She moved closer to Harris, Maya, and Ammara who were all sitting on the foot of the bed. "I'm part of Gaffer's team. My name is Stella, and I am one of Irene's close friends. She, Betty, and I worked together to get Gaffer to take on this mission. By looking at each of you, I can pretty much tell who you are. She looked first at Maya.

"You must be Harris's girlfriend, the nurse, you saved his life more than once! Is Maya your birth name?" asked Stella.

"No, my birth name is Amber, but as you know, they gave us new names when we were taken. I was born in London and studying nursing at the University in Bangkok. I was in my senior year, and I had applied for a job, a similar offer to what Harris received. I went to the interview and that was my last memory of the real world. I was sold to the Bossman as his camp nurse. I lived in the same building as the militia leaders and cooks. My duty was to keep certain prisoners healthy with the scant medical supplies we had. I had water, food, a bed, and a uniform I washed nightly. Also, I had a friend to talk to, Ammara. My greatest fear was being so near to Bossman. His behavior was unpredictable. Also, the young officers enjoyed pushing me around and frightening me."

"I am sorry you had to endure captivity. You are a brave woman. Even though you felt better off than the others, you were among the most dangerous in the camp. That, too, is a constant fear," added Stella, looking over at Ammara. "Ammara, is this your birth name?"

Ammara was definitely more confident and outgoing than Maya. She looked Stella directly in the eyes. "Yes, I was born Ammara, and I live in Thailand." Her cold look concerned Stella. "You were important in the role of helping Maya and Harris escape and for that, I want to thank you."

"They are my friends. I wanted to help, and I also wanted to escape. My story is different than Amber's and Harris's. Two years ago, a lady visited our home and talked to my mother about a job she had for me, the middle girl out of three. She needed an assistant cook in the kitchen of a camp for young men. My family was not poor. We all worked and put our money together to pay bills and buy necessities, but we couldn't get ahead. My mother offered my services to the lady. I packed a few belongings and left with the woman. Since then, I was never allowed to leave camp, and I was never paid. I do not know whether the camp sends the money to my mother or not. I became a prisoner too. However, I was around food and water and had only one boss, the lady cook. She was stern, impatient, but fair. Not like Bossman."

"That's an interesting story. Was your family large?" asked Stella.

Ammara gently smiled, showing off her one deep dimple. "Yes, I have six brothers and two sisters, plus me. That's nine of us."

Ammara intrigued Stella. Her beauty was captivating, just as Gaffer had described, but what exactly made her so alluring, was allusive. Was it her sharp intellect, her compelling rough edges, or her unique features: the one-dimple smiles, the perfectly proportioned eyes, the elegantly shaped nose, and her model-like body? Despite her lack of height, Ammara's long, shapely legs added to her mysterious charm.

"That is a large family, and they must be as anxious as you are to be together again," Stella moved toward Harris but not without seeing Ammara's unresponsive reaction to rejoining her family.

"And you are Harris, also known as Ricco. It's nice to meet you!" greeted Stella with a warm welcoming smile.

Harris's head had been gently bowed, but now he raised it high. "Hello, Stella. It is nice to meet one of Irene's friends and thank you for rescuing us. I owe my life to the team."

"And to Irene. She wouldn't give up on you! Harris, we have looked into your background, searching for information, so I won't ask you about your family or where you lived. However, do you need anything?" Stella asked in her most caring voice.

"To see my mother again or at least speak to her. Is that possible?" He smiled, a young, handsome smile.

"Yes, and hopefully by this time tomorrow, you and your mother will reunite. It's best if we do not use cells until we are in London," replied Stella.

Harris spoke urgently. "Ms. Stella, one more thing about what happened on the beach during our escape." Stella watched his face change from shyness or shame, to worry, maybe fear. "What is it, Harris?"

"What happened on the beach that night…" he paused. "When we were escaping, we encountered the 'Bossman' on the beach. He was yelling at us as he ran right toward me and the girls. I put my head down and ran like a bull, ready to attack. I knocked him down. We were wrestling on the beach. Maya had a gun, and when she had a clean shot, she shot him in the back. His body fell on top of mine. When the girls rolled him off of me, we looked at his face. He had the black ski mask on, which he never took off. He wouldn't let anyone see his face. When we pulled the mask off, we saw a man who was severely burned. His face was melted. But I thought I saw an image of my father. He burned to death.

Could he possibly be the Bossman?"

Stella looked toward Gaffer. How to answer this question was beyond her. Gaffer moved next to Stella.

"Harris, people have terrible accidents that they survive. I'm sure it wasn't your father," he offered with sincerity.

Ammara spoke up. "And I found this interesting piece of broken glass on the grounds of the camp right before we escaped. I saved it because the pattern was so pretty. Wait, I'll show you! Here!" she unwrapped it from a small towel and handed it to Gaffer.

"It looks English!" remarked Stella. "It has an unusual pattern." She added as she turned the glass to different angles and held it up to the light.

"I have seen that glass before," interrupted Harris. "My mother received a box from England a week after my dad's passing, and it was a set of glasses. That was the design on them. It's the last gift she received from Dad. Maybe that's the glass they used at the café, and he ordered a set for Mom. And maybe that café had something to do with the militia."

Stella and Gaffer looked at one another. "You could be right, Harris," added Gaffer, "but for now, until you get you yourself well again, let it be. Focus on life in the moment before you focus on life in the past. You will need strength and wisdom to learn more about your father. How about we take a little break: we have coffee, ice water, and fruits on the bed stand."

Stella took hold of Gaffer's arm and whispered in his ear, "Do think what Harris said could be possible?"

"I do," Gaffer responded, "but now isn't the time to dive back into the hell he just got out of. His overall health is poor."

As soon as they regrouped, Ammara brought up the past again. "And there is that leather bag," Ammara piped up. "Harris said his father carried one like it to work every day. It was in Bossman's office. It looked old and worn."

"It did look like Dad's." Harris looked at Gaffer for an explanation.

"Leather bags were common in those days. When you are ready, Harris, we can look into this further. I promise you that. But for now, all three of you need to take care of your bodies physically and mentally. Today and tomorrow are enough for all of you to deal with. Don't go beyond that point. Got it?" asked Gaffer, looking at all three with a face no one wanted to challenge.

They agreed.

"We had an interesting and pleasant visit tonight. Now we rest for what tomorrow may bring. At this moment, Amber, I do believe the airport has received papers from the embassy clearing you for the flight to London tomorrow. Harris, we do have papers for you also. And, Ammara, we are currently in the process of speaking with your parents about them meeting you at the airport in Bangkok. It will be a big day!"

Then he addressed Stella. "Will you help the girls, tomorrow morning, and I'll get Harris ready. Dog and Edge, you will be our eyes until we are off the ground, and the plane is at altitude and holding steady. With that said, let's get to bed!"

As they were leaving Gaffer's room, Stella stepped back for a moment and grabbed Gaffer's arm. Using a soft quiet voice she asked, "What about Ammara? She clearly does not want to go back to a home that sold her!"

Gaffer whispered back, "Not now, Stella. She's safe at the moment. Don't read any more into it, and that's an order." Stella read his face. One she had read for almost twenty years, and it said, "Listen," which was exactly what she was going to do and didn't push the issue any further.

## Chapter 27

# WHERE ARE BETTY AND IRENE?

**"I do hope Stella had a good flight.** I told her not to call unless she thought it was important," Betty babbled on about this and that as she and Irene ate breakfast.

"She also forgot to send us the list of questions. I am, however, grateful for that! I have my own questions for Maureen Smythe. How about you?" asked Irene.

"At the moment, my mind is drawing a blank, but I am sure that once we start chatting I will have several! I suppose we should request a black cab to take us to her home and also book a return. Have we decided what to bring? Flowers or chocolates?" questioned Betty.

"My opinion is both," answered Irene. "Flowers to remember us and chocolates to share."

"Well, aren't you the clever one today! When I arrange the cab, I will also arrange a stop at the bakery we found. They had small gift boxes of chocolates, and we can pick up a bouquet nearby," suggested Betty. "Irene, what is up with you? You are a million miles away!"

"I'm sorry, Betty, it's just that I can't stop thinking about Harris and what I should say when I see him," replied Irene.

"It's best not to plan a speech. Follow your instincts instead. He may be too weak to have a lengthy talk. That will come with time. For now, a few positive words would be enough," suggested Betty. "We need to get going! It's a lovely morning, cool, dry, and sunny! Let's get our work done, and then we'll think of something fun to do tonight. How does that sound?"

Irene smiled. "It sounds enjoyable. However, I am not leaving until I finish this fried bread and my coffee."

Betty sat back to relax. "Do you think we should buy milk chocolate or dark chocolate? Maybe white? I do believe white chocolate was mainly made for kings and queens."

"That's interesting, Betty, and now anyone can eat white chocolate!"

"There's white chocolate they sell for baking, but that tastes like wax. A lot of chocolate does! But a good white chocolate is irresistible! It has more cocoa butter and no cocoa."

Irene put her fried bread down. "If white chocolate is only butter, milk, and sugar, then why do they call it a chocolate?"

Betty's puzzled look said it all. "How can you even think like that about chocolate?"

"Because it confuses me! It would be a terrific debate question for school—the defenders of dark chocolate against the defenders of white chocolate." Irene dramatized her comment with arm movements and changes in the tone of her voice.

"Okay, that's enough about chocolate. We're buying a mixed box if they have one and if not, dark. Now, I will excuse myself to check with the concierge on a black cab. I'll be back shortly." Betty stood up, pushed her chair in, threw back her shoulders, and walked over to the concierge's desk.

Alone, Irene sat looking at her fried bread, thinking, 'This is not good for me, but why do I enjoy it so? Very perplexing. And I would have never ordered black pudding if I had known it was made from pork blood! Good grief! My mother would have killed for some tasty blood sausage, but not me, definitely not my cup of tea. I'm full. Time to join Betty." She stood up, pushed her chair in, and walked over to the help desk.

"Hi, Betty, did we get a taxi…I mean a black cab?" asked Irene.

"Yes, he booked one for us, and it will be here shortly. We can stand outside by their pick-up point."

Both girls walked out to the front of the hotel, taking the steps down to the street level where they watched people and traffic. The city was wide awake, bustling with tourists, workers, sounds, and smells. It was a scene to remember—different, yet similar to large American cities.

Their black cab arrived. The driver pulled close to the curb and checked to make sure he had the correct address and people.

"Just a minute, sir, I want to double check the address," requested Betty as she pulled out a nicely folded piece of paper from her purse and read the numbers. It was a match. "We're good. Thank you. Irene, don't forget the chocolates! I have the flowers!"

Forty minutes later, the cab stopped at the curb of Maureen Smythe's home. Betty thanked the driver and stepped out of the cab. Irene slid across the seat and stepped out next. Both were impressed with the quaint neighborhood. It was older, but tidy and well-kept, with plenty of trees, shrubs, grass, and flower gardens.

"It's quite lovely here, don't you think?" asked Betty.

"And quiet! I wouldn't mind buying a flat here. We aren't that far from the city center." Irene stood still, soaking in the friendly atmosphere.

"Well, are you coming?" asked an agitated Betty.

"Who's going to talk first?" replied Irene.

"Do you want to?" asked Betty.

"No! Absolutely not, but if I have to I will," said Irene.

"So I have to talk first? Do I give her the flowers and the chocolates, or do we introduce ourselves and then each give her a gift?" Betty's nerves and anxiety were building.

"Yes, you talk first. Introduce yourself, and then I will introduce myself. We can each offer her a gift. I'll give her the flowers," said Irene.

"No, flowers should be first and then the chocolates," stated Betty.

"Where did you read that? I don't think it matters!" answered Irene.

"Oh, for crying out loud, are we going to stand here all day making a spectacle of ourselves or are we going to walk up to her door?" questioned a nervous Betty.

"It's my nerves too! Let's go," answered Irene as she walked behind Betty. She felt Betty should always walk in front of her because Betty was short and thin, while Irene was tall and normal.

Betty pushed the doorbell.

"Can you hear her coming?" whispered Irene.

"Will you be quiet! She's probably looking at us through the peephole!" replied Betty.

"Maybe we should wave to her, like we do in Chicago!" giggled Irene.

"I'm going to step on your foot if you don't be quiet!" threatened Betty.

Irene was trying to get a handle on her nerves, but it was obvious that Betty didn't want any part of it. She straightened herself up and remained quiet. But not for long.

"Maybe she's not home!" whispered Irene.

Betty turned her head and gave Irene a look that could kill.

"Okay, okay!" Irene took a step back.

The door opened as far as the chain lock would allow. A sweet-looking, kind Asian woman, slightly older than Irene and Betty, appeared. She had a shoulder-length bob cut, with bangs, tanned skin, and sparkly eyes. She was a few inches taller than Betty, petite, with jet-black hair. Her peaceful and calming aura made Irene want to pick her up and give her a huge hug from Harris and herself.

"Hi, I'm Betty, and this is my friend, Irene. We are from Chicago, but your son has brought us here to London."

The lady stepped back. "My son doesn't live here." Her face turned ghost-like, and her aura was protective.

Irene spoke up. "We know that, Maureen. We have been working with a team who has found your son, Harris, and we have some good news. May we come in and chat?"

"You know Harris?" she asked, sounding confused and hesitant.

"I know him from the work I do and the work he has been doing. Maybe we can talk more and explain everything to you inside?" suggested Irene.

"And we bought you these flowers." Betty handed Maureen the bouquet.

"And a box of chocolates." Irene held out the box.

Maureen accepted both with gratitude.

"Please, come in." She slid the chain lock backward to open the door. Betty and Irene slipped off their shoes and entered.

**The flat was as adorable as** its owner. Clean, bright, well-kept, and artistic. Her walls were covered with modern art of flowers. It was scantily filled with furniture, displaying that of which was needed and nothing more. The walls were painted white with various accent walls to complement the colors of the art.

"My, what a lovely home you have, and the artwork is impressive! Did you paint them?" asked Irene.

"Yes, after Harris disappeared, I was lost. For what was there to live for?" Tears swelled in her eyes. "A friend said she had enough of me suffering, and one day, she drove me to the university to sign up for art classes. Something I had always wanted to do but kept making excuses not to. I didn't go peacefully, I complained constantly, but after two weeks, I looked forward to class, and now I can look at each picture and tell a story."

"Do you sell them?" asked Betty, admiring one of the rose paintings.

"No, not yet. The one you are looking at is from a picture Harris sent me on the day he landed in Bangkok. It was the last photo I received from him. But did you say you worked with him? I am confused," stated Maureen.

"I think it would be best if we sat down and had a talk," suggested Irene.

"We can sit in the kitchen, and I'll make some tea. Do you like scones? I made a small batch earlier this morning."

Maureen lead them to the kitchen where she put a teapot on the small oven top, placed cups in front of Irene and Betty, placed sugar cubes and cream in the center of the table and a beautiful glass plate with six skillfully placed fresh scones closest to her guests. By then the water for the tea was ready, she placed several tea bags in the pot and let it steep in the center of the table.

"Please, Maureen, come and sit with us," invited Betty.

"I believe everything is on the table—please help yourselves," replied Maureen. After pouring herself a cup of tea, she leaned in, bringing herself closer to Betty and Maureen and then asked, "Is Harris alive, or have you come to tell me you found his body and he was killed?"

Betty and Irene looked at one another. This was harder than they both realized. Irene took the lead. "Maureen, Harris is alive."

Maureen buried her face in her hands and wept. Irene placed her hand on Maureen's arm for comfort.

Minutes passed. "I can't believe this! It has been nearly two years. What happened to him?"

Irene cleared her throat. "After Harris visited the Botanical Gardens in Bangkok, he was abducted by the people that had offered him the job he came for. They were criminal actors. There was no job and no furnished apartment waiting for him. They were dangerous frauds."

"You mean it was a setup? Nothing was the truth?" asked Maureen in shock.

Betty answered, "Sadly, that is correct. The scam began here in London. He filled out several forms for work. Do you remember anything about them or where he received them from?"

"Let me think back." She closed her eyes, forcing a deeper concentration. "I do remember he worked on them for an entire week here at home, and he needed two letters of recommendation from professors. The forms didn't arrive through the mail. He must have picked them up at school or on the internet," offered Maureen, displaying concern.

"Would you happen to know which two professors he asked for a reference letter?" asked Irene, now with her notebook and pen.

Maureen was shaking her head no. "I never thought to ask. Harris was mature, and he lived his own life, although he called this home, it was mostly a safe haven to sleep and eat. He felt responsible for my well-being ever since he was fifteen when we lost his father."

"That was a terrible tragedy…it had to have been difficult for both of you. Did Harris reach out for help?" asked Irene.

"No, he hardly shed a tear. I felt he was in shock, so I called our doctor asking him to come to the house. He checked Harris and said he was fine, just not able to talk about it yet, and I needed to give him time. But instead, I decided to leave Chicago and move to London."

"At the moment, I didn't even think of how Harris would feel about leaving his small circle of friends. They were finishing up their freshman year in high school. I sold the house quickly. Harris had his records sent to the secondary school he was going to attend in London, and we left—with few possessions. Harris loves me, I know that, and I am fortunate to have his love, but I don't feel I was a good mother after his father's death. I was a ghost. He basically raised himself."

"But what was his childhood like in Chicago?" inquired Betty.

"At that time, I was an involved mother. He would go to work with me at the library, and while I worked on archives, he had free roaming rights to all levels of the library. He read samples of everything! Even romance novels! After work, we went to a small café where we had afternoon snacks and hot cocoa and then we rode a bus home. We were dropped off about a half mile from our house, so we walked and that is when Harris was the most verbal."

"What did he like to talk about?" asked Irene.

"He loved to talk about what he read! We had adult conversations, and he was only four," said Maureen as she reached for one of the gift chocolates and more tea.

"Do you know why Harris chose to work in Bangkok?" asked Betty.

"His father and I took Harris to Bangkok when he was around twelve years old. He fell in love with the culture of the city. His father knew Bangkok like the back of his hand. He had worked in Southeast Asia as a part of the Doctors without Borders. It is where we met." Maureen blushed. "He was a handsome American doctor, and I was an archivist identifying possible historical materials. The job was fascinating. It's an old country with history dating back to 1238."

"Harris enjoyed learning about both country's history—that of America and Southeast Asia, specifically Thailand. He also spent a spring break with his friends in Bangkok, as a sophomore in college."

Irene's thoughts began to change direction. "What did Harris like to do with his father?"

"His father was a quiet man of few words. He was a thinker and liked to be alone, but they enjoyed time together in his father's office. Harris would lay on the leather couch reading, and his father would be in his recliner, reading. They barely spoke, but both appeared to be comfortable, doing what they did."

"Harris would also attend sporting events with his father. That was one of the few activities that got him out of the house. Can we please speak more about my son? Where has he been? Why hasn't he contacted me? When can I see him or at least speak to him?" asked Maureen with a tone of immediacy.

"Maureen, some of what we can tell you is difficult to hear. Do you want to hear that now? Or you could wait until you meet with the commander of his rescue tomorrow."

"I want to know now! Do you have any idea how this has haunted me?" Maureen asked with a tinge of anger in her voice.

"I'll try to do my best." Irene watched Maureen's reactions. She knew she had to be straight with his mother. No frills. She straightened her posture and began. "Maureen, Harris was kidnapped by soldiers of a militia, drugged for two days while they moved him through Thailand. At some point he was sold to the leader of this militia to be a laborer in a small cyber scam camp near the border of Myanmar."

Maureen's face reflected utter dread, as if she had stumbled upon a ghost from her darkest nightmares. "My dear Lord! I should have gone with him. He wanted to take me with...did you know that? He is gentle and kind, why would anyone treat him with such violence?"

"Maureen, if you would have been there, they may have killed you, in front of Harris. I know that sounds harsh of me for saying so, but it could likely be the truth. While he was in captivity, he knew you were safe at home, that was grounding for him. Do you see what I am saying?"

Betty interjected, "The people that took your son are not good people. They have little love except for themselves."

"My poor Harris! What did they make him do at that camp?" asked Maureen, anticipating the worse.

"He was used to help the militia train other workers in the area of literature and computers. Then he had to scam people like me, to make money for the militias' needs such as weapons and recruiting more soldiers. That is how I met your son. He was selling me a package to print my first book."

"My son has a good heart. He would never do anything like that!" The information overwhelmed her thinking.

"Everything he did, he did to stay alive. To get back home to you. He wasn't a crook. He was a forced laborer.

He had no other choice except to be killed." Betty explained directly.

"Maureen, Harris met a nurse in the camp who was also imprisoned. Together, with the help of another friend, they escaped with assistance from a team of professionals who specialize in extractions." Irene felt Maureen needed to hear the good news now. More of the truth would come in time from Harris.

Betty, seeing the direction Irene was headed in, jumped in to help. "He will be flying home tomorrow, and you will be there with us to greet him!"

"I am going to see my son tomorrow. Is he okay?" Three words most parents would ask about their missing child.

"Harris needs medical attention. Nothing serious, but he is weak and dehydrated and he has lost weight. The rescue team wants him evaluated at a hospital here in London. I am sure he is much thinner than you have ever seen him, but his spirits are high. He is strong in mind! And you will be able to meet his girlfriend too. Her name is Amber. Her parents will also be at the airport."

"Harris has a girlfriend! He has always been too shy around girls. That makes me happy."

"It has also brought joy to both of them," added Irene. "What he went through may take years to mend and learn how to cope with, but he will have you, Amber, and all of us to help. We won't give up on Harris," answered Irene. "None of us!"

"How could this be a coincidence? His father died in London from a terrorist attack and now his son was kidnapped by a group of terrorists! Don't you think that is highly unusual?" Maureen spoke with skepticism in her voice. "I never accepted the death of his father as an individual attack against London. All the people in that café, on that particular morning, were doctors and scientists. In my eyes, it was a planned attack. Not a random bombing to send a message. And I still believe that! Why or how would Harris fall into such a terrible web of deceit?"

Betty looked at Irene. Irene looked at Betty. They both wanted Gaffer. Maybe he could answer this question, but not them! She made a strong point—maybe Harris's dad was somehow involved. It made no sense at all, and yet it made perfect sense...both at the same time.

**Betty and Irene returned to the hotel exhausted!**
"I think we did an okay job, but I wouldn't say we did our best. Stella would have kept us on a flow. We were jumping all over the place!" complained Betty. "A long shower, two glasses of wine, and a marvelous dinner is what we need tonight."

"It felt like a maze with no way out. Poor Maureen, she is now alone, trying to put everything we talked about in the correct order. Do you believe there is a connection between Harris's father's death and the kidnapping of Harris?" wondered Irene.

Laying on the small sofa in her room, with her shoes kicked off and a cold folded wash cloth laying on her forehead, Betty responded, "I truly do not know, and at this point, I don't want to. I need to think in a different mode—one more peaceful and secure—then I can return and analyze."

"If we don't hear from Stella in the next few hours, I will give her a call and read my notes to her. She'll have an interesting take on all of this, but for now, I will join you to destress and find 'normal' again. While you're showering, can I plop down on your bed and take a nap?" asked Irene.

"Knock yourself out!" Betty replied as she got off the couch and began walking toward her suitcase. "Irene?" she asked, but there was no reply. There, on her bed, was Irene, face-down and sound asleep.

## Chapter 28

# BACK TO LONDON

**The vibration of Gaffer's watch woke him up.** He laid in his makeshift bed on the hotel floor and listened to the stillness of a sleeping world. It was peaceful, and he wanted to stay where he was, mentally and physically, for a while—but time was not on his side. Today was the second most dangerous part of the mission, getting back on that plane and returning to London.

He walked over to Harris and gently rocked his shoulder. "Harris, it's time to wake up."

Harris rubbed his eyes. "I slept hard last night. I think it was the air-conditioning and the dry room. I even feel better."

"You have the rest of your life to enjoy the pleasures of sleep. Unless you join the military." Gaffer chuckled softly.

"No, sir, not me. I will never put myself in a situation where I could be imprisoned again."

Gaffer glanced at Harris. Tall, dark, thin, handsome, and a generally an all-around nice guy. He was going to have many more adventures! "Don't be too sure of that! We'll stay connected, Harris. Maybe have a celebration party once a year."

Harris admired Gaffer. He felt like a father to all. "I would like that! I really would."

"You better grab the bathroom. I'm waking the girls soon." He waited a few minutes and then opened the room darkening shades a few inches. Light streamed in. "Amber, Ammara, it's time to get up."

"That was not funny!" muttered a sleepy Ammara.

"Good morning!" Gaffer greeted them both as he felt the vibration of his phone in his pocket. He had turned off the ringer in respect of the kids sleeping longer. "What's up, Stella?" he asked.

"Nope, it's me, Dog, do you want to go down to the lobby and grab a coffee. They have fruit, rice, and grilled chicken. I'll stay with the kids. Stella is down there."

"Sure, coffee does sound good. Thanks." Gaffer left the room, and Dog entered.

**Immediately, Gaffer spotted Stella.** How could anyone not notice her? The hair, her height, her body, the clothes— she was a looker. "Good morning, Stella. I take it you didn't sleep last night."

"The sleeping arrangements changed – seems they all want to be close to Daddy Gaffer!" Stella gave Gaffer a big tease smile. "Actually, I did sleep well but woke up at four. My body has no timeline at this point. Have a chair." She slid one out. "I'll get you some coffee."

"And a banana…please and thank you."

"Yes, sir! Coming right at you." She picked up a banana and threw it to him. He always caught it. "Damn that man. Will he ever miss?" she mumbled to herself. She returned with a cup of hot coffee from the beans she bought at market. The hotel didn't serve coffee, so she showed them how to do a pour-over, and it was going over big with the tourists. Stella felt good about helping the hotel business and gave them the bag of beans, saving the other for herself.

"So what's your gut saying about the airport?" she asked seriously.

"I feel good. It should be easy. Direk said the papers that came in were legit and from the embassy. They can always detain us for nearly anything, a bug on the windshield, but legal papers from two countries is strong. We are going to get on the plane and fly away. It's going to be that simple."

"It will. I can feel it too. Gaffer, you have been so patient and forgiving in this mission. Thank you from my heart. I owe you!" A truly emotional Stella locked eyes with Gaffer's.

"I'm pretty sure I will come up with a rewarding offer," his smile just about knocked her off her feet, but she had learned how to kick herself internally over the years. She had known him since she was twenty-something years old, and he was thirty. Now they were both in their forties. Where did all that time go? How did they make it through all these missions?

"Cheers!" Gaffer slugged down the remaining coffee. "Stella, after you get the girls in their 'uniforms' and looking professional, do you mind coming down here until we have Direk's SUV loaded?"

"No problem. I'll take the rest of the coffee and let the kids share it." Stella slid the carafe into her hands.

"And take a few bananas too. I'll see you in a few. Harris should almost be out of the shower. I didn't want to rush him, but the girls… Hey, can you stop by my room and pick up the girls?" Gaffer asked. "They can shower in your room and don't forget to grab some extra towels. I have plenty!"

Stella walked carefully up the stairway, with the carafe held in one hand, and the three cups held with the fingers of her other hand, looped into and around their handles. When she reached Gaffer's room, she carefully used her booted foot to make a knock on the door.

"Who is it?" she recognized Harris's voice.

"It's me, Stella. Can you open the door? I have coffee in my hands."

The door opened, and immediately, Harris freed her from the cups. She looked up at the bed, and the girls were sitting, nervously, obviously concerned about something. "What's up, Amber? Ammara? You both look worried," inquired Stella, pouring them each a cup of coffee.

"This is delicious!" stated Amber. "I have dreamed about coffee! Every day it was tea. The same tea over and over. It tasted good, but it wasn't a cup of coffee!"

"I doubt that is what's bothering you," said Stella. "Ammara, what is your question?"

Ammara stood up and walked closer to Stella. "I am not worried about myself because I was born here in Thailand, but Amber and Harris, what if they arrest them at the airport?"

"What grounds would they have to detain them? The camp was illegal. They are closing these camps down whenever they can. Helping the people in them to get back to their homes is their duty. Also, Gaffer said the papers are legal, from the embassy. It's a good question, Ammara, and I am glad you shared it with me, however, let's keep being positive. Today is going to go smoothly. Now…grab some towels and come with me! I brought you your clothes for the flight and a few other goodies from London." Stella turned to Harris. "Drink up and have a banana. Gaffer will be up soon. Stay here!"

"I won't leave this room with anyone but Gaffer, no worries there!"

**The girls followed Stella** to her room. She could hear whispers between the two. Stella had bad vibes about Ammara. At first she thought it was due to Ammara hitting on Edge and Stella was protecting him like a big sister should. But after last night's introduction, it was something else causing her to be suspicious. At this point, in Stella's mind, Ammara was the only problem that could develop.

She unlocked the door and let the girls go in first.

"What is that soft flowery smell?" asked Amber.

Stella smiled; there was nothing not to like about Amber. "It's my new perfume. After your shower, you can put some on. A little goes a long way, so be careful!" Stella turned to Ammara. "You can use some also!"

Both girls expressed their gratitude. Then Stella took out their blouses, skirts, and black flats. She had also picked up two sport bras and underwear and laid them out on the bed.

"Well, what do you think? I couldn't buy anything to draw attention—that could create problems, so that is why they look so plain. However, the blouses, with the pleats in the back and the princess collars are adorable on, plus the fabric is to die for. Also, the skirts move with you. So comfy. Who's showering first? Grab your clothes. We need to move a little faster. I will put your hair up too. You will both look quite fashionable and professional."

Ammara raced to the bed. She felt the fabrics, looked at the shoes, and smiled, exposing that one unique dimple. "Thank you, Stella," and quickly entered the bathroom.

"Amber, how are you doing? You look worried," asked Stella gently.

"I am worried, Ms. Stella. I am worried about Harris. We haven't had any time alone, and now our parents will take us away and who knows how long it will be until we see one another again. Maybe my parents will send me to America thinking a change would be good. But I want to stay in London. I want to be near Harris. I am not a little girl anymore."

Stella's heart felt heavy. The look in Amber's eyes was all about love. "Amber, what you just said to me, you may need to tell your parents. With time, they will understand. You need to heal also and then return to a real nursing job. Maybe on the children's floor. You can go back to school and earn a nursing degree in pediatrics. I can see you doing that! You are no one's prisoner, but your own. Remember that!"

Amber gave Stella a warm, loving hug. "Will you keep in touch with me?" she asked Amber.

"Yes, most definitely! Gaffer and I will be harassing you and Harris for years to come."

Just then, Ammara walked out of the bathroom, looking like a young business woman.

"Wow! You look really…hot!" Amber shouted out..

"You most certainly do!" agreed Stella.

"Thank you. I feel like I can conquer anything!" Ammara twirled around while Amber quickly picked up her clothing and went to shower.

"Ammara, come and sit here on this chair. I am going to twirl your hair into a bun, and I bought these hair clamps. Which one would you like?"

"I would like the shiny black one," she politely stated. "Ms. Stella, you have been truly kind to me. I am grateful. But I do not want to return to my parents. I do not want to return to the farm and work in the fields. I want to go to school, a beauty school!"

Stella thought that Ammara's unknown strange behavior was now out in the open. She doesn't want to be captured again and forced to work at something she doesn't want to do. Now, this was going to be a problem. Stella had to think fast.

"Ammara, how old are you?" asked Stella.

"I am twenty-six years old. I should be married and have babies by now. But I want to fall in love after I am a beautician." She was firm in her decision.

"You are an adult. Maybe your mother will understand your goals," offered Stella in a rather clumsy way. Stella thought Ammara should have no problem talking with her parents, but then she remembered that it was her mother that sold her to the camp.

Ammara bowed her head. "No, my mother is mean, and my father is worse. I will have to run away at the airport. I had a friend in Bangkok. Maybe she is still there. She was a beautician. I will find her."

Slowly, Stella moved toward Ammara. "Ammara, here is my telephone number. If you need help, call me. Anytime. Will you do that?" she asked.

"Thank you, again, Ms. Stella. When I am trained, you can come to get your nails done!"

"I would love to do that and maybe bring Amber with too!" Stella handed Ammara a small mirror. "Do you like your hair?"

"It is so beautiful!" gleamed Ammara.

"You are so beautiful," returned Stella then called out to Amber. "Are you dressed and ready for your hairdo?"

Amber opened the bathroom door slowly and walked out like a fairy princess. She had such a naturally given beauty. "Do I look silly?" she asked shyly.

"No!" answered Ammara. "You look like a princess. Wait until Harris sees you!" Amber blushed.

"Okay, girls, I have Amber's hair to do, and then we need to get downstairs. Direk has arrived with the SUV." Stella put it in high gear. "For you, Amber, we are going to do a braid, wrap it in a circle, just above your neck, and use this hair clamp. Ready?"

Stella worked with ease as if she had done hair all her life, and she had. Her own wild head of hair was a daily routine.

With her bag packed and the girls looking like top professionals, Stella led the way down the steps and to the lobby where Gaffer was waiting, and the SUV packed.

"Girls, you look lovely! Walk with confidence. You are professional women who help others in need. Questions?" asked Gaffer.

Both girls shook their heads no. Maya remarked, "Pretending isn't hard to do after being held a prisoner because to survive, you need to master the art of pretending."

"Well said, Maya." Complimented Gaffer and then he moved to Stella, picking up her bags. "Why are your bags always heavier than mine or the guys?" he asked.

Stella shot a dagger grin at Gaffer. "Look here at this body, this face…maintenance requires care products, my love !" Afterwards she wished she could do a fast delete, delete, delete—but it was too late; instead, she put on her pouty look, which always cracked Gaffer up.

"Everyone is here, and it's time to roll. We'll be up in the air within the hour, that is if everything goes as planned." Gaffer wiped the sweat off his forehead from the heat and humidity with a handkerchief, then jumped in the front seat. "It's a go, Direk."

**They cleared the gate at the airport grounds,** allowing Direk to drive the SUV on the tarmac and close to the plane. Gaffer opened his door, grabbed his duffel bag, and walked to the pilot who was waiting at the bottom of the plane's steps.

"Hi, Frank! How was the flight here?" Gaffer shook Frank's hand. "This is Harris, a new trainee for our program."

"Nice to meet you," Frank greeted Harris with a solid handshake. "The flight was uneventful. It's a great day to get into the air. No storms predicted in the route to Bangkok. The control officer gave me an 'all clear' with the passenger list. I am going to board and start the preflight ritual. Are you sitting up front with me, Gaffer?"

"You know I love to fly planes! Thanks. I'll wave the guys over." Gaffer gave a thumbs-up wave and followed the pilot up the narrow steps into the cockpit while Harris sat in a passenger seat. His health was improving, but he continued to have days of severe headaches. This was one of those days. Harris tried to get comfortable, and Gaffer began helping Frank with the control panel.

Next, Amber and Ammara began their walk up the steps. Both quiet, focusing on one step at a time, and praying that they would not hear a whistle blowing from the distance, their hearts pounding in their chests and the sweat from nerves and heat beaded on their faces. The twelve steps felt like thirty, and time didn't want to move. Amber reached the top and turned right toward the passenger seats. She sat next to Harris. One look at him, and her fear was replaced with compassion and love.

Ammara entered next. She sat in the first seat she saw, placed her head down, and began to pray the rosary. Sounds of silence intensified.

Stella was behind the girls, just in case they needed to get on that plane in seconds. She surely was strong enough to pick them up and carry one on each side if she had to.

Also, Edge and Dog were following. Edge carried his duffel bag looking cool, calm, and carefree, a look that was definitely the opposite of his character. He sat across from Ammara, which didn't surprise Stella or the others. There was a shared energy between them.

Dog, last in line, moved up the plane's steps with a confident stride. Before he entered the plane, he turned to wave farewell to Direk, and as he cleared the last step, the pilot gave the okay for the steps to be pulled away. Dog sat across from Amber and Harris. His deep voice broke through the eerie silence. "Everyone…belt yourself in," he commanded. "We are not out of danger yet."

The runway was clear. There was no sign of the militia. They waited for the land controller to give them the "clear for takeoff" message. Time ticked. Their clothing wilting with sweat. Edge took out his gun. Dog followed suit. One looking to the right, the other to the left. Harris put his head down between his knees. Amber laid her head on Harris's back. Ammara remained, praying.

Gaffer was cool, calm, and composed as well as the pilot and Stella. The message arrived—cleared for takeoff.

The engines roared to life, slicing through the silence like a herd of wild buffalos. The pilot, with nerves of steel and intense focus, surged down the runway, the aircraft quivering as it clawed its way into the sky. At last, they broke free, soaring through a white cumulus cloud. The plane leveled, and the trembling stopped. In minutes, a burst of triumphant shouts erupted throughout the cabin.

Harris and Amber steadied one another, their arms draped protectively around each other. Exhaustion overtook them. Now they could dream.

Nearby, Edge embraced Ammara. Her quiet sobs escaped in shallow bursts, years of pent-up fear unraveling against his shoulder. When her tears subsided, her voice cracked through the still air. "Did anyone bring whiskey?"

Her remark shattered the solemn feeling and released a waterfall of laughter—a fragile reminder that they were still alive, still human, and now free. They were no longer owned.

Gaffer silently observed the loyalty, empathy, and strength of his team and the young adults that survived captivity. He swelled with pride, but he also realized there was a new life unfolding in all of them. Edge and Ammara, he and Stella, and Dog moving up to command a new team.

"Gaffer, what the hell! That was as smooth as a baby's butt!" Stella soared with relief and happiness. Trying to control her emotions to stay true to her image didn't matter. Not on this particular day.

"Hey, babes, we are flying like a bird. From here on, our problems will be small. Amber's parents will be at the airport in London as well as Maureen. Ammara hasn't told me her plans, but I think Edge will stay in Bangkok for the time being to see how it works out. Our group may be changing!"

"Gaffer, you say that after every mission, and one day it may be true, but not yet! We're still young! Come on back and have a shot," suggested Stella.

"Thanks, Stella, but not today. I am helping with navigation. We can share a drink in Bangkok while we wait for our London flight. Be my eyes back there!"

Stella wore a thinking grin. *Did Gaffer just call me babes? Nah, he must have been delirious with relief, but I rather enjoyed it.*

## Chapter 29

# ALWAYS TELL THE TRUTH

**Twenty minutes before landing, Gaffer joined his team and the others in the cabin** to go over new information he received from the Bangkok airport.

"How's the flight?" he asked with a hint of humor.

"It's the worst ever! Who's the copilot? We haven't been served drinks or food," Dog replied, clearly joking back.

"We do offer free parachute packs and a free push out of the plane," teased Gaffer. The comic line brought everyone to laughter. "Seriously, we are about to descend to the Don Mueang International Airport. For those of you who haven't landed there before, it is a primary airport with a dedicated terminal for private jets. The Customs and Immigration office moves swiftly. We will be stopping to have our papers approved for London and to refuel."

"What if they detain us?" asked Amber, saddened with the news as she thought everything was clear all the way to London and the horror stories about being detained frightened her.

"Amber and Harris, you will be fine. These Custom and Immigration officers are highly trained and have been helping us with your papers out of Ranong. Please don't worry."

Amber nodded and tried to relax. Harris squeezed her hand tighter, trying to reassure her.

"What about my parents? I don't think they would be allowed into DMK," asked Ammara, feeling that Gaffer pulled a fast one on her.

"Is seeing your parents and family what you are hoping for?" asked a sly Gaffer as he knew about her request of not returning home.

"You arranged this, so I didn't have to confront them?" she cautiously inquired.

"Ammara, your situation is yours alone, you have to make that decision, and I do not judge you for the choice you make. Here's what I know—Edge is going to stay with you. Think of him as your bodyguard. When we land, you can have him drive you to BKK to meet your parents. If you choose not to, you can go directly into the city. If you want to fly to London, that is an option open for you also."

Harris, Amber, Stella, and Dog looked on with a sense of shock. Edge going rogue and leaving the team couldn't be true, but it apparently was!

Edge took the floor. "Don't look so surprised! You've seen Ammara and I together at times. I want to help her find her way. Gaffer gave me a six-month leave to figure out what I want to do on one condition, and that was to check in with him, or one of you, every week. So it's not like I'm disappearing. You'll be kept in the loop."

"Do I need to decide now about which path I will take tonight?" asked Ammara, feeling not only excited to have Edge, but also frightened not to return to the fields and a life of poverty.

"No, and if you and Edge want to go to London, that can be arranged at a later date, right, Edge?"

"Absolutely!" He smiled and took Ammara's hand in his.

"This is a such a sad, descending story! I can't take anymore!" a visually teared-up Stella attempted to change the mood in the cabin.

"Right! For those of us moving on to London, I do not know the time of departure. Frank put in his flight request but hasn't been notified yet. We can leave the plane and enjoy the VIP lounge in the terminal. Any questions?" The cabin remained quiet, each passenger thinking of their new way forward. "With that, buckle up and prepare for landing. The weather near Bangkok is still hot and humid." It brought a little chuckle and a few smiles.

**As a group, they walked into the terminal raising** eyebrows and Stella embraced every second of it. Gaffer was wearing his pro golf attire, looking, and walking with an air of authority, one not to be messed with. Edge wore flip-flops, Bermuda shorts, and an expensive, loose-fitting golf shirt showing only a glimpse of his muscular body when his shirt sporadically shifted, hugging his chest. He had a carefree swag and holding onto his arm was Ammara—beautiful, intriguing, and professionally dressed. Dog held himself up with a strong, authoritative confidence that no one could match. He looked like a movie star you saw in a movie but couldn't remember his name. Next to him walked Stella. She had it all: the looks, the hair, the body, and a stunning sun dress of red and green. Harris appeared to be a young soldier who was with his new adorable young bride. And all together, they could be taken as a casting crew for a new movie.

They entered the VIP lounge and separated into various tables. The young lovers finding their private corners while

Stella, Gaffer, and Dog found a small round table looking out over the runways.

"There are some damn nice planes taking off and landing!" exclaimed Dog as he watched the airport activity with intensity.

"Agree!" stated Gaffer, doing basically the same thing. "Hey, Dog, before Stella comes back, I have to ask you a sensitive and difficult question," warned Gaffer, feeling a pit at in his gut.

"Which is…?" asked Dog in wonderment, rarely hearing Gaffer speak in such a secretive manner.

Gaffer stalled. "Man, this is hard. I'm just going to spit it out. Will you consider replacing me, becoming the new commander, and putting together a new team?" Gaffer sat back and watched Dog's reaction.

"Are you toying with my head? Why would you step down? Is there something I don't know…for crying out loud…you're sick. Cancer?" Dog was flabbergasted. Gaffer was a poster man for good health and a strong body.

"Nothing like that, Dog, I am tired. The daily training, the stress, lack of sleep, being responsible for three more lives, even more during rescues, for twenty years? I need a change. Besides, I have someone incredibly special to me that I want to spend more time with, and I am not getting younger. I'm unloading to you and only you, so 'mum' is the word. I had to let you in because you are a natural-born leader. You're an expert at your work. And you're younger."

"Have you given any thought to a temporary break, like maybe six months off like Edge?" asked Dog, concerned that his best friend may not be making the best decision.

"I have thought of every angle I could take. I wouldn't mind helping in an occasional rescue if needed. Like Direk does. But that's as far as I would take it," replied Gaffer.

"And a lady? You never talk about women. I have never seen you go on a date. Who is this mystery lady?" asked Dog eagerly. "No, wait! You sly fox in sheep's clothing! It's Stella, isn't it? You two have been playing the dance of the birds since training. Oh my gosh! Do the others know?" Dog was elated. It was the best news he had ever heard!

"Dog, quiet down, Stella doesn't even know. I plan on telling her tonight. Either here or in London, which would be tomorrow. We have been on missions beyond dangerous, more like deadly and impossible, and I kept my cool. But talking seriously to Stella is making my blood pressure rise. Sometimes I get dizzy because of my nerves. I need to open up, get it off my chest, and hope she sees me like I see her."

In a faint whisper, Edge questioned, "She doesn't know yet? Oh, man, you are not in command on this mission! Should I take over now and offer you some advice?" Dog asked with confident pleasure.

"Make it short," replied Gaffer, leaning in attentively.

"Be honest. Always be honest. That's it! My folks have been married for fifty-five years, and they say honesty leads to trust and trust leads to love," Dog romantically offered his advice from one commander to the other.

Gaffer nodded in agreement. "Thanks, Dog. You've earned this advancement, and you'll be one of the greatest. You can always reach out to me…about anything. Congratulations, and I'll have the paperwork ready for you before I leave London."

"I'll be calling quite often," replied Dog as he smiled and shared a firm handshake with Gaffer. "You never speak of where or how we get money to finance our extractions and constant training, and there always seems to be an abundance. Will I be working with the same investors?"

"Great question! Yes, you will have the same investors plus me. We will be arranging a private conference with you in the near future, and all your questions will be answered there. The money is never talked about with the team, as you know. And the investors are kept secret. Money is their job. The extraction is yours and the team. Here comes Stella. Act normal. If you can."

"What are you boys shaking hands over?" asked Stella inquisitively.

"Just a bet, Stella, on whether or not Edge will come back. I say yes, Gaffer thinks differently," answered Dog smoothly, avoiding the truth of their handshake.

Stella made herself comfortable and gazed at the two men. "I agree with Dog. I think he will help Ammara become successful enough to support herself and then return to the team. But there's always that word…but…he may become a father very quickly, and that would put an end to the missions," she added.

Dog and Gaffer looked surprised. "What are those looks for? Haven't you ever heard of two people in love getting pregnant when they least expect it?" questioned Stella.

"How about we change the topic?" asked a nervous Gaffer.

"Well, I am going to take one of those VIP rooms and grab some shuteye. How long do you estimate until a runway opens up?" asked Dog.

Gaffer checked his watch. "It's hard to say. Frank mentioned at least two hours. I'll wake you up when I get a call. Want any food to bring on board?" asked Gaffer.

Dog stood up, ready to go. "Nachos, salsa, and a few cold Modell beers. That's it! Thanks. See you later!" he said as he backed up to turn around.

Stella watched. "That was weird, don't you think? At first he sounded as if he just inherited the world and its problems, then he grew all shy and awkward as if he were going on his first date!"

"He's tired. It has been a hectic few weeks putting this mission together, but the outcome was worth every minute, and I feel as if I may have gained a son." Gaffer smiled. "I genuinely enjoy talking with Harris. He's knowledgeable about so many topics."

"According to his mother, he spent his first twelve years growing up in a library where he read something about almost everything," stated Stella as she played with the umbrella stick in her drink.

"How are the girls, Irene and Betty?" inquired Gaffer. "I haven't heard you mention them. Do they not enjoy London?"

"Just the opposite, Irene wants to move there, close to Maureen, and Betty said she would follow but would choose a different area closer to downtown. They did find an interesting lead about Harris's father. Maureen believes the bombing was intentional and that the café was full of known scientists and doctors, but the investigation shut down early, laying the blame on a specific stand-alone crazed person. She believes it was a terrorist group. Harris's father was a quiet man, always busy, but she didn't know with what. There could be something there," informed Stella as she watched Gaffer's uninterested facial expressions. "What's up, Gaffer? Is it about Edge?"

"In a way…it's about the team. Stella, I asked Dog to replace me as commander." He was speaking the truth and building up the strength to continue. Now it was his turn to watch Stella's reaction.

"You…are…kidding! Right! I mean, did you wake up this morning and say to yourself, 'This would be a great day to retire from my twenty-year career of saving the world!' No wonder Dog had that look!" reamed Stella with nothing but unbelief in her voice.

"No, that's not true. What is true is that I have been interested in a woman for an exceptionally long time, and I care about her. I deeply care about her, and I want to spend many healthy years as a part of her team. Just me and her." His eyes stayed locked into Stella's. He saw tears starting to form as she blinked them away. His heart ached, feeling he had really messed this whole conversation up.

"Now, wait," Stella addressed him with hurt and pain but did not allow herself to show it. "You haven't talked about your family. I don't even know if you have a mother and father. Maybe you hatched from an egg found in the sand on a beach! I have given in to the idea that the military found you and raised you as one of them! Now you tell me there has been a woman in your life for…like decades…and you're in love? Well, that's a tall glass to drink! Who is this mystery woman. You owe me the truth, Gaffer!"

He didn't know what to say because he was looking at her, and then Dog's words came to haunt him… always be truthful. Gaffer looked up at Stella, admiring everything about her and gently said the truth. "I'm looking at her."

Stella, not a person known to be without words or opinion, was now speechless. All she could do was breathe. Throughout her career, she had to forget her feelings for him because he was her commander. All the nights of drinking and dancing, even singing karaoke together, she knew when the night was over, he would walk one way and she the other. After years of flirting, she accepted that he couldn't love anyone because of his work, and that she could accept, as long as they remained friends. But tonight hit her like a close-ranged missile.

"Stella, I know we have been interested in one another since we met. On that very first day, there was electricity. Our currents were strong, and I still feel that way toward you. I want to be with you more than being with my job. Will you please say something? Anything?" he asked, not knowing if this was going to be the best moment of his life or the worst.

One thought of Stella, not in his life, was one thought too many. He felt his heart pounding. Under the table, his leg was shaking. And across from him was the woman he loved who could not confirm her love for him. Maybe he was wrong all these years.

Stella moved closer to the table and leaned inward, placing her hand in the center. With locked eyes, Gaffer moved his hand slowly over hers. The currents they shared created a sensual warmth. "I don't know what to say! But that I have always loved you too!" She tried to smile, but she was caught in his stare.

"That's all you need to say, Stella," he said, comforting her with his slow smooth voice. "I've avoided loving relationships my entire life. The word *love* didn't exist in my vocabulary until I saw you on the first day of training, and that feeling is as fresh now as it was then. I guess I am afraid of being vulnerable."

"Don't worry, you'll love feeling vulnerable. Leave that worry to me," Stella replied in a soft, sexy whisper and a strong come-on smile.

The romance and heated moment was shattered by Gaffer's ring tone. "Hold that look," he said to Stella and picked up his phone. "Gaffer here, what's up, Frank?" he gazed over at Stella who was now wearing a look of redemption.

"We have a runway, time to say your goodbyes or hellos. We need to make one fuel stop so if you want to bring drinks or food on board, order that now. We will load in thirty minutes at Gate B33. Questions?"

"Nope, we will be there. Thanks, Frank."

Stella stood up and walked closer to him. He moved closer to her. "Stella, I…" She placed a finger on his lips and brought them both back to reality, saying, "Not now, we have a job to finish."

With that, she walked up to the bar to place an order. Gaffer followed. "Stella, Dog wanted chips and salsa with a few cold Modell beers. I'll round up the others." They shared a longing smile.

## Chapter 30
# BACK TO LONDON

**The flight to London, being twelve hours long**, messed up days and nights. The fuel stop was appreciated by all, as they were able to walk to the terminal, use restrooms, grab snacks, and drinks. Stella moved almost robotically. She was still swirling from Gaffer's offer. During the flight, he stayed in the cockpit as usual, coming out occasionally to have a coffee break. They talked like they always did, but it was difficult for them to stay focused and business—like now that they had ignited their electrical currents. One touch or a sweep of their clothing touching the other would turn the fire on.

Finally, the announcement came that they would be descending soon and to prepare for landing at Farnborough Airport near London.

Stella took on the stewardess role by holding an open garbage bag for others to throw their garbage and left overs in. When she came to Harris and Amber, she picked up their mess not to disturb their sleep. Amber laying with her head on Harris's shoulder, and Harris sleeping with his head next to hers. Stella smiled. That would be her and Gaffer one day soon. And then it hit her. What was his real name? She doubted it was Gaffer. Their new world was open for many unexplored questions.

As Stella began putting her seat belt on, Dog swiftly slid in next to her. "Stella, did you hear anything from Edge or Ammara?" he asked, concerned for his best friend.

"No," she said. "And Gaffer hasn't mentioned a word. When we land, we can turn on our phones, and I am sure that he has left a note to one of us. I am anxious to hear from him too!"

Dog continued to fill in Stella, "Ammara had to make a hard decision in a short period of time, and I am not sure if she realized the consequences of each. Edge does. He talked to me about it."

"What did Edge think she should do?" inquired Stella.

"He believes her family is involved with not-so-pleasant people. At least the men in the family. And that her fear from exposure to that type of living could keep her from making the best choice, which is to leave the family now while the opportunity is present, and she has support. Her family will not accept Edge—too American and ex-military. And Edge doesn't want to be any part of their business. He wants to save Ammara, but he understands that she must save herself first. He wanted to be there for her in case she chose that path. There is no one else in her life she could lean on," explained Dog in defense of his best friend.

"I get it, Edge is right. If Ammara wants to begin a new life, she knows only one kind, and that is a life of others controlling her. She has no idea who she is. I hope that when she does discover her talents and beauty, that Edge is a big part of it. He's fallen hard for her."

"If that happens, he has us. We're family, and speaking of family, what are you going to be doing once we depart London? Edge is gone, Gaffer is gone, and I'm taking over a team, which brings me to you. Are you interested in joining me?" Dog subtly asked, knowing damn well that she was going to go with Gaffer, but he had to ask to keep her believing he didn't know anything.

There was an uncomfortable silence between them. "Edge, I can't give you that answer at the moment. There are several questions I need to find answers to. Betty and Irene would love if I would retire and join their circle, and Betty wants to do more espionage—specifically looking for information. They are fun. Blizzard and I would be happy and together more often," answered Stella, not knowing if Dog knew about her and Gaffer or not, so playing it safe was the best way to go. "We're going to be landing! I am freaking out! I cannot wait to see Harris with his mother and to meet her. And Amber's family being there too!" Stella intentionally moved the conversation in another direction.

"I'm taking photos," said Dog happily. "There have been more memories of this mission than any others we have been on. I think it's these young kids and their resilience and camaraderie that hits home," explained Edge as they were lightly tossed about in the landing. "That landing was a little rough, don't you think?. Frank is burnt out too from these long flights to Thailand. I think we all need time to reboot," suggested Dog.

**The group gathered outside, near the plane** waiting for Gaffer. He had the latest updates, which they were all anxiously waiting for.

"There's our man," said Dog, pointing to Gaffer coming down the steps. "Hey, Gaffer, bumpy landing. Was that you behind the wheel?"

"Sush, of course it was me. I haven't landed a plane for quite some time...how could I resist the offer? Was it really that bad?" he asked, feeling confident about his abilities in flight. "Stella, what did you think? I can't go on Dog's opinion!"

Stella smiled at Gaffer. It was a different smile than her usual, more of a kidding grin. "Gaffer, honestly, that was one of...your worst! Sorry, but you said the truth is important!" Harris, loving the humor, added, "She's right, Gaffer, it was pretty rough. Amber thought we were going to crash or roll over."

"Come on, you guys! Give me a break. It was at least fair!" He caved in to admitting it wasn't his best.

"We have news from Edge...Ammara did not find her family anywhere. She took it hard. Family is family—even when they aren't perfect, but she didn't expect them to completely abandon her. She and Edge are in a nice hotel tonight, and next week, they will begin looking into careers she may like to pursue," informed Gaffer to the group.

"Please tell Edge to have Ammara call me when she can. I would love to stay in touch and help her as a friend," asked Amber as she nervously twisted her hands and fingers, being anxious about the long-awaited reunion with her parents.

"I will do that for you Amber." Gaffer became more serious. "Your parents are waiting in a private room in the terminal."

Then he addressed Harris. "Your mother is also waiting in a private room. And when you are ready, Irene and her friend Betty would like to have time with you and your mother. Afterwards, we will have a dinner and"—Gaffer choked, wiping his eyes—"and go our own ways. Except you, Harris. We have arranged a medical crew for you at St. Thomas Hospital. They will come to pick you and your mother up after the dinner. We want to make sure there is no infection."

Then Gaffer held up his cell. "And if any of you don't have my number, or Stella's, make sure you do before our goodbyes. Right, Stella?" he asked, admiring her fortitude. "Stella and I are going to be a team of two, and Dog is replacing me." Gaffer's eyes brightened as he walked to Stella and took her hand.

There were celebratory cheers and hugs from Amber, Harris, and Dog, creating one tightly formed circle of love.

Laughing, chatting, and full of life, the five of them entered the terminal and headed to the room where Amber's parents awaited.

**Gaffer slowly opened the door for Amber**, and the minute she saw her family, nothing happened slowly. Tears of joy, hugs of love, expressions of unbelief, and words of gratefulness filled everyone. Gaffer, Dog, and Stella watched. "This is why we have done what we did for twenty years, and Dog, this is what you are in command of—bringing good people back together."

"Gaffer, you're a hard act to follow!" added Dog. "Hey, I think they want us to come over."

The three joined Amber and Harris, who were waiting to introduce them to her family.

**Instead of five, there were now eight, setting out** to meet Harris's mother and reunite with Irene and Betty. Stella held Gaffer's hand tightly as she spoke softly to him, "I'm worried about Irene and if she'll be able to handle this!"

"Stella, Irene may fall apart, but it will be momentarily. At first she didn't believe herself, and when she did, she felt humiliated. Then you and Betty saw what she saw, and it was supportive, giving her hope. Now comes fruition. That's a lot for both Irene and Harris to take in. Harris is holding up, but he's still not 100 percent. I'm grateful that the doctors will be giving him a full medical exam. Let's stand back and soak it all in…together."

Gaffer turned to Harris. "Are you ready or do you need a minute?" he asked.

"You couldn't open that door fast enough!" answered Harris. "Amber, can…"

"Go!" she said, her eyes filled with tears. "I'm right here when you want me." Even her mother and father were motioning him to go.

Harris closed his eyes, threw back his shoulders, took a deep breath and let it out. "Okay, Gaffer, I am ready."

Gaffer opened the door; Maureen was standing by the window and saw her son's reflection. Immediately she turned, opening her arms to greet him. Harris began walking towards her. His pace continuously increasing, until he was in a full jog toward embracing his mother in his arms. They met and entwined one another as tightly as the threads woven into a cherished tapestry.

Harris pulled back and wiped the tears from his mother's face. "I can't believe I'm here with you. This was only a dream, but it's real. You are here! I love you so much, Mom!"

Again they embraced, this time Maureen reassuring her son that the moment was real.

"You are never leaving London again, without me!" Her feisty voice declared.

Harris grinned, looking at his mother, adoring her being as a whole, grateful they were together again. "I do not think you need to worry about that!"

"A little bird told me you had fallen in love!" Maureen spoke with pride.

"I have! Her name is Amber. She was the nurse at the…" Harris choked, not able to say where he was.

"That's alright, son, I know where you were, and I know that is where you two met. Can I meet her now?"

Harris moved swiftly to the door, opening it and seeing Amber anxiously waiting for him.

"Would you like to meet my mom?" he asked with pride.

Amber's smile was bright, "Absolutely!" and she grabbed his open hand.

He walked Amber to his mother. "Mom, this is my golden light. This is Amber."

Maureen took Amber's hand in hers and looked deeply into her eyes. "Thank you, for saving my son's life. Thank you for seeing his goodness." And then they gently embraced.

Gaffer quietly entered the room. "Harris, it's time to meet Irene. Are you up to it? She doesn't want you to feel pressured. She can see you when you are released from the hospital if you would prefer that."

Harris turned to his mother and Amber, "Mom, what do you think?"

"Irene is a lovely person. She believed in you. It was her determination that led to your freedom. I think a short greeting is just what she needs to feel her freedom. I will introduce you two."

"But what do I say to her? I scammed her. It's embarrassing. I hate…." The last word was where Maureen put a stop to his sentence.

"Harris, she understands, just like you do, in your heart. You know you had no choice," lovingly Maureen addressed her son, while holding onto his hand.

Gaffer and Amber allowed the two to decide without any interruptions.

Harris walked over to the large windows looking over the runways. He stood in deep thought, realizing that after his imprisonment, life didn't come back to you as you were when you left. That he had changed. There was a new and old Harris. The new Harris allowed to analyze what he had done. He broke Irene's life. And now he needed to give it back to her – that was the message from the old Harris.

He turned around, "Okay, let's do this. Mom, will you introduce us? And then I would like to be alone with her."

**Irene moved toward Maureen** and Harris. Maureen introduced them. "Harris, my son, this is Irene."

Irene had tried to stay composed, but the dam that held back her river of emotions broke, releasing a storm of tears. Tears of joy, sadness, and gratefulness. "Harris, I am so sorry. I wish I knew earlier. I'm so sorry," she shakily spoke as she held his face in her hands.

Harris reached up, taking both of Irene's hands in his. He brought them to his lips, and he kissed them. "Irene, sorry isn't a word you can say again. You were hope, you were trust, and that is why I am here." Harris's voice cracked, fighting back his emotional tears. "I thought so long about what I would say to you, and now all I can do is wipe my tears. Thank you, thank you." He gripped her hands tightly in his. "When I am ready mentally and physically, I would like to help you publish your story correctly. That is, if it is okay with you."

"Okay? It would be an honor! If it takes months or even a year, I have no problem waiting. For now, we will both work on the present! Does that sound good to you?"

"Thank you Irene." Harris gave her a big hug. "Now, how about you introduce me to Betty? I was told she is your cheerleader!"

"What does one say about Betty? She is a tall glass of water, however she's quite petite. Do you know how some people refer to small dogs acting like large dogs, and large dogs acting like a small dog? Betty is that small dog that never believes, for a moment, that she isn't big!" Harris smiled at the comparisons.

**Betty entered the room** with the biggest smile on her face and her arms stretched out ready for a warm hug. "Harris! Oh my! You are quite tall! And extremely handsome!" she fussed over him like a mother hen. "When Irene first told me about you, I thought she was seriously having an emotional breakdown, but after I read a few of your latest emails, I quickly became her first supporter. We have been friends since middle school. Are you staying in London for a bit?

"Yes, Betty, I am staying with my mother, Maureen, until I get my feet back on the ground, my strength back, and a job."

"That's wise! No reason to rush! Let Irene and I know if and when you need help. We would love an excuse to return to London and do some sightseeing with Maureen. We have lovely visits! Who knows…"

Tears that fell from the dark heavy clouds disappeared; replaced by smiles from the sunshine that had broken through the storm.

**Gaffer brought everyone** to a larger room that was set up for dinner and a party. It was decorated with a welcome home theme.

The reunion continued well into the night, singing along with the karaoke machine, enjoying food that did not include any possible resemblance to what Harris and Amber had been eating and drinking. Every face was lit with smiles and life was in the moment. A grateful moment full of love. Gaffer approached Maya, "May I have this dance?" Blushing, Maya accepted.

When the dance ended, Gaffer reached inside his suit coat pocket and slid out a white envelope. "This is for you and Harris."

She opened the envelope, and within it was a stack of hundred-dollar bills. "Gaffer, I don't understand."

"On the beach, Amarra gave me an envelope of money to keep safe, which I did. Once we were rested on the boat, I returned it to her. She counted it, took half, and asked me to give you and Harris the rest. She said to think of it as a thank you gift and her half was going toward beauty school."

"She will be a fantastic beautician! I will thank her," said Maya.

"Gaffer? Do you mind if I ask you a question?"

"Not at all! What is it?"

"It's about Harris. I am worried he will return to the camp. He believes Bossman is his father. I told him no father would have allowed his son to become seriously ill from a beating. Then he pulls back from the idea, but only for a short time. I do not know what to say to keep him safe and to focus on our future instead."

"Maya, trauma is a haunting beast," replied Gaffer. "It likes to be one's lead; always noticed and in command. It takes time to put that beast behind who you currently are. A lot of therapy and practice. And I will be involved in his treatment. His father could have been linked to the militia, but I need to have that carefully researched. Don't give up on Harris. That's the worst thing anyone can do. Talk about this with your therapist too. And Stella! We are all here and we have all had to heal from trauma. You and Harris fit right in! One big healing family!" Gaffer warmly hugged Maya.

"Thank you." She dried the edges of her eyes. "Look at him! He is so happy tonight. Then he sleeps in the hospital and has to go through test after test. My mother and I will be there with Maureen. Right now, it's difficult to think about being alone or *leaving* anyone alone.

Gaffer was watching Harris laughing with Betty and Irene. "He's strong, Maya. I get that part about being alone. My life has not had 'family' as most peoples do. It too has been lonely, but now Stella and I are going to grow a new family, which you and Harris are the most important members."

"She's looking at us! Thank you, Gaffer." Again, her eyes swelled with tears, as she tried to keep them from falling with a table napkin. She hugged him, kissed him on the cheek, and returned to Harris.

**Gaffer and Stella were on opposite sides of** the room. They walked toward one another, meeting in the center. He took her hand. "I don't like big goodbyes, do you?"

"No, I prefer to slip out unnoticed," she whispered in his ear.

Gaffer gave her that look…you know the one when the guy you were flirting with all night finally notices you. He swaggers over, with a gleam in his eyes, and then says something truly corny, while you save him embarrassment with one of your best smiles. That look.

They slipped out the back door.

# Chapter 31

# HARRIS AND MAUREEN

**Three months later.**

"Mom, how are you doing? We haven't talked about therapy this week." Reminded Harris as he refilled his coffee cup.

Maureen watched his every move. She promised she would never take another day for granted. The moments they now shared were memories she placed in her forever lobe. "It was a busy week for all of us! I started a new painting and finding the right color palette has been tricky."

"What colors are you using?" he curiously inquired, carefully taking a bite of his scone.

"Amber is the main color!" she smiled.

Harris looked up at her. "Are you painting flowers for Amber?" he inquisitively asked.

"I am. I thought it would be a thoughtful Christmas present."

"But Christmas is three months away!" Harris paused. "That is going to be strange." His voice slowed and dropped to a quiet whisper. "Mom, I just realized that I missed two Christmases. It never crossed my mind before. Every day was hot and humid. The idea of seasons and holidays left my thoughts. I didn't even think about my birthday!" Another pause, as he ran his hand through his thick hair.

Maureen saw his anxiety increase. "Harris, many people do not celebrate Christmas, birthdays, or holidays. You aren't alone in that category. At that time in your life, they weren't necessary. But here in London they are! You get to live through holidays and birthdays again!"

"What if I can't handle it?"

"What if you can?" she shot back.

Harris thought about that, and his troubled face began to light up again. "I'm putting the cart in front of the horse again," he smiled. "Which doesn't get me anywhere! So finish telling me about your painting. I think it will be her favorite present!"

"Once my palette is finished, I am going to use the theme of the Calendulas flowers. There are many species which will make an interesting pattern to work with, don't you think?"

He looked at his mother with pride. "All you have been through and here you are, creating beauty from nearly a life of pain. You're to whom I look up to. You and Gaffer."

"Thank you, Harris. You'll find your niche. It takes time and risks."

"Actually, the risks are becoming depressing. Any type of work with a computer creates such anxiety I can't type. Computers were my life and now they are my nightmare. Thank God for Gaffer. When I am asked to leave one company, he has me in another the next day."

Maureen knew this was the biggest mountain for her son to climb: finding a new profession without going back to school. "You said nothing about last week's work at the Archives. Are you going to give it another week?"

"I am. My partner is leap years wiser than me. I want to be like her! And she 'gets' my restrictions. Instead of rolling her eyes or talking about me behind her back she sits down and asks me to tell her what I found easy and what was difficult. I told her running around that huge building searching for the right books and articles was easy, challenging, and enjoyable. But when I have to fill in the flow chart I start sweating and shaking, then I lose my focus."

"What did she say?"

"She said, "I want you to try using a different keyboard. It's amazing and simple to use with several built-in features. I'll have your desk set up for you on Monday. And she told me to have a nice weekend. Now, I feel I have to return."

"She's a leader! I think you found your match! She sees how gifted you are in research which doesn't surprise me. Why you have been doing that since you were four years old!"

"I didn't think about that, but you're right! I remember all those days I went to work with you and then joined you after school. Mom! I am remembering something fun about my past! I have to call Amber!"

"Hold on, son! Before you leave for the day, how is Amber doing?"

"She has moved from three hours of nursing a day to six hours and she definitely does better on the pediatric floor. She loves nursing and is finding it easier to return to than me with computers, which I am grateful for. I would be more of a mess if she were too. It helps to have us in different places during our re-introduction to society."

"You are both making great strides." Maureen handed the berries over to Harris. "Will you finish these up for me? The doctor said, 'berries every day'!"

"Ya, ya!" He begin to pick the blueberries out of the bowl and then moved onto the strawberries. "I spoke with Robert last week. Remember, I sat with him on the plane?"

"Yes, he visited you in the hospital. I believe he is a doctor?"

"Yes, he and his wife are having their first child. He's a nervous wreck. I suggested therapy." Maureen and Harris shared a chuckle. "Anyway, he wants to get me going in a health club. I told him my head injury doesn't allow much, and he laughed. He said we can do bikes, treadmills, and weights. That's his routine. I told him I'm in."

"That's great news!" Maureen sighed. "I'll clean up. You get ready. I believe you and Amber are going clothes shopping?"

"We are and it will be fun. Amber and I understand each other. We always have fun we are together. I think we were born for one another."

Maureen stopped cleaning up the kitchen and looked up at Harris. "I couldn't agree more." She smiled, feeling a massive tear cloud swelling up behind her eyes.

"Oh, and mom, I don't believe that dad was the head of that camp. Gaffer hasn't found any connections, and it has been three months. I have let that go! And so should you!"

He kissed her on the cheek and went to his room to prepare for the day. A freedom he now enjoyed immensely.

# Chapter 32

# BACK TO BETTY AND IRENE

**"We need another bottle of wine!"** droned Betty.

"Do you really think that will give us *more* energy?" Irene asked squinty eyed, trying hard not to slur her speech.

"Well," remarked Betty. "Maybe not energy, but it will help sleep come quicker!"

"Sorry to say this, but we can't even think about sleep yet! The movers are going to be here tomorrow morning at 10:00!" Irene waved the waiter to their table.'

"Yes, ma'am, how can I help you?" he politely inquired.

"We would like one of those appetizer trays with the cheese, salami, olives…do know which one I am referring to?" Irene was frustrated by her forgetfulness of its proper name. Lately, that had been happening when she was overly tired. And today she was past being overly tired. She was exhausted.

"Yes, I do. I will bring it right out. Would you like to order a main dish also?"

Irene looked at Betty who was staring out the window at a tree. "Yes, we'll have the Mediterranean pizza with pepperoni."

"Thank you." And he left like the Mad Hatter.

Addressing Betty, Irene continued, "Food will perk us up. Fook and some caffeine."

"Loads of caffeine and chocolate. We may as well give our last night in this gorgeous city of Chicago one last big hurrah!" Betty turned and faced Irene. "Do you believe we are doing the right thing?"

"No doubt about it! And we can always come back and visit whenever we want. Now that my book is doing so well and I have signed an Option Contract, money is comfortable once again."

Betty smiled at Irene. "You look ten years younger than a year ago. It's nice to have you back to being yourself…an even better self! More confident and less timid."

"Less timid? I haven't heard that one before, but you're right. I am not afraid to use my voice anymore! Have you heard from the kids?" asked Irene.

"Which ones? Edge and Ammara or Harris and Amber?" Grinned Betty, proud of how her family had grown.

"Both, or either one!" replied an equally happy Irene.

"Edge is thinking about helping out Dog for one job to make some extra cash. Ammara is finishing up her training. She has done a good job at networking and has a position at a well-known spa in Bangkok. And they will adjust her schedule to work with a newborn."

Excitedly, Irene leaned forward on the table, "Betty, do you think we could fly to Bangkok and help take care of the baby for a couple of weeks?"

"Take care of a baby? Which one of us knows how to do that?"

Irene sat back giving the comment some extra thought. "It can't be that difficult and we can read up on it. Oh please give it consideration before saying 'no.'"

"I won't say 'no'! It's Edge and Ammara! That baby is going to be gorgeous and we have spoiling rights!" giggled Betty.

The waiter approached with the appetizers. He set them down in the center of the table, stood back and advised, "Perhaps another wine?"

Both women replied with a stern, "No Thank You!"

He left quickly.

"I think we offended him!" stated Betty. "I'll explain when he returns. Thank goodness we only had to completely empty your condo."

"Do you think you will ever sell yours? It doesn't seem right to leave it as it is without anyone to enjoy it!" advised Irene, looking quite serious at her friend.

"I understand how you're feeling, but I can't let it go. I love it, and besides, when we come back to visit we will have my comfy beautiful condo to stay in. The memories will be there to flood our minds. Someday I may sell it, but only to someone I know. It has to stay in our circle."

Irene was listening attentively as she devoured over half of the appetizer tray. She looked up at Betty, "I'm sorry that I ate some of your half, but I'm starving! Do they have pizza in London?"

"Of course they do! But it has more of a true Italian influence. Around here we eat American pizza!"

"Hm, well Chicago is known for their pizza, American or Italian, I don't know, but I know a Chicago pan pizza!" Irene continued, "I wonder what trouble you, me, and Maureen will get into! I do love her neighborhood, and we were fortunate to find a two bedroom, two bath flat that quickly. Guess it was meant to be."

"I agree. That area has such healthy energy and many people our age! Maybe I will actually meet my Prince!" smiled Betty.

"I hope you do!" replied Irene. "I'm content being surrounded by friends. We'll see Harris and Amber. Even Stella and Gaffer. You know she still can't get him to tell her his birth name! She's starting to investigate, and I told her to stop. Gaffer will tell her when it's time. She needs to trust him. He is too calculated about everything! I wonder how he is in bed?" Irene whispered the last sentence with a devious chuckle.

"Irene Watkins shame on you for even thinking of such private matters!" Betty straightened her napkin and whispered back, "But it's hard to see anyone taking over Stella. She probably has him tied up while she works on an extraction!" Both girls broke out in laughter.

"Seriously," Betty continued, "are you definitely done with counseling?"

"I am," answered Irene. "My last session was last week. I don't like to think where I would be if Harris hadn't connected me with his former employee. That opened up doors for success. I heard he is still struggling. Maybe with two more doting mothers around he'll make bigger strides. On the other hand, Maya is pushing the green light with nursing. She loves pediatrics."

"We are each unique and time will heal us all. Harris seems to be enjoying his job working with the archives and he's doing better in therapy. I feel he's finding his new self, and he'll snap back quickly. Not having a purpose or direction in life makes it tough to be happy with yourself. Don't you agree, Irene?"

"I sure do! He went to hell and back. But Gaffer has his back and won't rest until Harris is strong on his own two feet. He has truly become a dad-like figure for Harris." Let's eat up and finish packing those boxes! We may be able to catch a few hours of sleep before our flight."

"Betty, how do you feel about a tiny dog, like Blizzard?"

"Are you kidding me? We would spoil that dog beyond the definition. That's an idea we will discuss when we are settled in."

"Thinking back, do you still feel that Harris's father could have been the Bossman?" Irene casually asked Betty.

Betty stopped eating and glared at Irene. "Don't you even go there! That's a dangerous falsehood that does not need any more recognition. No father would have allowed his son to nearly die in such horrid conditions. Irene, are you sure you are done with counseling?"

"Of course I am sure, Betty! It crosses my mind occasionally and talking helps me put it back to where it belongs. I would never say anything to the kids! Just you. Always 'besties,' right?"

"Absolutely! And no more Bossman talk," added Betty.

## Chapter 33

# MEANWHILE IN THAILAND

"**Bossman, you are not well enough to be worrying** about the camp. The doctor said you are a lucky man and that the bullet Maya shot you with narrowly missed your spine, and if you want to walk again, you must heal first. *My* job is to worry about the camp. We lost the building for the laborers. It was old, and now it is time for a new one with proper bunk beds. We can double our numbers and hours. I have found a crew from town to help us build and buy materials. It will be done in two or three months. We can add a shower room. If you could draw me a floorplan of how you want it to look, I will take care of the rest. I have placed paper and pencils on your bedstand."

"Have you stopped looking for survivors?" Bossman asked weakly.

"Why should we stop? We do not understand that order?" the soldier spoke with a conflicting tone.

"The storm was worse than we thought. We left them to fend for themselves, and the ones that did make it out have earned their freedom." The boss rested and then continued in a raspy voice, "Any news on Maya, Ammara, and Ricco?"

"No, sir, no news. We believe they were swept out to sea."

"I didn't want to hurt them, but to save them. They did not know that."

"You would have let them run with the rest?"

"Yes, I would have," he slowly nodded his head.

"Boss, now we start over, do better, and make more money!"

"Yes, a new building, new laborers. I am tiring, but before you go, bring my metal box on the shelf. Later I will draw a floor plan when I am able to."

The soldier walked to the shelves in his room, picked up the metal box and brought it over to the Bossman.

"May I ask what is in here?" questioned the soldier.

The Bossman replied, "No, you may not. Now go! I am tiring!"

**The soldier left, and Bossman studied his metal box.** It was beautifully etched with flowers. He briefly opened it up and looked through its belongings. Then he closed it, latched the metal hook, and placed it on his bed stand.

His weary eyes drifted into a restless, haunted sleep. The stormy night replayed in his mind: the desperate struggle with his only child, Harris, on the beach. He could still feel the frailty in his son's body—so diminished, so vulnerable—a stark reminder of the suffering they both endured. Yet, in Harris's hollow, dehydrated eyes, there flickered a fierce determination that refused to yield. Maya's quick thinking had saved him; without her, he surely would have lost hope. His son was no longer a boy, but a resilient young man, shaped by hardship and sustained by love worth fighting for.

The old way was now gone, and with it, the recognition that a new beginning was waiting.

# Facts and information about Cyber Scam Camps

<u>Cyber Scam Camps</u> – **also known as scam centers and fraud compounds.**
   -run by well organized criminal groups with international connections (criminal actors or cybercriminals)
   -controlled by militias and warlords
   -house approximately 300,000 young people forced to work 16 hours or more a day with limited food and no medical care. If not obedient, they are subjected to beatings, starvation, and electric shocks.
   -has been referred to as 'modern slavery' since their key element is human trafficking– people who were simply seeking better economic prospects but lured to these compounds on false pretenses and robbed of their identity. (passports and cellphones taken from them)
   - examples of jobs they were lured away from are tech support, call centers and beauty salons.

<u>Where are they?</u>
   -remote, border access, low law enforcement areas of Southeast Asia are the primary locations. Scam camps have been expanding into Latin America and West Africa.
   -countries such as Myanmar, Cambodia, Laos, and the Philippines
   - cyber scam camps are now a global reality

**How did they get their start?**
- Chinese crime syndicates, posed as investors, shifted their operations from illegal gambling houses to online fraud. This shift began in the 2000's but took a strong hold during COVID.

-it is a new form of crime that the US is only now becoming more aware of as a threat to our security. The camps can be shut down but reopen in new locations as the business is lucrative.

- American's lost $12.5 billion to cyber fraud in 2024 according to the FTC.

- Globally, scams and frauds will cost approximately $10.5 trillion annually in 2025.

**How do they work, from my experiences and research?**
-initially, and under duress, they begin to cultivate trust from their victim becoming like a friend who knows you well. It is referred to as 'fattening up the pig'.

-once trust is emotionally strong the criminal actors offer a scheme – it could be an investment, tech support, even romance.

-once a purchase has been made they 'groom the pig' by calling weekly, sending positive feedback, and continuing the friendship/trust connection. During this grooming stage the cost of their investment plans usually increase.

-when they get you to take a big bite and sink your teeth into their proposal/s, they completed their mission and 'butchered the pig'. By this time the consumer usually realizes what happened and begins trying to get their charges reversed, which is difficult to do if cryptocurrency was used. Crypto is difficult to trace. The consumer is worse off than when they began.

### How can you tell if they are scammers? (From my own experiences)

-criminal actors are professionally trained. They use real names, real photos, and closely replicated logos. Hire a lawyer to read any contract. Right from the start share conversations and offers with someone you trust.

- do research on any name or company.
- if the deal is too good to be true, beware!
- if you feel you are being pressured to move quickly, because there is only one spot open, or the deal lasts for only a day or a week, hundreds are waiting behind you ... hang up.
- never give out personal information – if they ask ANYTHING personal... disconnect.

-If you do believe that you were scammed, report the experience to the local police and to our government -ftc.gov, as soon as possible.

### Can you live beyond being scammed?

-YES! It is embarrassing and shameful. It creates havoc with one's finances, but there is help out there...and use it! Reporting gives you hope and power. Talking to your partner or an understanding friend rebuilds trust in yourself. **If in need of emotional support, text or dial 988- it offers free, immediate, confidential support.**

-Go to your bank if you need help paying off the credit cards and try to have the charges reversed. Do Not Beat Yourself up! There are millions in the same situation, or worse!

-Take the negative and create a positive. Start a support group. Write about your experience, engage in public speaking.

-Look into systems one can have added to their phone that blocks spam calls.

-Block all my credit cards. Close accounts and reopen with a new number.

-Change your phone number and email address, if possible.

-Focus on the little things that make you smile and feel loved. You can become wiser and feel more confident after being a victim of fraud or scams.

Remember, nothing gets better for the hundreds of thousands of cyber scam camp laborers who are being forced to do what they are doing to innocent civilians. These laborers are living in poor conditions and under constant threat of beatings, starvation, being electrically shocked or becoming gravely ill with no medication.

Sources:
- Gemini
- www.Cybersecuritydive.com BEC scams…
- www.ice.gov Cybercrime…
- www.fbi.gov FBI Releases A….
- www.boisestate.edu Cybercrime to ….
- www.kbtx.com/2025 Texas A&M University police say cyber scams….
- www.yahoo.com>news March 9-2025 Associated Press. They were forced…
- www.darkreading.com/program/dr-global
  - Robert Lemos, contributing Writer/ 6-11-2024
- www.csis.org Cyber Scamming….
- themekongclub.org Forced – Labor…
- enactafrica.org Human trafficking
- www.interpol.int INTERPOL issue…
- www.ohchr.org Hundreds of th…
- www.indiatoday.in Operation Cyber…
- www.interpol.int NTERPOL operation….

# BOOK CLUB DISCUSSION QUESTIONS:

1. Criminal actors professionally scammed Irene. Does anyone have an experience of being scammed, or have heard of someone else's scam, and would like to share? How are the scams similar? Different? What emotions were felt by Irene during and after the scam?

2. Of the three female characters, Irene, Betty, and Stella, which one would you like to play the part of in a movie? (Do tell why!)

3. Every story has a theme, such as: Good vs. Evil, Love, Friendships, Coming of Age, Redemption, Courage and Perseverance, Revenge, Family, Identity and Self-Discovery, Power and Corruption, Survival, Prejudice, Individual vs. Society.

4. After reading Between Lines, discuss two or three themes that as a group, you felt stood out.

5. The author was a teacher and enjoys continuing to educate others through her writings. Make a list of what you learned or were surprised about after reading Between Lines.

6. In the story, the reader travels from Chicago to London and then Thailand. Of these three locations, which one would you like to win a free trip to? Explain your decision.

7. In the last five years, 80 million people in the United States lost money through scams. In 2024 it is reported that $47 billion dollars was lost to adult Americans through fraud and scams. What do you think is causing this increase and what could be done?

8. Is there anything that stands out about the style, or voice, of the author?

www.ingramcontent.com/pod-product-compliance
Lightning Source LLC
Chambersburg PA
CBHW020453030426
42337CB00011B/104